THE DOOR OF FAITH

SERAFINO M. LANZETTA

The Door of Faith
When Reason and Love Meet

AROUCA PRESS

Copyright © Arouca Press 2022
Copyright © Serafino M. Lanzetta 2022
All rights reserved:
No part of this book may be reproduced or transmitted,
in any form or by any means, without permission

ISBN: 978-1-990685-02-6 (pbk)
ISBN: 978-1-990685-03-3 (hc)

Arouca Press
PO Box 55003
Bridgeport PO
Waterloo, ON N2J 3G0
Canada
www.aroucapress.com
Send inquiries to info@aroucapress.com

To my grandmother Ines,
who, in teaching me to pray,
handed on to me the Faith.

Contents

INTRODUCTION XIII

PART ONE: FAITH AND REASON 1

The Current Challenges for Faith:
Between New Myths and Old Leftovers 3
   1. If the God of the Philosophers Is
      No Longer the God of the Bible. 3
   2. If the God of the Theologians Is
      No Longer the God of Revelation. 14

I Believe: Reason, Faith, and Doubt? 23
   1. What Do I Mean When I Say "I Believe"? . . 23
   2. Is It Rational to Believe or Is It Just
      an Illusion? 26
   3. I Believe in God, but I Believe
      Only in God 28
   4. I Doubt, Therefore I Don't Think 30
   5. "I Believe" Is to Trust in a Testimony. 34

"We worship what we know" (Jn 4:22):
Faith and Religious Belief 37
   Introduction. 37
   1. Worship of God after Knowing Him 39
   2. Faith and Belief:
      Distinctions and Distance. 43
   3. Revelation in Christ as Fullness 49

    4. Errors Concerning the Failed Distinction
       between Faith and Belief 51
    5. Conversion as "Passage" from
       Belief to Faith. 57

The Tension between Faith and its Proclamation:
Act of Faith and Believed Truths 61
    1. Searching for the Start of the Act of Faith . . 62
    2. Faith and Proclamation on the
       Threshold of Vatican II 66
    3. The Crisis of the Church in the
       Post-Conciliar Period 71
    4. If Faith Subsumes the Problematic
       Fact of Existence 73
    5. Faith between the Informative and
       Performative Aspects. 76

Does God Punish?:
Reflections on God and the Problem of Evil 82
    Introduction. 82
    1. Does God Punish? 83
    2. If God is Good, Why Does He Punish? . . . 99
    3. If God Were Not to Punish. 103

PART TWO:
THE CIRCULAR NATURE OF THE SOURCES: 107

Veritas and *Caritas*:
Two Wings of the Human Spirit 109
    1. The Truth about Charity for a
       Charity of Truth 109
    2. Reason and Love as Rational
       Presupposition 114
    3. Faith and Charity as
       Revelatory Fulfilment 117

  4. Doctrine and Pastoral Care in
    a Circular Relationship 124

The Truth about Love for Love in Truth:
 The Paradigm of Deus Caritas Est 130
  Introduction 130
  1. *Deus Caritas Est*, an Apologia of Love . . . 132
  2. Love in Truth for a Love of Truth 143
  3. The Apologetic Discourse: Giving Truth
    to Love in Love of Truth 146
  4. A Sketch of the Contemporary
    Philosophical Panorama:
    Two Nihilisms Compared 164
  5. A Contemporary Risk for Theology 188
  Concluding Remarks 194

The Good Shepherd:
 When Logos and Love are One Person 198
  1. The "Good Shepherd" in
    Sacred Scripture 199
  2. The "Good Shepherd" in the
    Reflection of Benedict XVI 200
  3. A Theology between the Lines 203

"Sacramentum Caritatis" in *Veritate*:
 The Logos-Love is the "Bread of Life" 209
  1. The Food of Truth 210
  2. The Eucharist Draws Us into
    Christ's Oblation 212
  3. The Eucharist as Spousal Gift 214
  4. The Intertwining of Faith, Liturgy
    and Life in the Eucharist 216
  5. Eucharist and the Church's Mission 219
  6. The Eucharist, Truth of Love 221

PART THREE: THE OBLIVION OF FAITH. 223

   When Reason and Love Do Not Meet:
      Beyond Post-Modern Levelling 225
         1. If Reason and Love No Longer Look
            at Each Other. 225
         2. Religious Freedom Compared with
            Reason and Love 229

CONCLUSION. 239

INDEX OF NAMES .241

Introduction

FAITH AS A DOOR IS A FASCINATING image. A new horizon appears at precisely the moment when a man decides to cross the threshold and look out at the reality that is beyond his doorstep. Our life is a continual looking out at reality through many doors, both open and closed, the latter often leaving us dissatisfied. Our life is marked by mystery. Either mystery or nothing: we must choose. Either choose the truth, and therefore the faith, or resign ourselves to wade through the waves of our continual foundering.

Faith is the door[1] that opens the mystery of God to us and through which God gives us our raison d'être, reasons for things and for the world. Faith is necessary and attainable. It is a human act; it is not a dive into the sea of existence where you desperately grab onto a life jacket or a blind wandering around the streets of the world, believing that you can see something when in reality you only see darkness. Here, the illusion of seeing would be the comfort of faith, but faith itself would be thick darkness and therefore a waste of time. This is the world in which many people dwell. Faith is an illusion. They believe in order to find comfort in something. On the contrary, faith is an act of our intelligence and will moved by grace; it is an act that is part of us and marks our life.

---

[1] See Acts 14:27.

How many human acts of faith we make in order to live! For example, when traveling, if we do not believe we will arrive at the pre-arranged destination, and if we do not hope to arrive safe and sound, then we must refuse to set out. Supernatural faith is the most important journey. It is the only journey which is worth undertaking.

However, it is essential to set out on a journey well-prepared. Faith in God is not an irrational or involuntary option. One must start at the foundation: reason and love. Reason tells us who God is and love impels us toward Him, as the Good to be embraced and possessed. Faith, then, always works through charity[2]: it is driven toward and stretches out to the love of God. Faith alone is not sufficient but must be completed by love, by the possession of the Good in which a man has believed and hoped. Faith and charity work together like reason and love although the two pairs are on different levels. We will learn to see these two levels — one natural and the other supernatural — in harmony so that with reason and love, faith and charity, we can truly embrace the whole of reality and give a definitive response to our life.

With how many doubts must we contend! Doubt is not a threat to truth, or to the act of faith, but a wound to our intelligence that prevents us from fully consenting, as we would like, to the truth. "Ten thousand difficulties do not make one doubt," says Newman.[3] Doubt torments the people of our time, and the problem of truth remains buried. This intellectual climate allows them to remain in doubt and to overlook or neglect the religious question, confirming, then, the prevalence of doubt by

---

2 See Gal 5:6.
3 John Henry Newman, *Apologia Pro Vita Sua* (Oxford: Clarendon Press, 1967), 210.

Introduction

the multiplicity of religions or religious offerings. Now, in place of truth, stands humanity and its desires. A bizarre idea of "humility" toward truth stops the human person from attaining happiness. As G. K. Chesterton noted, we suffer from humility in the wrong place:

> A man was meant to be doubtful about himself, but undoubting about the truth; this has been exactly reversed. Nowadays the part of a man that a man does assert is exactly the part he ought not to assert—himself. The part he doubts is exactly the part he ought not to doubt—the Divine Reason. Huxley preached a humility content to learn from Nature. But the new sceptic is so humble that he doubts if he can even learn.... The old humility was a spur that prevented a man from stopping; not a nail in his boot that prevented him from going on. For the old humility made a man doubtful about his efforts, which might make him work harder. But the new humility makes a man doubtful about his aims, which will make him stop working altogether.[4]

Refusal to shake off this principle-doubt — which in fact is not a principle — sets up doubt as an epistemological principle to justify one's cognitive hesitancy, while only embracing what is most convenient. The fact that many religions exist is used as justification to forgo the religious question or leave it in a state of general uncertainty in which each person chooses what is most pleasing to them. The atheist settles for his or her atheism, perhaps occassionally asking a question about morality

---

4   G. K. Chesterton, *Orthodoxy* (London: The Week-End Library, 1934), 53–54.

or human behavior. The believer chooses his or her God in the religion that is most closely aligned to their ideals. The problem of truth is absent, and therefore, so is the problem of true religion. But the issue is not avoided by the multiplicity of truthful offerings, even when one is of a religious background. In this panorama of prevalent subjectivism, truth is always the one real problem that cannot be avoided. The dangers of relativism are incalculable because they corrode the truth from within consciences, simultaneously soothing them. The dangers make consciences defenceless.

Jesus, too, doubted on the Cross. So says the current theological fashion, as it explains that Jesus, symbol of humanity, experienced deep down the failure of human existence, which is nothing more than the struggle between an act of faith and an act of desperation. If this were true, life would be a mixture of contradictions; even in the believer, a dual soul would reign — that of the devout, faithful person and that of the non-believer who rebels against God. Jesus's doubt would be well-disposed to reconcile what some Protestant theologians, such as Paul Tillich, see as the inexorable decadence of human existence in the search for its own destiny imbued with non-meaning and contradictions.[5] The problem here is the rejection of reason. Faith would be nothing but an embrace of the irrational, justified by the Lord's Cross. In truth, the Cross is not Jesus's descent into contradiction, but love *to the end* in the certainty that Jesus is God the Redeemer. Jesus does not have faith because He is God. Instead, all those who start with Jesus's doubt erroneously claim that He had faith. Jesus is God, and therefore, He need not believe

---

5   See Antonio Livi, "La deriva irrazionalistica nella teologia cattolica e le sue radici luterane," *Fides Catholica* 2 (2016): 94–113.

Introduction

in Himself. Once we have understand this, He helps us to believe in God without contradictions.

Unfortunately, faith is humanity's problem. God is everywhere men and women suffer — where they are uncomfortable, where tears are shed over their distress. In a certain sense, this is true. However, God is only where the Cross of Christ is adored or at least desired. He suffers only in Jesus and in His Cross. If God suffers beyond the Son's Cross, it means that the pain suffered for us, for all of us, is in vain. The pain will never be redeemed. If God is where men and women are with their problems, He will only be the redeemer of the problem of humanity, as placed by humanity. Men and women pose God as a problem, by posing their own problems. Where humanity's problems are missing, God is missing, too. This current way of thinking about faith and God, which theologians claim began with Auschwitz hides a great misunderstanding: God becomes simply a hypothesis of necessity, entirely post-modern and uncertain; He is no longer the *One who is*, recognized by reason and love. Faith thus becomes the justification of all the faiths of men and women and loses its value. God is dimmed at the twilight of the myths and the gods.

To believe in God again, we must become aware of the contradictions that result from denying Him. Today the post-Christian culture wallows in contradictions, but enjoys being stuck in them: it is more convenient, less demanding on reason. It is always more difficult to enter into the world — one must be selected at the door of entry — and it is always easier to leave, for when we are deemed useless and cumbersome, we are dispatched like parcels. We often speak of *privacy*, a word that has become social dogma, while in reality, we have never been so exposed to the public as we are today. From credit cards to mobile phones to Facebook, everything is public. Anything but privacy! Instead, so-called privacy is preserved only in one's own faith relationship with God. No one should get involved; it is a subjective and inner choice. Not even God can tell man how to live. This so-called privacy helps one to hide himself from His sight, like the first Adam, rather than to preserve his inner freedom and discretion. One loves everything; everything is love; everything is justified by love, apart from God, who, instead, is challenged most of the time. He is an enemy. Along with Him, other individuals are enemies, too — those who instead of personifying the ministries of love would seek to poison the world's eros with signs adverse to morality and doctrine.

Of course, the problem of evil remains the primary question and a great mystery. Faced with the persistence of evil, modern man desires to see therein the absence of God, if not His proven negation. The only way out of the problem of evil seems to be the denial of God's existence. Mere denial, however, not only does not explain the problem but creates another one: who will be able to give us an answer? To resolve the problem of evil is it sufficient to say that God does not punish? How many forms of atheism are disguised as false beliefs! The question still grips modern humanity: if God exists, how is it that He remains powerless and mute in the face of evil, especially in the face of innocent suffering? The reality of suffering creates another opportunity to pose the problem of God and usually to deny His existence. In fact, the real problem is overlooked. Yes, suffering remains a mystery. However, if evil speaks to us about God, reminding us of Him, why does goodness not tell us anything? Why should evil alone

Introduction

be the catalyst to speak about God and perhaps even deny Him? Is it not essential to start from goodness and thus give a satisfactory answer to the problem of evil? Is it not necessary to start from God? Sentiment dominates over reason and love. If evil is the way to deny God, then men and women will love evil, or hate it, contrary to reason and opposed to God and themselves. Love is without reason; sentiment is against reason and faith.

The problem of faith is not its denial, which can happen in the name of reason. Reason is never against faith. In fact, faith rests on it. Of course, faith does not begin in reason but is something beyond. Its origin is in supernatural revelation, but reason is its noetic prerequisite. Faith will only accept what is in harmony with reason; it will never accept contradictions or fables. Faith, therefore, as a human action, starts from reason. In other words, it is an action rooted in reason, and therefore, in the human capacity to welcome truth in the knowledge of reality. Faith is real, not a mere ideal. It speaks to us about reality. It enables us to welcome the most truthful reality, that which is hidden behind things and which reason intuits as necessary, even without seeing its face or understanding its meaning. Life's battle is not that of reason against faith, but a battle between reason and faith on one side against sentiment and whims or moods on the other. Moods change, but reason is constant. If one's faith is based on moods, then it is possible to lose it, as they say. One cannot even be a pure atheist unless he has overcome the temptation to entrust every certainty to moods rather than to reason. If certainty rests in the present state of his soul—i.e., emotional and not rational evidence—then he must even renounce his atheism. A genuine atheist entrusts themselves to reason and not to sentiment. C. S. Lewis saw this clearly, stating that what took away faith was imagination and emotion, not reason. He wrote:

> For moods will change, whatever view your reason takes. I know that by experience. Now that I am a Christian I do have moods in which the whole thing looks very improbable: but when I was an atheist I had moods in which Christianity looked terribly probable. This rebellion of your moods against your real self is going to come anyway. That is why Faith is such a necessary virtue: unless you teach your moods 'where they get off', you can never be either a sound Christian or even a sound atheist, but just a creature dithering to and fro, with its beliefs really dependent on the weather and the state of its digestion. Consequently one must train the habit of Faith.[6]

Reason is allied to faith. Faith and reason paired together are the life of the human person. Reason has allowed itself to become sentiment which has, in turn, replaced the rational act of judging. For this reason, it has become arid. The principle axiom of modernity — the goddess reason — has in fact produced a sublation of reason with sentiment, often with religious sentiment, which then casts aside reason in favor of love. Such weak thought gives rise to relativistic dogmatism: truth divides, and it is impossible to find because it is either fluid or does not exist, while love unites by igniting the heart and making people more sympathetic. Love is thus juxtaposed to truth. The real problem, which the dogmatics of relativism do not see, is that reason needs to be accompanied as it

---

6   C. S. Lewis, *Mere Christianity* (London: Harper Collins, 2002), 140–141.

Introduction

moves toward the truth; it is not something cold acceding to truth, because truth itself is not a cold syllogism or a mere mathematical calculation, but it is what humanity was created for — the origin of a person's being and their fulfilment. Truth embraces all the spheres of existence: logic, mathematics, the sciences, thought, choice, and life itself. Truth is the reason for the existence of humanity, and human beings reach out toward it in all that they desire and choose, not in a cold or passive manner but with zeal, with the desire to find it. The point is to find it in the correct place. Even the person who sets out from the premise that truth does not exist (and it will not because of an absolute pluralism) wants their premise to remain solid; they love it and so choose it as the foundation of their relativism. More faith is required to be an atheist than to believe in God.

Reason must be accompanied by love. Reason is for love, and love lives within the confines of reason. Reason and love are the two dimensions which together constitute the great human horizon: everything is tangible through these two directors of the human spirit. Reason and love suggest the correct relationship between truth and freedom, intellect and will. The great philosophical question about the relationship between truth and freedom must return to a harmonious circularity in which truth guides the will and freedom, which is the most beautiful and most noble *proprium* of the human person and which moves the intellect in knowledge, for the will is able to distance itself from the intellect without having to follow it in a slavish manner. The will is free not because it is against reason but because it goes beyond reason: it exceeds it and thus completes it. This book aims to shed a new light on the need to include the role of love in the discourse concerning the role of reason. In this way, I hope to integrate an understanding of truth and the intellect as director of the act of the will instead of underlining the precedence of the will and its freedom in following what the intellect has previously known as true.

Intellect and will, reason and love, must guide men and women as a firm and truthful premise of the faith that leads to charity. Together, reason and love are the natural and cognitive premises for the faith, which is fulfilled in charity. Faith and charity constitute the two wings of the Christian life. We can never have faith alone or charity alone, for one always implies the other. There is no charity without faith—and therefore truth—just as there is no authentic and formed faith without charity.

Christianity's historical development brought about a sort of displacement, one of the decisive factors being the Protestant Reformation. Today, we no longer have a Lutheran faith without works but works without faith. We are pressured to be committed to so many social causes, to engage in so much voluntary work, but all without faith. Many questions (Who is Jesus Christ? Is it still necessary to belong to the Church of Christ, the Catholic Church, to be saved?) are no longer seen as important and substantive but have become superfluous, because they have been overtaken by the sentiment of being good Christians. One assumes that this goodness will produce good actions—a term that commonly replaces the works of faith, at the center of which is charity.[7] The teachings of the faith do not matter much. Doctrine, even to men of the Church, seems a heavy burden. Moreover, such a burden seems to cause isolation and Pharisaism, that is, pointing fingers. Love,

---

7 Cf. Gal 5:6.

on the other hand, passes over all dissension. It unites us. We rediscover ourselves as exiles on the same boat, and so we seek to do good to each other, as much as possible. Charity seems to rise in accordance with the Christian life, but it rises in opposition to faith, without faith. We encounter the problem of a culture that defines itself as post-Christian. Truth divides while love brings together. Ideas divide us, but we try to overcome our division with a love that makes us companions on the journey. We are left with a loving relativism, a relativistic love.

Although we once had a faith without charity, we now have a charity without faith. These are two faces of the same Protestant coin, whether it crowns the Reformation or adorns the collar of Catholic jackets. It would be better to put this coin away in a drawer and forget it. Reason and love cannot be set against each other, just as you cannot choose either faith or charity. They either stand together or fall together. A Catholicism that only thinks about bringing people together and cultivating charitable sentiments but no longer teaches correct doctrine and the true faith, as received from the Fathers, is simply illusory. We condemn ourselves to indulge in all the vices of postmodernity and to renounce the supreme function that the Church alone can exercise, i.e., condemning vices and cultivating virtues. When a vice is proclaimed a virtue, the virtue, as with faith, quickly becomes a vice. As Chesterton says, it becomes a virtue gone mad. The modern world is not evil; rather, it is in some way excessively good. "It is full of wild and wasted virtues.... The modern world is full of the old Christian virtues gone mad."[8] When reason is lost, faith becomes an old virtue gone mad.

---

8   Chesterton, *Orthodoxy*, 50–51.

Where has faith gone? Can we once again cross the threshold of this blessed door which opens to the horizon of true life? Where has reason ended up? It had been lost in the twists and turns of love, and so charity has swallowed up faith. Faith has disappeared, but charity has disappeared, too. We are faced with the supremacy of love without or against truth. When love no longer has any dimension, it becomes rejection of God, the Church, and the sacraments. Christianity becomes the other face of a loving non-governmental organization; everything is justified, but there is no longer room for Christ and His doctrine of salvation. Benedict XVI writes in *Caritas in Veritate*:

> A Christianity of charity without truth would be more or less interchangeable with a pool of good sentiments, helpful for social cohesion, but of little relevance. In other words, there would no longer be any real place for God in the world. Without truth, charity is confined to a narrow field devoid of relations.[9]

"A Christianity of charity without truth" is the most terrible snare: it only leads to charity without faith, compassion and mercy without truth, and love without reason. It is to Benedict XVI's merit to have raised the Church's awareness of the contemporary uneasiness and derived profligacy in the name of an intoxicated but empty eros.

In the following pages, I will highlight the indissoluble knot which unites reason and faith, and then I examine the vital circularity of reason and love, faith and charity. The natural and fundamental bond of reason and love acts as

---

[9] Pope Benedict XVI, Encyclical Letter *Caritas in Veritate* (June 29, 2009), 4.

Introduction

a paradigm for circularity in the knowledge of reality. The whole of reality is embraced by two premises: intelligence and the heart, that is, thought and sentiment disciplined and elevated by agape. They are the source of knowledge and experience, of mutual relation and true judgment. In the supernatural setup, the bond of truth and love opens the door to mystery, which itself is dual. Mystery is justice and mercy, from which we infer the true and vital link between doctrine and pastoral works, between faith and charity. The attempt to incorporate faith into charity, paves the way for Christian do-goodism or good feelings; on the other hand, incorporating charity into faith leads to the individualist option of do-it-yourself. In either case, the two unbalanced aspects end up united in sentiment. This undisciplined eros wrecks God one minute and humanity the next — faith one minute, and charity the next — simply in the name of humanity and their own sentiments, which seem to be either fideistic or altruistic sentiments. Yet, only these very sentiments can generate one of the greatest dangers inherent in a religious freedom that justifies religious pluralism (or even at times syncretism) over and above the effort to seek out the truth about God and religion. A true religious freedom, possible for everyone, is founded on the pillars of the true God and the common good for society, not simply friendship among humans.

In this book, I have collected several essays originally written in Italian, which I have published separately. I have organized them into three main sections, each dealing with a specific aspect. Beginning with an examination of the relationship between faith and reason, we then tackle the circularity of reason and love, faith and charity, eventually reflecting on a possible danger caused by the abandonment of reason and love, especially the theological problem of religious freedom. The first section of the book highlights the fundamental relationship between faith and reason from the viewpoint of fundamental theology. The discourse is concerned with the topic of doubt in relation to faith and the distinction between theological faith and religious belief. Also, the two dimensions of faith as *informative* and *performative* will be clarified by refusing to conflate the doctrine of faith with the subjective act of faith. The final topic in this first part will be the problem of evil: does God punish? I will bring this question back into the theological realm, challenging our solution to the mystery of evil in general with the living presence of God in history and in our life. A divine *chastisment* (from *chaste, pure*) aims only at effecting our purification from sin so that the door to eternal salvation might be opened for us. When faith is supported by reason (and love) the understanding that Divine Providence leads both history and each man's life fills us with great hope, even in times of distress.

The second section examines the circularity between reason and love as a natural foundation for the theological interrelation of faith and charity. The circularity of truth and love immediately impacts the right relationship between doctrine and pastoral care. Doctrine is the prerequisite, while the pastoral effort to reach out to all people for their salvation is the goal to be achieved. A paradigm for this discourse will be offered by the Encyclical Letter *Deus Caritas Est* by Benedict XVI, whose core teaching might be condensed into one phrase: *a love in truth for a truth of love.* Two more topics in this second part will help the reader see this paradigm as much nedeed for the Christian life, which was, in a sense, made flesh in the Logos-Love, the mystery of the Word Incarnate, and ultimately in the Bread of Life, the Holy Eucharist.

Introduction

Finally, the last section shows the side effects of a discourse that might fail to take the vital circularity of reason and love into account. If there is no virtuous encounter of the two, religious freedom will only be concerned with social peace among religions and people but will ignore the very reason for freedom, which is the discovery of the truth that makes man free, namely, the true God and the true religion. Can we still speak of *religio vera* — a true religion? With this in mind, let us approach the various topics, starting with the cause of an extended loss of faith.

PART ONE

Faith and Reason

The Current Challenges for Faith:

BETWEEN NEW MYTHS AND OLD LEFTOVERS

WHAT IS THE MAIN CAUSE OF the present loss of faith, which is becoming increasingly subjective and intimistic? In my opinion, this crisis is generated largely by setting aside the question of God and rejecting any (strong) thought about God. When the thoughts of men and women are no longer capable of understanding God, they become non-thoughts and they head toward decline. Along with thought goes faith. This chapter examines the slow but gradual loss of thought about God to restore reason once again to our faith.

1. IF THE GOD OF THE PHILOSOPHERS IS NO LONGER THE GOD OF THE BIBLE

1.1 Forgetfulness about the certainty of God and the entry of weak thought

Miguel de Unamuno (1872–1970) summarizes the history of divine thought well: "On this side of the barrier, everything is explained without Him; on the further side, nothing is explained, either with Him or without Him; God therefore is superfluous."[1] Unamuno, a fervent Catholic in his adolescence, read Kant's *Critique of Pure Reason*

---

1 Miguel de Unamuno, *The Tragic Sense of Life* (North Chelmsford, MA: Courier Corporation, 2012), 161.

as a young university student and discovered atheism. Kant blew his convictions apart. In fact, the influence of the Könisberg philosopher can be discerned in the statement above; for, according to Kant, what is in itself is not knowable, and on the further side of the barrier there is no true knowledge. How do the *a posteriori* proofs of God's existence show that the first uncaused cause is the One we call God? Kant perceived an insurmountable chasm between the First Cause and God. Thus, Kant explored other means to obtain knowledge of God, which he called the moral path, having to postulate its existence as a premise for the categorical imperative. But if God is merely the moral necessity of humanity, does He not soon become an enemy of freedom? Why moral necessity?

God is seen as an enemy of humanity, of the vital space of men and women; they are forced to choose between God and their own existence. But the question remains in the background, like a specter of thought: Is God really necessary? Or is He simply a construction of our thought? To what does the word *God* allude? Does the word refer to an ordering cause of everything or to the One who invites me into the dimension of the sacred? Philosophers describe the two possibilities as exclusive alternatives. The god accessible by reason alone is not really God. Only faith can generate an encounter with God, which means that there is fatal divide between faith and reason. The truths known by reason do not correspond to the teachings of faith. Further, matters of faith are longer supported by reason. Thus, the path toward scepticism, which appears as fideism in matters of faith, is opened. The risk today is not the lack of faith but fideism, that is, sentimentalism and subjectivism.

We think of Pascal, who appealed in a vehement fashion to the God of the Bible — the God of Abraham, of Isaac, and of Jacob — and not to the God of the philosophers and the wise. God — that is, Certainty — is found only in the Way of the Gospel.²

Heidegger, too, says: "[. . .] the god-less thinking which must abandon the god of philosophy, god as *causa sui*, is thus perhaps closer to the divine God."³ The idea of God *causa sui*, which is not borrowed from Augustine or Thomas Aquinas but from Cartesian rationalism, is abstract because it demotes God to the level of the existent. Further, according to Heidegger, being is not God and God is not even the foundation of being, since being is only itself. God is subordinated to being because He exists. "Man can neither pray nor sacrifice to this god. Before the *causa sui*, man can neither fall to his knees in awe nor can he play music and dance before this God."⁴ Following this line of reasoning, Richard Rorty (1931–2007) and Gianni Vattimo (b. 1936) say that the God of metaphysics is dead. There is no truth by which intelligence can express a compelling judgment with certainty. There is only a multiplicity of partial truths that are surmountable by new truths posited by men and women. But truth is no longer recognizable. God as absolute is unthinkable. It is necessary to find God elsewhere, through other means. According to Rorty and Vattimo, He is found in Christianity in a practical way in doing good and in charity. Therefore, weak thought says it is necessary to free the Christian faith from the leftovers of Greek thought, which imagines God as absolute and suggests absolute truths, and to free the Church from the arbitrary act of imposing its own truth. Men and women

---

2   Blaise Pascal, *Il Memoriale. Pensieri*, ed. P. Serini (Turin: Einaudi, 1967), 421–422.
3   Martin Heidegger, *Identität und Differenz* (Pfullingen: Neske, 1957), 71 (English translation: *Identity and Difference*, 1969).
4   Ibid., 70.

must wallow in the great sea of the most contradictory pluralism, which without doubt quickly leads to nihilism as the logical haven of relativism. Religion will be able to regain its ground if, leaving aside thought of God, it is dedicated to doing good, that is, to voluntary work. It will be, therefore, a religion without faith. We observe a gradual drift from Luther's faith without reason and therefore without works, to works without faith and therefore without reason. Today, the Church is faced with a problem that is not secondary to pastoral care. We are witnessing an ever-increasing demand for voluntary work but often without faith. The charity of so many Christians is no longer animated by faith in the God who has saved us in Jesus, or by the desire to bring everyone to Him through the works of our own hands, but is more and more often marked by good actions while hiding one's adherence to Christ and the fear of revealing a crucifix or another religious symbol, which could offend those with different religious convictions.

When God is no longer recognizable as the foundation of being, as the One who is on whom everything that is depends, then faith can only limp along, torn between the desire for good and the limitation which reaches out toward Him, because it will be a good without a name, anonymous. God as *causa sui* does not put a limit on faith — almost a vagueness dangerous to life — but attests that reason is capable of God and that the God known through reason is the God of everyone, the Logos recognizable by everyone. Thus, the universality of religion, the *religio vera* accessible to all, when married to faith will ensure Christianity's place as a universal religion. The Church's missionary character is the natural consequence of every man's rationality and of the God who is Logos for all peoples. Faith's object is to see His face, to know *who* this Logos is; it is not about knowing *if* He really is; it is not about knowing *whether* there is a reason for everything from the beginning or merely a primordial chaos that is cause of itself.

The criticism of the philosophy of the rational God that collides with faith highlights an interesting feature for theology, one that should be welcomed to push philosophical inquiry into God to a more in-depth examination. Reason alone is not sufficient to truly know God. The human person is not only reason but also and above all love, the heart. Thus, it is essential to unite reason and love to know God. Only the God known through both reason and love is the true God because He is the fullness. He Himself is Reason and Love. This union illustrates a valuable circularity. Reason reveals God as the supreme being, love as the fulfilment; reason affirms that God necessarily exists, love that the God who is necessary has a heart and unveils His heart; reason brings me to God through the things that I am not, love makes me experience His presence as the presence of love in fullness, as the experience of gift. If the Logos is love, then men and women, who are made of reason and love, have their very foundation and life only in Him. Consequently, the only true religion is the one where God is the fullness of reason and love, to which must correspond faith and charity. Together they can be great things. William of Saint-Thierry (1075–1148) studied and explained this valuable pairing in his treatise *On the Nature and Dignity of Love*, wherein he identifies charity with the vision possessed by the soul to see God, saying that charity has two eyes: love and reason. If one of the two works without the other, it will not have much success. But together they can accomplish much, as they become more and more one eye.

Reason becomes more what it is by passing through what it is not, namely, through denial. Love remains what it is, shedding what it is not; it arises from what is not, but moves toward what is. Reason is simpler, while love leads to happiness. If they help each other — if reason teaches love and love enlightens reason, if reason converts to love and love allows itself to be bound by reason — the two together, according to William of Saint-Thierry, can do great things.[5]

Reason and love reveal all things; they reveal creation as harmony, as a deed accomplished for humanity, and because man lives in it and can find his place and vocation. God, the maker of everything, is in Himself the reason for everything that exists and is the One who is lovable. He is the reason for love. If love is rational, that is, if it is rooted in reason, then it is possible, and men and women can live. Reason cannot exclude love by restricting it to a mere mathematical, factual setting; in turn, love cannot ignore reason by hiding in the meanderings of sentiment, the pure basking in existence that does not bother about the why or the fundamental questions. We will return to these concepts in a more systematic manner later.

A false understanding that explained God as the cold existence of a supreme computer led men and women to seek Him in their sentiments. On the one hand knowledge rules, as factual and programming reason. On the other, the constant effort to limit religion to the confines of reason transforms Christianity into an ethical, world community. There are theologians who applaud this. Having lost sight of the realistic approach to God as uncaused Supreme Being, reason has tried to take the parallel path

---

[5] See William of Saint-Thierry, *De natura et dignitate amoris*, especially III.21. 6–8. In the second part of the book we will examine this work in detail.

of the moral good and has been forced to accept the challenge since God remains an imperative of reason and the life of men and women. It must be repeated that the God perceived by reason is not different from the God believed by faith; the division posited by philosophers is not valid. If it were, reality would manifest as divided in a testable factuality and in a *plus* of unachievable meaning; between the two there would never be any possibility of communication. Such a division is a return to the material distinction between a *res cogitans* and a *res extensa*. If it was so, human beings would be divided between what they consume and what they desire to be. But man's consumption is always accompanied by hope — the hope of living. Reason and faith lead to God Himself: reason led by love tells me who God is, that is, Love who creates; faith tells me that the Creator God is also my Savior, the One who has revealed Himself and who has a wounded heart. The two have the same face. Identity is situated in the truth of Logos and Love. God is Logos and Love. Only the Love-Logos is God.

1.2 The constant temptation to reduce Christianity to its essence, and faith in doing good

The reason of the philosophers often thought it could see in Christianity, in addition to the religion of the spirit, the religion par excellence and its own proper essence. Thus, although it was once believed to be incapable of accessing God, philosophical reason soon declared the overthrow of dogma, Sacred Scripture, and the Church's Tradition. This line of thought was encouraged by the philosophical approach of Hegel, then of Schelling, Kierkegaard, and Feuerbach.[6] Each expresses the desire to define

---

6   A. Schultz, Preface to *L'essenza del cristianesimo*, by Ernesto

what Christianity is, but none of them are willing to listen in silence to the truth about Christianity. "Actually, the Essence of Christianity is not something to be defined, but to be received and accepted.... It must be tradition which tells us the truth."[7] This statement offers an important lesson for all those who think their intellectual powers have found the *Kern* of the problem.

Adolph von Harnack, in particular, systematically attempted to reduce Christianity to its essence, acknowledging it as an ethical message rather then the supernatural principle of the Christ-God made incarnate for our salvation. Harnack writes: "This is the third head, and the whole of the Gospel is embraced under it: to represent the Gospel as an ethical message is no depreciation of its value."[8]

According to Harnack, early Christianity divinized Christ. There was an ethos against external worship and a morality against religion, which Harnack would join in humility, which as pure receptivity expresses the inner need and its openness to God. The unique foundation of ethics is love,[9] a position that became a model to many. Those who were inspired by Harnack's stance include A. Sabatier,[10] A. Loisy,[11] and E. Buonaiuti.[12] Each attempted his own reduction of the Christian faith to its essence. Ultimately, the religious philosophy of Vito Mancuso (b. 1962) also falls into this category. One of the few things

---

Buonaiuti (Vatican City: Lateran University Press, 2009), 5–26.
7   Ibid., 24–25.
8   Adolf von Harnack, *What is Christianity?* (San Diego, CA: The Book Tree, 2006), 70.
9   Ibid., 111–113.
10 See Auguse Sabatier, *Esquisse d'une philosophie de la religion d'après la psychologie et l'histoire* (Paris: Fischbacher, 1987).
11 See Alfred Loisy, *La naissance du christianisme* (Paris: Nourry, 1933).
12 See Ernesto Buonaiti, *L'essenza del cristianesimo.*

Mancuso does not question in his philosophical-religious system is the incarnation of God, but he reduces faith and Christianity to doing good. He negates reason to the point of the extreme power, and faith becomes a deviation of knowledge and a necessity "for the wreck of reason in the face of the sea of life." Before publishing his very successful book, *L'anima e il suo destino*—at the cost of calling a dozen or so dogmas of faith into question[13]—Mancuso, in an earlier and preparatory work, did not hide his daring intention to refound faith.[14] Like Simone Weil, he was convinced that faith had to be rewritten. He was tormented by the idea of freedom and strongly conditioned by the power of evil in the world, from which liberation had to be sought by fighting for freedom. In this great confusion of evil, which distresses and divides the human person, God is either a simple spectator or entirely absent. Mancuso denies the providence of a creator God, and therefore His intervention in history (in a sophisticated way he says that God intervenes in humanity). Further, he denies the dogma of original sin defined as a crime committed by an original couple and handed down by way of generation. This author is a *dialectic I*, who, unable to explain why an innocent child should inherit a fault they have not committed, confirms the inconsistency in two children—one baptized and the other not—who have fun, play, laugh, lie; they both do the same things. From their similarity, he concludes that there is no original fault (sic!).[15] The greatest mystery for Mancuso is why God did not intervene to preserve the ancestors from falling into sin. He

---

13 See Corrado Marucci, "*L'anima e il suo destino secondo Vito Mancuso*," in *La Civiltà Cattolica* 3 (2008), 256–264.
14 See Vito Mancuso, *Rifondazione della fede* (Milan: Oscar Mondadori, 2008).
15 Ibid., 89–90.

answers the question symbolically, with an "appropriate clarification," which helps us to assess the way in which his thought is dressed up:

> God did not intervene in order to give rise to freedom, and his non-intervention then is the symbol of his *never* interfering in the history of the world. God does not intervene with Adam when the serpent comes into play, because God never intervenes on this world's stage, at the natural level of this world. If God wanted to intervene and govern, he would have done it there, in that primordial scene where everything was contained. But God desires freedom, and so throws our souls into the unpredictable game of life.[16]

Obedience is not owed to God because He does not command, and He does not command because He is absent; to God is owed freedom. History is not governed by God but by a "mocking two-faced Janus who makes fun of us and our need for terra firma under our feet."[17] Furthermore, a dual principle, good and evil, reigns from the start, where the "divine sphere, the demonic sphere, the cosmic sphere, the sapiential sphere, in reality, all together, are nothing but the broadest sphere of life which envelops men and women on every side and confuses them...."[18] We are firmly in Manichaean-Gnostic territory.

Faith, too, must be considered no longer as obedience but as freedom. In Mancuso's opinion the fact that the Church obliges one to believe God's revelation is a subjugation of intelligence to a precept. However, the foundations of faith in a man and in history, with is the "product par excellence

---

16   Mancuso, *Rifondazione della fede*, 98–99.
17   Ibid., 23.
18   Ibid., 111.

of freedom,"[19] need to be rethought. Faith ought to be founded on the idea of goodness: "unconditional adherence of the soul to goodness" is the "sole reason for adherence to faith."[20] Faith is addressed to goodness because truth — i.e., being — is not knowable. God is not necessity and omnipotence. The Cross of Christ, the negative moment, which by virtue of evil had divided goodness from omnipotence in God, now transcribes this relationship based on the concept of good.[21] In other words, the Cross of Christ abolishes the necessary God, replacing Him with the good and loving God. Thus, God is recognizable in good actions, and every person who does good not only draws close to God but becomes divine: "In fact the soul of the human person can become divine, and does so when it acts like God, that is through love, according to the interested logic which moves nature and history."[22]

Is love an alternative to sanctifying grace and therefore to faith? If Mancuso is consistent with his reasoning the answer must be yes. Faith as freedom becomes faith as love but without faith. Every person, if he does good, is divine, despite what he believes, because the foundation itself — the idea — is good. Good is more universal than truth! This is not only a new attempt to reduce Christianity to its essence, but, since Mancuso describes himself as a theologian, it is also the beginning of his naturalization. This shift allows him to overcome what he judges to be an aporia of

---

19 Mancuso, *Rifondazione della fede*, 107.
20 Ibid., 37.
21 Ibid., 211. Here the Hegelian background is obvious. Mancuso devoted his doctoral thesis, supervised by P. Coda, to *La salvezza della storia. La filosofia di Hegel come teologia*; it was published under the title *Hegel teologo e l'imperdonabile assenza del Principe di questo mondo* (Casale Monferrato: Piemme, 1996).
22 Ibid., 213.

the day — to believe that Christianity is superior to other religions while unable to proclaim it in good conscience without denying the humanity of others. Good triumphs, but only in a relativistic world in which people will have as many ideas about God as there are about goodness — ideas which are occasionally born or demanded by the time. An examination of Mancuso's ethical-moral consequences reveals the demeaning result of his idea of good — an apparent idea of good — which, according to him ought to be respected and proclaimed. This *good* supports euthanasia, contraception, and artificial insemination, among others. Obviously, Mancuso's good is no longer compatible with faith because there is no longer even reason. Love without truth is false. Good without truth is empty.

It is a great temptation to bring Christianity back to its essence and to reconcile diversity in charity without faith, diversity in love without reason. Instead, it is essential to hold firm to both reason and love, faith and charity. The God whom I encounter in the good must correspond to the God who is and who lives, and His living must be the reason for everything that can live. The God of the philosophers, in the words of Ratzinger, is the God of men and women. The God of men and women can only be the God of reason-love and of revelation. Otherwise, there would only be a god made on a human scale.

2. IF THE GOD OF THE THEOLOGIANS IS NO LONGER THE GOD OF REVELATION

Another idea that weakens faith, taking it to the very brink of extinction, results from interpreting the passion of Jesus as an entry into the suffering of God, and understanding His cry on the Cross as a prayer addressed to the Father through Psalm 21 — a sort of manifestation of the Son's abandonment and God's silence. Hence, Christ would have experienced every possible type of abandonment, even that solitude which is Godless. In that cry Jesus would become the God of the Godless, of those who do not know what to say about God and therefore prefer to remain silent. In the distance of the Son from the Father, in that very solitude, redemption would cause the shortening of the distance of God from the sinner, and men and women would be redeemed. What distance is between Christ and the Father? Is there really an abandonment of the Son?

A number of authors — including Moltmann, von Balthasar, Kasper, and Forte — claim that Jesus's cry on the Cross[23] marks the moment Christ was abandoned by the Father; the Son becomes sin, separating Himself from God, and it is precisely in His separation that the separated human person is reunited. Jesus's abandonment manifests God's love. God sets Himself against Himself: love against omnipotence. Moltmann takes the claim one step further. According to him, God is against Himself, in the sense that the three divine Persons partake in a dialectic dispute. In the end, on the Cross, God becomes what He ought to be, finally knowing how to comply to the needs of men and women, realizing how to bridge their solitude, doubt, abandonment.

Above all, it seems that the post-Auschwitz God (Why not the post-gulag one?) can only be the God of abandonment and silence, who redeems because first He was subject to tragedy. The book of H. Jonas, *The Concept of God after Auschwitz*, argues that after the scandal and the slaughter of Auschwitz, we must realize that an omnipotent God is either lacking in goodness or totally incomprehensible.

---

23 See Mk 15:34.

According to Jonas, God deprived Himself of omnipotence in granting freedom to humanity. If, however, we look at the concept of God after the gulag, more easily and perhaps more spontaneously our mind turns to the responsibility of people. Their moral misery, from an idea or idealogy, reached the point of exploitation and horrific slaughter in the name of that same humanity they wanted to save.

If we look more carefully, God does not appear as impotent but as the One who, granting us freedom, has in some way limited His power of intervention, His range of action. He looks at us as a father beside the son who is learning to walk. The father leaves the son; he lets him walk so that he can learn, but he stays alongside him with his advice, with his word. He picks him up if he falls, but he will not stop him from walking. What often escapes us is that the true God has compromised with us. He Himself became vulnerable by becoming man, by becoming a child. God remains that Child set down on the straw of a poor manger. It is precisely in His compliance that He shows us who He truly is: Love. The One who does not oppress us in His infiniteness, does not impose Himself. He does not desire to receive but only to give, and He can only give because there is nothing He could receive. He can only humble Himself to come to us. All this implies His acceptance of derision and perceived weakness. But love is never weak, even when it forgives. It is precisely in its giving that one sees its true strength, its essence. On the contrary, undeserved strength and arrogance prove to be presumption. If God's love, His freedom, does not stoop down to us, we could not heal our own wounds, wounds of pride and presumed self-sufficiency. His staying silently and discreetly with us, means that God always remains the Child. God made man remains that Child. Only those who enter into this logic of smallness, of dependency, can accept this unique mode of omnipotence. It is God's way. The presumed human omnipotence tells us up to what point God's image can be discerned in humanity. When this image is dimmed, God is lost from view.

Freedom is therefore a risk in humanity, one which God in His love has decided to take. He always warns us against a perverse use of freedom and the deceit of the devilish serpent who directs us against Him and therefore against ourselves.

God is not silent but speaks in His Scriptures, which are always a topical word in the affairs of humanity. The problem is not a mute God, who is weak according to the logic of the world, but a deaf humanity. God speaks, but men and women do not know how to listen to Him. They do not recognize His Word, confused by a desire for greatness without Him and the emptiness of freedom without truth which impoverishes humanity. How could a God who has chosen to make Himself Eucharist for us be silent? Thus, we return to the problem of the God who should speak. What is our concept of God when we attribute to Him simply a sort of muteness imbued with an inexplicable grief? What God are we talking about? The words of J. B. Metz, a theologian from Münster and disciple of Rahner, who then set out on the path of political theology, are highly appropriate. With great shrewdness he said, "However, if there is no God for us in Auschwitz, how can there be a God for us anywhere else?"[24] God was there in that camp of horror and slaughter. Since one could pray there, so — Metz

---

24   Johann Baptist Metz, "Auschwitz: termine locale irrinunciabile di un discorso cristiano su Dio," in Benedict XVI, in *Dove era Dio? Il discorso di Auschwitz*, by **Pope Benedict XVI** (Milan: Oscar Mondadori, 2012), 62.

says in reply to the Czech philosopher, Milan Machovec — it will also be possible to pray afterwards, post-Auschwitz.

Often there is an attempt to redeem this apparent omnipotence of God by introducing the mystery of suffering and death into God Himself (no longer only in Christ as true man). This is also a revolution against self to re-discover oneself more capable of self, more present in the history of the world alongside all those who are suffering. With a discourse which should make many other theologians inclined to reflect on the undue suffering of God, Metz adds:

> I have never believed that the discourse about the God who suffers, or about the suffering *in* God, represents an adequate way to confront the theological scandal elicited by the question of theodicy. For me, the *pathos* of Christian hope is always inserted in the suffering that refers *to* God, not to spill on the daily experiences of suffering a religious suffering too, and not to add to the secular history of suffering a mystical suffering too, but rather to bring together in this negative figure of hope, as suffering which refers back to God, all our contradictory experiences of grief and thus to tear them from the abyss of despair and forgetfulness.[25]

2.1 God's silence as absence?

Let us turn our focus to one aspect of Christ's suffering, Jesus's cry from the Cross: "*My God, my God, why have you forsaken me?*" (Matt 27:46). Christ's abandonment on the Cross remains the symbol of God's silence. It leads

---

25 Metz, "Auschwitz: termine locale irrinunciabile di un discorso di Auschwitz," 60.

The Current Challenges for Faith

men to conclude His absence, an absence which remains against the background of a silent presence and almost a continuous threat for some; an absence which, for many others, proves the truth of His silence. The Son has been abandoned, and it seems that God is silent, distancing Himself. But is that truly the way things are?

G. Rossé writes:

> Christ's abandonment on the cross presents itself as God's answer to the scandal of the suffering of humanity, of the death of the innocent, of the anguish and all the 'why's' which have no answer. It is God's definitive 'yes' to failed humanity, far from God. A yes which does not remove this suffering, does not explain it nor justify it, but inserts it into the Trinitarian Mystery of God, in the relationship of Father-Son love experienced and revealed on the cross. Now, every cry of abandonment involves the Trinity, every 'why?' belongs to the very Mystery of the Divinity.[26]

The abandonment of the Son by the Father would be the descent of Christ into the existential failure of humanity. He would be divided from God, especially in the rejection by God of a man who is thus afflicted by his own self-doubt. Rossé continues, in a way truly symptomatic of this line of thought, which is one of the causes of the decline in faith: "In his abandonment Jesus is the God of the God-less; he presents himself in a special way as the response to contemporary atheism."

Relying on Moltmann, he adds:

---

26 Gerard Rosse, *Il grido di Gesù in croce. Una panoramica esegetica e teologica* (Rome: Città Nuova, 1996), 131.

Christian theology will have to understand the abandoned Jesus, even identify itself with this cry, if it does not want to fail in the face of the problems of the protest atheism of an Ivan Karamazov and a Camus. The God who reveals himself in the abandonment of Christ is not the 'cold heavenly power' and does not 'hover over the bodies', but, continues Moltomann, "is known as human God in the Son of God crucified", a God who takes on deep down the 'why?' of men and women, a God also capable of communicating a totally different existence, beyond Good Friday, on the morning of Easter. More generally, Jesus in abandonment is probably the God of our time, a time in which wars, concentration camps, totalitarian ideologies and many other factors seem to cry out that God is dead. Perhaps today more than ever God's silence has made itself acute, noticeable by human conscience, and men and women are searching for their God. More than ever, men and women today can identify with the face of Christ on the cross, abandoned by his God.[27]

In Orthodox theology this cry of Jesus on the Cross is interpreted differently. Apart from Trembelas, who sees it as a withdrawal of the paternal protection of the Father — the two natures in Christ always remain united in one divine hypostasis — many read it, as a true separation of the Son from the Father, though with different nuances. Metropolitan Kallistos Ware interprets Jesus's exclamation as an authentic experience of spiritual death and a separation of Jesus from God. Paul Evdokimov sees in the cry of the crucified Jesus the moment when the Father

---

27 Rosse, *Il grido di Gesù in croce*, 137–138.

abandons the Son and the Son finds Himself without God; only thus can Christ die for the Godless, even for atheists. S. Bulgakov goes even further in this separation of Jesus from God. For him, the cry of Jesus on the Cross represents the final extremity of the destruction of the crucified divinity. Jesus would no longer be aware of His divine Sonship. On the Cross there is a distancing between the Father and the Son, between the Holy Spirit and the Son, an estrangement that is the painful co-operation of the whole of the Trinity in the death of Christ. The Triune God participates in the suffering of this death. Otherwise, according to Bulgakov, God would remain indifferent. The Holy Spirit is co-crucified with the Son; Love is crucified.[28] Thus, a raised sophiological emphasis leads us to consider in God what is right only in humanity.

It ought to be about a more precise exegesis of the words of Jesus on the Cross. That is, it is essential to ascertain, through the whole of the exegetical tradition, the theologically correct manner of interpreting this abandonment, remembering that the only begotten Son is oriented to the Father,[29] always sees the Father, and only thus reveals Him. This remains true on the Cross. The Lord suffers abandonment in His humanity; He experiences the mortal effects of the separation of sinful humanity from God. He has taken on Himself such disastrous consequences to atone for sin through His suffering and death. Only through this is the person who abandons God through their sin reconciled in Christ with the Father. If abandonment marked the ontological separation of the

---

28 Telesphora Pavlou, "Il cristocentrismo nella teologia ortodossa contemporanea," in *Cristocentrismo. Riflessione teologica*, ed. Paolo Sarafoni (Rome: Città Nuova, 2002), 140–143.
29 See Jn 1:18.

Son from the Father, then either Christ would not be God or God would not have truly redeemed us.

If instead we want to carry out a more à *la page* exegesis, and so see in Christ the teacher of a believing atheism and of a faith continually threatened by denial of God, we must also have the courage to ask ourselves if this abandoned God would be the true response to men and women of our time, in which more and more believers are atheists and atheists are believers in a different way. Often, although one embraces the precarious human existence with all its doubts, one seems to still believe, even if *de facto* he rejects faith. Therefore, is doubt a means to believe? This question will be the subject of the next chapter.

I Believe

REASON, FAITH, AND DOUBT?

THE THREE WORDS IN THE SUBTItle become evermore insistently a harmony of perspectives, of inseparable worlds. Faith entails reason but confronts doubts; doubts deny faith and hold reason in check; reason seeks to encourage faith in an understandable God but due to systematic doubt must suspect the very principle of reasoning and therefore of faith. So, it seems that one is stuck in this triangle which threatens faith one minute and reason the next. Faith is experiencing a crisis, even if reason was the first to renounce its decisive role and leave us frightened by the anti-reason that seems to be a consuming doubt, a fundamental and prevalent scepticism. Let us examine the correct harmonization of reason and faith so that we can understand doubt and separate it in our unconscious from truth and faith, recognizing that it belongs to the uncertainty of our poor reason and is therefore treatable.

1. WHAT DO I MEAN WHEN I SAY "I BELIEVE"?

Faith is a theological virtue and is offered to me freely by God as a gift. But at the same time it is an action proper to humanity. It is a human action — to believe is profoundly human — which surpasses reason and allows me, through God's grace, to welcome a truth that surpasses me, but also gives me self-reason and reason for everything that exists. To believe is to welcome God's Revelation, namely the truth introduced by God for my salvation. To believe is an act of obedience to God, moved by His grace. Otherwise, faith would fall into sentiment. If faith is not obedience, it simply becomes subjective experience. Belief is not subjective necessity matured into knowledge that sees in Jesus the ideal medicine or satisfaction of one's own desires or inner spiritual needs: that kind of faith leads to subjectivism. It is not a theo-logical faith but a human sentiment. We confuse the two all too easily.

Theological faith is a virtue instilled by God into my soul through baptism, which makes me respond to His call, that is, to the fact that God makes Himself known through His Word and His teachings. This invaluable treasure, which is indeed the Revelation of God, is looked after by the Church and is offered to me in a didactic way in the catechism. To believe therefore implies knowledge of the catechism so that I might profess the correct faith in Jesus, my Lord, and through the correct faith foster charity — love for Him — and the hope of possessing Him one day in eternity. I cannot think of loving the Lord correctly without knowing His Word, His Revelation, and therefore, by way of a compendium, the doctrinal catechism. There is not, nor should there be, a divide between faith understood as concepts to learn and faith lived in a personal encounter with the Lord. They are two aspects of the same faith: objective faith (truth to be believed) and subjective faith (a personal act of faith). A subjective faith lived without an objective, doctrinal content quickly becomes illusory, unfounded in the truth or in obedience to the Church. Today, it is fashionable to have a bespoke faith, like a suit. Sadly, the subjective aspect of belief has prevailed against, or to the detriment of, objective faith. Often, even in catechism classes, the notions of faith are not taught to children, but time is spent playing games and designing posters. The underlying reason is that faith should not be *content-led* for the content — the notions of faith — would lead to faith itself drying up. Obviously, this prejudice will lead the child, as he grows up, to develop a faith according to his own vision of Christ and the Church. We must recover the true faith and the harmonious relationship between the two aspects we have mentioned. *In other words, faith in the experience of Jesus cannot be absorbed, nor can personal experience be detached from the correct faith.*

Faith, in fact, is an intellectual and loving assent to supernatural truth. The living encounter with the Lord is realized in the sacraments and especially in the Eucharist, where, in the words of Benedict XVI, there is "a personal encounter with the Lord Jesus in the sacrament."[1] The movement of the living encounter with the Lord to the believing moment of the act of faith implies not just a gradual secularization of the sacraments, which has occurred to a great extent, but also the introduction of subjective experience into faith itself, determining its becoming. Of course, faith is also an encounter with the Lord understood as a loving 'yes' to His Truth, which occurs by virtue of the bond between faith and charity, but it cannot become the fruition of the presence of the Lord: this is not the moment. Usability is given to faith by charity, and charity is nourished by the presence of the Lord in the Eucharist. It is right and proper to order faith and the sacraments in a just relationship. Faith prepares man to receive the sacraments, and the sacraments allow man to truly communicate in the grace of the living God.

---

[1] Pope Benedict XVI, Post-Synodal Exhortation *Sacramentum Caritatis* (February 22, 2007), 50. See also 19.

2. IS IT RATIONAL TO BELIEVE OR IS IT JUST AN ILLUSION?

Is it still possible for people in the twenty-first century, who are increasingly sophistical experts in reality and processing subjects, to believe? Is believing truly rational and human, or is it self-deception turning the mind to abstruse and indemonstrable things?

It is necessary to begin with reality, with things that exist. As soon as I observe things, I realize that reality is greater than me. I become aware that I am not the center of the universe, nor the reason for what exists; I am not even the reason for myself. My reason is not everything. This gives me the opportunity to reflect on the fact that I must necessarily go beyond the finite, beyond myself and beyond my own reason. To question the rationality or the deceptiveness of faith is already a sign that I posses a desire to understand, and this desire is profoundly human; it is the desire for transcendence. To ask the question of God and of faith (even the atheists pose the problem they then deny) is to accept the evidence that something is beyond what is tangible in my experience of life; human intelligence opens itself to the mystery that I grasp in some way as presence but ultimately surpasses me. I either choose the mystery or nothing. There is no alternative. Faith means choosing God and everything. It is the only true alternative to nihilism.

The great Albert Einstein said: "Anyone who does not acknowledge the unfathomable mystery cannot even be a scientist." One day Count Kessler asked Einstein: "Professor! I hear that you are deeply religious." Einstein replied:

> Yes, you can call it that. Try and penetrate with our limited means the secrets of nature and you will find that, behind all the discernible concatenations, there remains something subtle,

I Believe

intangible and inexplicable. Veneration for this force beyond anything that we can comprehend is my religion. To that extent I am, in point of fact, religious.[2]

Einsten provides us with an excellent proof of theodicy, in other words a rational theology of God, rather than a true revealed religion. Faith is a demand of reason. Faith gives a meaningful response to our lives and to all problems, even to those economic ones which seem to have absolute primacy today. One forgets that economic problems cannot be resolved with the euro. The root of the crisis is anthropological and existential. Today, at a time of great social confusion, are we simply faced with the problem of GDP, the sovereign debt? Or the problem of reason apart from God? Is it perhaps true that we are living in a less human, if not at times inhuman, world? It is always more difficult to be born, and it is always easier to die. There is consumption but not production, and so there is importation. With the decline of the GDP, our capacity to be people declines, too, while despair and the most horrendous crimes increase. We are experiencing one of the greatest economic crises, but before becoming a monetary crisis it was a crisis of human and Christian values. The economist Ettore Gotti Tedeschi summarized the problem in the following words:

> We are faced with a new world economic order caused by the fall in birth rates in the West, by the rapid globalisation which has out-sourced too much production in Asia, dividing the world between consumer nations and non-productive and productive but not yet consumer nations.

2   Denis Brian, *Einstein: A Life* (New York: J. Wiley, 1996), 161.

The new current scenario is due largely to unsustainable debt consumer growth, in the Western world.[3]

Is this terrible inversion of reality related to the absence of God or not? If we reflect, we will discover that taking away primacy from God and faith — from reason — and placing humanity at the center, ultimately ends in self-destruction in all the spheres of human life. The myth of omnipotent reason becomes the experience and outcome of a miserable humanity. The inversion of faith in God into a faith in science and the economy has caused the miserable fall of the first principles of human life. The economy stands on true human values, and the human person is based only on God. If God and faith in Him is lacking, the human edifice collapses.

3. I BELIEVE IN GOD, BUT I BELIEVE ONLY IN GOD

If you believe in God with reason and love, you believe only in God and in no one else. The title of this section takes up an expression from the rustic philosopher G. Thibon. It highlights the risk of believing in everything when you do not believe in God — the true God. Man cannot not believe. Men and women accomplish acts of human faith continually, throughout the whole day. If I did not give human credence to what I do not see, I could no longer plan my life or have trust in the future. Thus, to believe is profoundly human. The militant atheist is also a believer but in the opposite; he believes in order to demolish faith, but he won't succeed, for then his own endeavours would lose meaning.

---

3   Ettore Gotti Tedeshci, "Solidarietà tra le Nazioni. Stati Uniti ed Europa insieme per vincere la crisi," *L'Osservatore Romano*, January 20, 2012, 1.

In the words of Fabrice Hadjadj, a young French philosopher and son of Tunisian Jews, who converted to Christianity as an adult: "The reprimand that can be made to atheists is that of not being what they expect to become. By definition an atheist is someone "godless", one must get rid of all idols, trying not to make his atheism an idol."[4]

In addition to the militant atheists (a minority) there are, vice versa, believers who deny reason in faith and make God a shield for themselves. Faith can also be used to one's own advantage or as an ideology. Between the militant atheists and the believers who make God their own private property are those who, in the words of Benedict XVI, while not having faith try to approach God with a sincere heart, that is, those atheists who deep down are seeking, who are at least open to God, initially as someone unknown:

> I think that today too the Church should open a sort of 'Court of the Gentiles' in which people might in some way latch on to God, without knowing him and before gaining access to his mystery, at whose service the inner life of the Church stands. Today, in addition to interreligious dialogue, there should be a dialogue with those to whom religion is something foreign, to whom God is unknown and who nevertheless do not want to be left merely Godless, but rather to draw near to him, albeit as the Unknown.[5]

The pope commented on such people in his address at Assisi in October 2011, during the meeting with different religious leaders for the day of reflection and prayer for peace:

---

4 Lorenzo Fazzini, ed., "Caro laico, non idolatrare l'ateismo. Colloquio con Fabrice Hadjadj," in *Studi Cattolici* 610 (2011), 863.
5 Pope Benedict XVI, "Address to the Roman Curia," (December 21, 2009): *AAS* 1 (2010), 40.

> [These people] take away from militant atheists the false certainty by which these claim to know that there is no God and they invite them to leave polemics aside and to become seekers who do not give up hope in the existence of truth and in the possibility and necessity of living by it. But they also challenge the followers of religions not to consider God as their own property, as if he belonged to them, in such a way that they feel vindicated in using force against others.[6]

There are atheists open to the values of the spirit, to eternal values, who demonstrate once again that believing in God is the only true alternative to a profound confusion of meaning. Through our sincere testimony of faith, they would encounter what they seek and have not yet found.

The Holy Father's proposal to enter into dialogue with the non-believers, who are asking the question of God and are approaching Him in the meantime as one Unknown, was certainly not a canonization of atheism or an attempt to let God remain as Unknown, but rather a suggestion to help them discover the Face of God revealed in Christ and resolve existential doubt by seeing faith not as a dark tunnel but as the only true answer. It is necessary to read this text in light of the whole of his theocentric Pontificate.

4. I DOUBT, THEREFORE I DON'T THINK

Or, I think little, so there is little to doubt. The problem lies in discerning the truth from doubt. Today, it is increasingly predominant, even in Catholic circles, for the starting point in seeking the truth to be doubt. The Cartesian claim

---

[6] Pope Benedict XVI, "Day of Reflection, Dialogue and Prayer for Peace and Justice in the World," (October 27, 2011): *AAS* 11 (2011), 762.

is transformed into *dubito ergo sum*, because deep down the French philosopher was doubting his own existence. As Heidegger highlighted well, behind Descartes' *cogito* is hidden a *volo*, read by Nietzsche as the will to power: man shapes reality through knowledge, therefore he decides. No longer does reality precede the human person, but it is first the human person and then reality.

However, to start from doubt to affirm the truth, if one arrives there, is gnoseologically incorrect. One cannot doubt in order to affirm, since doubt is the denial of a truth which can be doubted only if it exists. It is essential to start from truth, which means starting from reality, from what *is*. One cannot doubt his existence: it is an immediate and obvious truth. The Cartesian *cogito* is not a methodology for knowledge, but rather the affirmation of a new truth: the primacy of the knowledge of being. Therefore, one cannot start from doubt, or he remains a prisoner in a vicious circle, a prisoner of his own doubt. No knowledge, no truthful inquiry about the mechanisms of nature or the laws which regulate it, could begin with doubt but only with the verification of a fact, which is what can be verified. If one postulated doubt as a principle of knowledge, one would not know the law of gravity, for example, nor could we split the atom. The doubt which assails intelligence through lack of due knowledge presents a different case. Here, it is not about a problem of reality — it is not creation which is a defective being in our sight — but a defect of intelligence. The whole dominates my little horizon and sometimes provokes an uncertain judgment or confuses my understanding. In this case, the problem is of a spiritual or metaphysical order in me and not a defect of creation or an error on the part of the Creator. Doubt in faith could arise in me, especially involuntarily, only due to the imminent extent of the mystery to which I give theological assent but not due to the defectiveness of the truth of faith. Doubt does not prove the inconclusiveness of my faith so much as a defect of my intelligence, i.e., its uncertainty. Thus, it is not a check on faith.

There are not two souls fighting within me, that of the believer and that of the doubter, which occasionally give me a crisis of faith. Instead, original sin, which caused a wound to my intelligence, dwells within me.

But one could object that it is false to say that the believer is not burdened by doubt, just as it is false that the non-believer is always calm in their atheistic faith. Cardinal Martini, in fact, said he was inspired by the words of J. Ratzinger in his *Introduction to Christianity* to create in Milan a chair of non-believers, which was equivalent to putting the non-believers in the chair. In 1968 Ratzinger wrote:

> Just as the believer is choked by the salt water of doubt constantly washed into his mouth by the ocean of uncertainty, so the non-believer is troubled by doubts about his unbelief, about the real totality of the world which he has made up his mind to explain as a self-contained whole. [. . .] Just as the believer knows himself to be constantly threatened by unbelief, which he must experience as a continual temptation, so for the unbeliever faith remains a temptation and a threat to his apparently permanently closed world.[7]

Of course, the rationale of the believer is tempted by doubt, as is that of the non-believer. But once again, doubt is an anxiety of reason, not of faith, or to be more precise,

---

[7] Joseph Ratzinger, *Introduction to Christianity*, trans. J. R. Foster (San Francisco: Ignatius Press, 2004), 45.

of reason in the investigation of the truth which surpasses the confines of the immediate and the perceptible, first in the field of the finite and then the transcendent. Of course, I am tempted to dismiss faith, but that temptation is an illness of the intellect which can be cured by an extra dose of reason, by greater steadfastness in seeing that the mystery towers over my little world — that the finite is not *my* world nor the *whole* of the world — and by prayer to Almighty God, through which I ask for my spiritual infirmity to be healed and to be made to see. But to leave faith at the mercy of doubt and doubt at the mercy of faith — to leave the two dimensions to live side-by-side — means to determine the contradictoriness of faith, and soon its uselessness. This was certainly not the tenor of Ratzinger's thought.

Like the man born blind in the Gospel, through humility we, who cannot see, can begin to see. The person who believes while not seeing Christ, is blind.[8] Doubt, therefore, is a sickness of intelligence and is comprehensible only in relation to it and in relation to the truth, just as evil is explicable only in relation to good, or illness in relation to a healthy body. A philosophy or even a theology of doubt, which in the final analysis proves the possibility of being atheistic believers or believers continually threatened by atheism, is simply a rejection of thought. It is an illness of reason and not of faith, an epistemological error. Ratzinger, with some profound words, also wrote about why it is necessary to believe instead, dispelling doubt: "Belief is the conversion in which man discovers that he is following an illusion if he devotes himself only to the tangible. This is at the same time the fundamental reason

---

8   See Jn 9:35–39.

why belief is not demonstrable: it is an about-turn; only he who turns about is receptive to it."[9]

In very clear words John Paul II, in the Encyclical *Fides et Ratio*, summarizes the problem of people who seek truth and never doubt, even when they think of hiding:

> The natural limitation of reason and the inconstancy of the heart often obscure and distort a person's search. Truth can also drown in a welter of other concerns. People can even run from the truth as soon as they glimpse it because they are afraid of its demands. Yet, for all that they may evade it, the truth still influences life. Life in fact can never be grounded upon doubt, uncertainty or deceit; such an existence would be threatened constantly by fear and anxiety. One may define the human being, therefore, as *the one who seeks the truth*.[10]

5. "I BELIEVE" IS TO TRUST IN A TESTIMONY

The Catholic faith is based on the *testimony* of those who lived together with Jesus, those who saw, touched, and heard him and therefore handed that on.[11] They imparted the Lord, giving to the Church, first through their preaching and then through the Gospels and New Testament writings, the historical and supernatural truth of the Lord Jesus. We believe that Christ suffered and died and has truly risen because there are credible witnesses — the apostles — who saw and testified. They gave the supreme witness of their lives through martyrdom. The Apostles

---

9   Ratzinger, *Introduction to Christianity*, 51.
10 Pope John Paul II, Encyclical Letter *Fides et Ratio* (September 14, 1998), 28: *AAS* 91 (1999), 27–28.
11 See 1 Jn 1:1–3.

were succeeded by the bishops, and so the living testimony of the Lord Jesus is perpetuated until the final coming of the Risen One. We can believe only *in communion* with this living testimony. This testimony which extends in time is precisely the Church as the Body of the Lord.

The concept of the transmission of faith, which comes from on high and reaches us by word of mouth, from heart to heart, is implied. To believe is to rediscover the Tradition of the Church so that one might believe *with* the Church. Faith is possible only in the living assembly of the Risen Christ, the Church, and through the living faith of the Lord's Mystical Body. Faith is a gift which comes from on high and which incorprates me with my brothers and sisters into the community of the saved. The Church is the place where I learn the faith, profess it, and celebrate it. Just as there cannot be a faith without the testimony of those who have seen, so there is no faith without the Church. Our faith is individual insofar as one believes with the whole Church, with the whole of the Church's Tradition.

Whoever believes can never be alone. Believing is always as the *body* of Christ. This communial reality preserves us from loneliness, from individualism, from the do-it-yourself faith that prevails in today's culture. To believe today, in a certain sense, is more urgent than yesterday; it is the only true restoration of a shattered world.

May the Lord deign to increase our faith, and with the father of the epileptic child in the Gospel, may we also say with humility: "I believe; help my unbelief" (Mk 9:24). Echoing the words of the blind Bartimaeus (Mk 10:46-52), who represents every person fallen into a servile condition of mendicity, we will be able to ask the Lord: "Help me to see You with reason, to desire You with love, to believe with faith, to unite myself forever with You in charity."

In order to clarify what an act of faith is, we must now turn to another subject: the essential distinction between supernatural faith and religious belief.

"We worship what we know" (Jn 4:22)
FAITH AND RELIGIOUS BELIEF

INTRODUCTION

Faith and belief, two aspects which concern the religious dimension of the human person, converge in some respects but remain substantially different. Let us begin this reflection on them by turning to London physicist and cosmologist Paul Davies, a well-known researcher and respected scientific popularizer. In a work entitled *The Mind of God,* Davies sketches out the discourse on reason and faith:

> Human beings have all sorts of beliefs. The way in which they arrive at them varies from reasoned argument to blind faith. Some beliefs are based on personal experience, others on education, and others on indoctrination. Many beliefs are no doubt innate: we are born with them as a result of evolutionary factors. Some beliefs we feel we can justify, others we hold because of "gut feelings". Obviously many of our beliefs are wrong, either because they are incoherent, or because they conflict with other beliefs, or with the facts.[1]

Davies presents a very precise analysis of what belief is. Beliefs are often in conflict, so much so that the early

---

[1] Paul Davies, *The Mind of God* (New York: Simon & Schuster, 1992) 19.

philosophers were inspired to investigate on a common, rational level, removing all possible mythical constructions and thus providing some irrefutable rules, such as logical deduction. Davies, as a non-religious person, remains open to the philosophical question which postulates a meaning and a truth that surpasses the finite and the measurable — a question which explains the why of the universe's existence and why I am in the universe, too. Davies argues that

> only in science, and especially mathematics, have the ideals of the Greek philosophers been upheld (and in philosophy itself, of course). When it comes to addressing the really deep issues of existence, such as the origin and meaning of the universe, there is a strong temptation to retreat into unreasoned belief. Even scientists are not immune from this.[2]

Science, with its rigor — first inductive and then deductive when formulating a universal law — is a useful tool for understanding the universe without seeking refuge in a belief, which often turns out to be a rejection of thought. The same logical structure which constitutes measurable things — Davies is profoundly convinced — contains within itself paradoxical limitations, by which we could never grasp the totality of existence through observation. There are questions which lie outside and need a more perfect knowledge of a superior order. While Davies does not grasp this, we will see that it is the only way to give reason to belief and definitively surpass it in the knowledge of the truth, and of God, through faith. Faith, which is in an order of superior knowledge, is seen and desired by reason and by science. In this way faith satisfies the demands of

---

2   Paul Davies, *The Mind of God*, 19-20.

philosophy to find a common terrain on which to sketch out a rational religious discourse that is valid for every person and religion, thus avoiding a priori conflicts and dogmatization. True faith provides a common base, of a rational and supernatural order, so that all religions can meet beyond what is solely factual or socially useful and work toward peaceful co-existence. And so, we examine the merits of our topic.

1. WORSHIP OF GOD AFTER KNOWING HIM

In our reflection on the fundamental distinction between faith and belief, let us turn to the Gospel episode of the Samaritan at Jacob's well, that splendid conversation with Jesus which reveals Him as the longed-for Messiah[3] Among the numerous requests the Lord makes of the woman, one is most important. The Samaritan woman's thirsting for truth moves from ignorance of the profound meaning of Jesus's words—"Give me some water"—to a true understanding, and she can therefore worship the true God. The Lord interrupts His profound discourse for a moment and says to her, "Call your husband." The lady, who was living in a morally disordered situation, replies, "I have no husband." Jesus goes on, in an ironic fashion, "In fact you have had five husbands and the one you have now is not your husband." The Samaritan woman did not have a husband and so could not bring him to Jesus. St. Augustine's comment on this passage is very interesting, and brings us to a greater understanding of the value of honest faith in the knowledge of God. The saint from Hippo explains in highly allegorical fashion the meaning of the five husbands and of the one who the lady should have presented to the Lord. The five symbolize the five

---

3   See Jn 4:7–29.

senses of the body, which point to knowledge of material things and lead us to see only the things of this world; the husband is the symbol of the intellect, which, enlightened by wisdom, moves us to see eternal things and so to believe in God. The soul, which is led by these five senses — that is, moves under the protection of these five husbands — is still weak. As it matures, if it accepts the teaching of wisdom, something true and legitimate will happen to those five husbands: wisdom will guide them toward eternity. At the start, the Samaritan woman was not capable of giving way to the true husband. Still dominated by the senses, her intellect was at fault. St. Augustine describes this truth in a wonderful passage:

> This husband had not yet succeeded to those five husbands in that woman. And where he does not succeed, error sways. For when the soul has begun to be capable of reason, it is ruled either by the wise mind or by error: but yet error does not rule but destroys. Wherefore, after these five senses was that woman still wandering, and error was tossing her to and fro. And this error was not a lawful husband, but a paramour: for that reason the Lord says to her, *You have well said, I have not a husband. For you have had five husbands.* The five senses of the flesh ruled you at first; you have come to the age of using reason, and yet you are not come to wisdom, but art fallen into error. Therefore, after those five husbands, *this whom you now have is not your husband.* And if not a husband, what was he but a paramour? And so, *Call*, not the paramour, but *your husband*, that you may receive me with the understanding, and not by error have some false notion of

me. For the woman was still in error, as she was thinking of that water; while the Lord was now speaking of the Holy Ghost. Why was she erring, but because she had a paramour, not a husband? Put away, therefore, that paramour who corrupts you, and *go, call your husband*. Call, and come that you may understand me.[4]

"That you may understand me." The Lord asks the Samaritan woman to use her intelligence, led by wisdom, to believe in Him as the true Messiah, that is, to "understand him." From understanding one reaches worship of Him. Faith needs to understand correctly and reject error to know the truth, so that worship of God might be in spirit and truth. It is not material, not tied to the senses, because God does not have a body, but it is spiritual and enlivened by the living Spirit.

The dialogue between Jesus and the Samaritan woman turns to the debate between the true temple of the Jews and the true mountain on which to worship God for the Samaritans. The woman, who has recognized Jesus as a prophet, questions Him about which is the true mountain on which to worship God. In this way she wishes to resolve a bitter dispute, one which divided and antagonized two neighboring peoples — the Jews and the Samaritans. However, it was a dispute still tied to the old husbands, St. Augustine says. In fact, "Both peoples contended in ignorance, because they had not the husband: they were inflated against each other, on the one side on behalf of the temple, on the other on behalf of the mountain."[5]

---

[4] St. Augustine, *Commentary on the Gospel of John*, Homily XV, 22.
[5] Ibid., 23.

Now, as the woman begins to reason better, Jesus guides her to knowledge of true worship and to becoming a true worshipper of God. Led by the intellect enlightened by faith, she must understand that God is spirit. God is the only inaccessible and immaterial one — therefore omnipresent — who asks us to seek Him and allows Himself to be found in the true faith that worships in spirit and truth. If God were to have a body, we would have to worship Him on the mountain because the mountain is a place, or worship Him in the temple because the temple is material; but God wants to be worshipped by every man and woman in the temple which is themselves, enlightened and guided by the Spirit of truth. Thus, Jesus reveals the true God to the woman, the God who will topple the wall of separation which divided the Jews from the Greeks.[6] Now there is no longer a wall but a common foundation: the cornerstone which is the Lord Jesus Christ.[7] In fact, in John's Gospel, Jesus presents Himself as the true temple of God, in which the Father is to be found — "The Father and I are one" (Jn 10:30) — and the one Lord is to be worshipped — "Destroy this temple and in three days I will raise it up." The Evangelist soothes the perplexity of his listeners by clarifying: "But he was speaking of the temple of his body" (Jn 2:19–2). God can only be worshipped in Christ, the One who is the "foundation" of all possible access to God. He is the mediator between God and humanity.[8] Thus, we arrive at the universality of faith in Christ and therefore the substantial distinction between faith and religious belief on which we will now focus.

---

6 See Eph 2:14.
7 See Eph 2:19; Pet 2:1
8 See 2 Tim 1:5.

2. FAITH AND BELIEF: DISTINCTIONS AND DISTANCE

What is theological faith? It must be defined precisely to reveal its foundation and thus the reason to believe. The Catechism summarizes the issue as follows:

> Faith is first of all a personal adherence of man to God. At the same time, and inseparably, it is a free assent to the whole truth that God has revealed. As personal adherence to God and assent to his truth, Christian faith differs from our faith in any human person. It is right and just to entrust oneself wholly to God and to believe absolutely what he says. It would be futile and false to place such faith in a creature.[9]

The act of faith begins in the human person since God is unchanging truth, does not deceive, and cannot nor does not want to deceive.[10] This, then, is the reason for the personal adherence of men and women to God—adherence with their intelligence and their love guided and enlightened by grace. Intellect and will are accompanied by actual divine grace, which precedes and helps, enlightening the eyes of the mind and moving the heart toward God.[11] So, faith can also be defined as an inner enlightenment provoked by God through His Spirit (cf. Matt 16:17).

From *adhering* to God, that is, from this becoming *contiguous with* Him and with His Word of infallible love, flows the free *assent* to the revealed truths, to the whole of God's Revelation. Faith takes shape as a human response to God Who reveals Himself. It is fully human because reason

---

9   *Catechism of the Catholic Church* 150.
10 See First Vatican Council, Dogmatic Constitution *Dei Filius*, c. 3: DS 3008.
11 See Second Vatican Council, Dogmatic Constitution on Divine Revelation, *Dei Verbum*, 5.

and will are not abolished or humiliated but empowered by grace to welcome a greater gift, a truth of a superior order. Therefore, faith is essentially obedience to the revealing God. *Ob-audire*, the etymology of the word "obedience," makes us understand that we cannot believe without listening to God, to His truth. A careful listening to the truth transcends us to move us to faith. So, without a prior turning to truth with reason, it is difficult to conceive of faith as obedience. If faith is not obedience, it becomes simply a personal and intimate experience. Often it becomes, even according to some theorists, a *constraint* to change into *freedom* because faith lives in the now. If you scrutinize the origin of faithful thought, you discover that that deep-down human access to the truth, the very cogency of truth for life, is denied. The Catechism clearly states:

> To obey (from the Latin *ob-audire*, "to hear or listen to") in faith is to submit freely to the word that has been heard, because its truth is guaranteed by God, who is Truth itself. Abraham is the model of such obedience offered us by Sacred Scripture. The Virgin Mary is its most perfect embodiment.[12]

Therefore, faith implies entrusting ourselves to the Word of God, to God as a Person who speaks to us. The Catechism tells us that entrustment — or better yet, closeness to God — does not stem from purely subjective motives or the short-lived needs of the heart, but from His placement of His Being as the foundation of the reality of His Word. Once again, it is worth underlining that faith requires the foundation of reason to be open to truth. Otherwise, it risks being confused with one of the many

---

12   CCC, 144.

sentiments which crowd the heart, and the greater risk is confusing God with our heart.

Instead we ask ourselves, "What is belief?" This question was analyzed systematically in John Paul II's Encyclical *Fides et Ratio*. To shed some light on this concept we must recall the fact that the human person is a being who naturally seeks the truth. One cannot live without the truth or without reaching it at least partially, namely by sketching out responses to the many questions which crowd the mind. Merely to raise questions of a strictly existential, philosophical, or religious order is a sign of the need to find a foundation, that is, a truth. What's more, men and women do not live alone, and no one can live for themselves. Every person is born and grows in a specific social, cultural, and religious context. Many traditions shape people's feelings from their infancy. Much information received from the world and from one's own environment can be verified, with the growth and passage of time, in light of reason, the scientific method, and facts themselves which contradict or prove previous facts. People want certainty, and so they scrutinize their knowledge via a critical attention to reality. Thus, many truths become irrelevant and new ones are acquired. But not everything is verifiable, and it is not desirable — not even properly human — to doubt those things which are communicated to us by trustworthy people, like parents and teachers. Which individual is able to trace the historical and experiential path of the great religious traditions of humanity and so sound out all their details with the aim of having a certifiable knowledge of them? Who would be able to verify all the scientific hypotheses and claim that they had found the only reliable one? Whoever thinks of believing only after carefully scrutinizing all the religions is like the person looking for a needle in a haystack. It is better to simply buy a new needle; it is better to start from the truth.

"This means that the human being — the one who seeks the truth — is also *the one who lives by belief.*"[13] Many things are accepted as belief, which is therefore no less human than reason. Belief is about seeing its intimate explanation.

Therefore, *belief* is the act of entrusting oneself to the knowledge of other people. In this regard, *Fides et Ratio* observes a tension between a still primitive aspect of knowledge and a more positive aspect which opens to human interrelationality. Belief, while it still seems weak because it makes us accept the word of another without verification, allows us, in this way, to establish a friendly and interpersonal bond with so many others. After all, one does not have isolated or self-referential knowledge of things. One knows believing and entrusting oneself to the knowledge of others involves, as John Paul II writes,

> an important tension. On the one hand, the knowledge acquired through belief can seem an imperfect form of knowledge, to be perfected gradually through personal accumulation of evidence; on the other hand, belief is often humanly richer than mere evidence, because it involves an interpersonal relationship and brings into play not only a person's capacity to know but also the deeper capacity to entrust oneself to others, to enter into a relationship with them which is intimate and enduring.[14]

Belief, then, implies an inter-personal relationship, namely, trusting in the veracity of another person. It can

---

13   Pope John Paul II, *Fides et Ratio*, 31.
14   Ibid., 32.

therefore be open to a very fruitful human interrelationality. In fact, "knowledge through belief, grounded as it is on trust between persons, is linked to truth: in the act of believing, men and women entrust themselves to the truth which the other declares to them."[15] Belief unites the search for truth and trust in another person. Man entrusts himself to a person when that person is believed to be worthy of the greatest trust. Belief moves toward faith but remains in the preliminary stage until there is proof — echoing Johannine vocabulary, we might say "knowledge" — that the one who speaks to me is truthful and worthy of my trust, that he is one to whom I can give the whole of my existence.

So, belief and faith agree that both trust by means of a testimony; both are an acceptance of a truth which I cannot directly verify but which I receive based on the word of others. The substantial difference consists in two premises which together lead to a third:

a) The believer must verify, above all, the truthfulness of the witness, who must be credible in their own life. One thinks of the martyrs for the Christian faith, beginning with the Apostles, who attested to the truth of the Gospel by giving their own lives for love of Christ and of the oppressor, to be saved;

b) the witness must speak to us about God with God's words and not simply their own human words. It is essential to move with *prophetic* direction, in which the messenger confirms their word with the signs that accompany it, that is, by miracles[16];

c) finally — and here we see the singularity of Christ and therefore of Christianity — the witness must identify him or herself with their own testimony; prophet and

---

15 Pope John Paul II, *Fides et Ratio*, 32.
16 See Deut 18:18–21 in relation to Jn 10:36–38 and Mk 16:20.

prophecy must necessarily be one thing. Only the One who is recognizable as coming from God, equal to Him, is credible and brings the word of truth. Only the One who manifests Himself as mediator between God and humanity,[17] offering the definitive sign of God in our midst with His own life, passion, death, and resurrection[18] and carrying out God's work, is the true witness.

Belief therefore stops before faith. Faith can be professed only in God and in the One who is the Son of God, equal to the Father: "Believe in God, believe also in me" (Jn 14:1). Without deceit you can believe in the Word of another, but you can only truly believe when the One who is speaking is not really *another* but God Himself in our midst who gives witness to the Eternal. The Son has come to dwell with us. In Christ we have the unity between witness and testimony, between author and object of faith. Every prophecy can only find its fulfilment in Him. Whoever welcomes Christ has the fullness of truth, for in Him, in His Person, there is immediate access to God. Beyond Christ there is no prophet; beyond Christ there is no faithful witness (Rev 1:5). He is fullness.

Therefore, faith requires a fundamental pairing: the One who persuades me to believe through His word and His testimony is my Lord. There is not, nor can there be an intermediary between God and humanity other than God Himself made man. Christianity therefore claims to be the only salvific way that leads to God because there is no other outside of Christ or what He has established, namely, His Church and His sacramental body.

Through faith, which is rooted in the definitive testimony of the Son who reveals the Father, we have a breakthrough

---

17 See 1 Tim 2:5.
18 See Mt 12:40.

regarding belief. Faith alone makes us adhere personally to God and makes us infallibly believe in His truth. It reveals to us the only credible God who by virtue of His being-with-us and His effective testimony, is the true God. Belief remains at the human level of testimony and is often nourished by the great religious traditions that are fruits of human experiences and real treasures of popular wisdom. If belief were to "prove" the supernatural nature of its testimony, it would necessarily decide in favor of Christianity, because it could not yet ascend alone to the supernatural level. It is necessary to cast one's lot in with the full and definitive truth.

We can summarize the whole matter with the following warning, taken from the Declaration *Dominus Iesus* by the Congregation for the Doctrine of the Faith:

> For this reason, the distinction between *theological faith* and *belief* in the other religions, must be *firmly held*. If faith is the acceptance in grace of revealed truth, which "makes it possible to penetrate the mystery in a way that allows us to understand it coherently," then belief, in the other religions, is that sum of experience and thought that constitutes the human treasury of wisdom and religious aspiration, which man in his search for truth has conceived and acted upon in his relationship to God and the Absolute.[19]

3. REVELATION IN CHRIST AS FULLNESS

This reflection has led us to an important milestone. We must now carefully distinguish between faith and belief and then see the errors, still recurrent today, related to religious syncretism. Systematic reflection on reality arose

---

19   Congregation for the Doctrine of the Faith, Declaration *Dominus Jesus* (August 6, 2000), 7.

in response to the need for the verification of numerous human assertions fostered by a religious-mythological vision. Philosophy is born through the separation from myth, that is, from a totality of knowledge derived from the divinization of things and natural phenomena. How was it possible to believe in those things created by human fantasy, or in any case, the fruit of human traditions? Philosophy — rational enquiry about the real — was cut loose from the concept myths offered about God, not by creating an alternative myth but by using an element common to everyone and verifiable by everyone: human reason. The birth of philosophy testifies to the fact that God, if He exists, must be recognizable by reason and so can only be at least as universal as human reason. Religion, at least partially, was thus purified of imaginative, and especially blasphemous (if not truly devilish), elements. The Greek philosophical context, in search of the true logos which alone can satisfy humanity, allowed the Church Fathers to open a courageous discourse with pagan interlocutors, an intercourse not founded on faith but on that common element which is the human logos. The dialogue with religions cannot be founded on individual religions or religious traditions but only on the universal basis common to all, namely, human reason. Christianity was able to compete in the challenge because it proclaims that God is the Logos, the Reason, the Meaning of all that exists, the Creator, and that this Logos became flesh, coming into our midst. If God is everything, He was also able to allow Himself to be seen by humanity, to reveal Himself. Christianity surpassed religion by presenting itself as the religion of all and offering to everyone the Savior, the God recognizable by all because, in the words of St. Paul, "in him the whole fullness of deity dwells bodily" (Col 2:9). Christianity is

"We worship what we know"

about explaining precisely what this fullness consists of.

Christianity must be understood as attestation of the divinity of Christ communicated in the personal union of the Word to humanity. Jesus is God, and between God and Jesus there is no division, just as there can be no division between the salvific work of Christ and the mission of the Holy Spirit in the Church.

All that God has said finds its finality, its revelatory fullness, in Christ the Son. Christ is the Word; by saying Son, God has said everything. After Christ, God does not nor cannot say anything else. Anyone looking for more beyond Christ is like one who wanders around endlessly without ever finding their goal. As the illuminating words of the Catechism proclaim, "Christ, the Son of God made man, is the Father's one, perfect and unsurpassable Word. In him he has said everything; there will be no other word than this one."[20] All is created and revealed in Christ and through Him. The Church believes there will be no other revelation beyond Christ and that the revelation of Christ brings to fulfilment every word of God. Anyone who welcomes Christ welcomes the way, the truth, and the life.[21] Revelation is thus complete. Now "it remains for Christian faith gradually to grasp its full significance over the course of the centuries."[22]

4. ERRORS CONCERNING THE FAILED DISTINCTION BETWEEN FAITH AND BELIEF

We have just alluded to the syncretistic confusion about religion. Above all, it stems from a failure to distinguish correctly between belief, which leaves us in a natural and

---

20 CCC, 65.
21 See Jn 14:6.
22 CCC, 66.

human state, and faith, which implies supernatural Revelation and therefore requires from men and women an assent of theological faith. All religions cannot be placed on the same level as Christianity, as if it were merely one among many. Rather, following the path of reason and truth, it is essential to side with the true religion. On the threshold of the new millennium, *Dominus Iesus* highlighted an important problem that arises when due account is not taken of the right distinction between faith and belief:

> This distinction is not always borne in mind in current theological reflection. Thus, theological faith (the acceptance of the truth revealed by the One and Triune God) is often identified with belief in other religions, which is religious experience still in search of the absolute truth and still lacking assent to God who reveals himself. This is one of the reasons why the differences between Christianity and the other religions tend to be reduced at times to the point of disappearance.[23]

The fundamental error in this case is to believe that God ought to be beyond every historical event, every religion, and so beyond Christ, too. Religions, then, are a partial manifestation of God.[24] From here, it is a small step to postulate equal rights between all religions, that is, syncretism. Thus, many believe that

> the theory of the limited, incomplete, or imperfect character of the revelation of Jesus Christ, which would be complementary to that found in other religions, is contrary to the Church's faith. Such

---

23 CDF, *Dominus Iesus*, 7.
24 See Congregation for the Doctrine of the Faith, *Notification on the Book Toward a Christian Theology of Religious Pluralism*, (January 24, 2001).

a position would claim to be based on the notion that the truth about God cannot be grasped and manifested in its globality and completeness by any historical religion, neither by Christianity nor by Jesus Christ.[25]

This position results in a Christological problem — a depletion of the mystery of Christ. To understand what is at stake, we must ask ourselves whether a separation between Jesus and the Word could ever be possible. Can we consider a presumed action of God beyond the Son? The question stands or falls if Christ is the Word of God, the Son consubstantial with the Father. Already the outdated and surreptitious distinction between Jesusology and Christology, in other words between the Jesus of history and the Christ of faith, which began with R. Bultmann but found compelling opponents in other Protestant theologians, (one thinks especially of W. Pannenberg and J. Moltmann[26]), resurfaces in the divide between Jesus and God as Logos. Jesus would be a historical manifestation of the Word but not the Word of the Father, the One who brings the whole of Revelation to fulfilment. Along with the Christological Councils of antiquity, we must affirm that Jesus Christ is the Son and Word of the Father.[27] For that reason, a Christian must firmly believe that Jesus of Nazareth, Son of Mary and Savior of the world, is the sole-begotten Son of God — who was made flesh, died, and is risen — and is the sole mediator of salvation for all people.[28] Through the unity of the salvific plan and the

---

25   CDF, *Dominus Iesus*, 6.
26   See René Latourelle, *Finding Jesus through the Gospels* (New York: Alba House, 1979), 82–88.
27   See First Council of Nicea (325): Denz. no. 125; Council of Chalcedon (431): Denz. no. 301.
28   See Council of Trent, *De peccato originali*: Denz no. 1513;

mystery of the incarnate Word, salvation is accomplished *in* and *through* Jesus Christ without divisions. For that reason, John Paul II, in the Encyclical *Redemptoris Missio* declared:

> To introduce any sort of separation between the Word and Jesus Christ is contrary to the Christian faith. St. John clearly states that the Word, who "was in the beginning with God," is the very one who "became flesh" (Jn 1:2, 14). Jesus is the Incarnate Word—a single and indivisible person. One cannot separate Jesus from the Christ or speak of a "Jesus of history" who would differ from the "Christ of faith." The Church acknowledges and confesses Jesus as "the Christ, the Son of the living God" (Mt 16:16): Christ is none other than Jesus of Nazareth: he is the Word of God made man for the salvation of all.... In the process of discovering and appreciating the manifold gifts-especially the spiritual treasures-that God has bestowed on every people, we cannot separate those gifts from Jesus Christ, who is at the centre of God's plan of salvation.[29]

Similarly, the Declaration *Dominus Iesus* reiterates, contrary to J. Dupuis's erroneous ideas of religious pluralism:

> It is likewise contrary to the Catholic faith to introduce a separation between the salvific action of the Word as such and that of the Word made man. With the incarnation, all the salvific actions of the Word of God are always done in unity with the human nature that he has assumed for the

---

De iustificatione: Denz. nos. 1522, 1523, 1529, 1530. See also Second Vatican Council, *Lumen Gentium*, 8; 14; 28; 49; 60.

29 John Paul II, Encyclical Letter *Redemptoris Missio* (December 7, 1990), 6.

salvation of all people. The one subject which operates in the two natures, human and divine, is the single person of the Word.[30]

Therefore, it is necessary to correctly consider the theandric tendencies of Jesus Christ, which, although he is human and therefore limited, are the actions of the one divine Person, and have as subject the divine person of the incarnate Word, who is "true God and true man,"[31] according to the Chalcedonian formula. For this reason, the salvific actions of Christ "possess in themselves the definitiveness and completeness of the revelation of God's salvific ways, even if the depth of the divine mystery in itself remains transcendent and inexhaustible."[32]

The logic of religious pluralism, portrayed as the possibility of dialogue with other religions beyond the salvific uniqueness of Christianity, would also see the work of the Holy Spirit as parallel to that of Christ, although more extensive. The Holy Spirit would act where Christ does not reach with His grace — beyond the confines of the economy of the incarnate Word — and would encourage a more universal salvific vision of God beyond the particular.

In truth, the Holy Spirit who acts since the Resurrection is none other than the Spirit of Christ, the Spirit sent by the Father in the name of the Son,[33] who guides man to the whole truth.[34] The verb used (*odegései*) indicates guiding to the truth along a path (the *odós*), which can only be Christ, the way which leads to life in truth. The

---

30 CDF, *Dominus Iesus,* 10. Here the doucment refers to St. Leo the Great, *Tomus ad Flavianum:* Denz., no. 294.
31 Councile of Chalcedon, *Symbolum Chalcedonense*: Denz., n. 301. Cf. St. Athanasius, *De Incarnatione,* 54, 3: *SC* 199, 458.
32 CDF, *Dominus Iesus,* 6.
33 See Jn 14:26.
34 See Jn 16:13.

Spirit takes from Christ and proclaims Him and thus glorifies the Son, because all that is the Son's is the Father's.[35] So, there is one salvific economy which is realized through Christ in the Holy Spirit, leading everything back to the Father.[36] Just as Christ is of God, so the Holy Spirit is of Christ. There is no Holy Spirit beyond Christ, just as there is no place of salvation outside Christ and his Church.

There is no other name under heaven through which we can be saved.[37] All that is good, even if it is insufficient and imperfect — such as truths traceable in other religions — can only be a reflection of the one truth which is the incarnate Logos. These partial elements, dispersed here and there, cry out for their fullness, which is present only in Christ and His Church. All followers of other religions are therefore ordered to the Church and are called to become members of it for salvation.[38]

In conclusion, it is useful to notice that the now normal expression in theology, "the God of Jesus Christ," risks fostering a conception of the diastasis in Christ between Jesus and the Word equal to the Father. Further, the phrase could lead to the conception of a possible action on the part of the Word of God apart from Christ. All that is outside Christ is outside God Himself because Jesus is God. In the end, to consider all religions as only flashes of a divinity that transcends them simply means pushing the question about the true God and about how we can know His Face further away. God the Father, while remaining transcendent and immeasurable, has given the Son, so that through Him we might return to God in

---

35   See Jn 16:13–15.
36   See CDF, *Dominus Iesus*, 12.
37   See Acts 4:12.
38   See *Lumen Gentium*, 13, 16; See also CDF, *Dominus Iesus*, 20–22.

His Spirit of truth. It is essential to turn to the truth and embrace it in love. The question is about verifying whether Christianity is capable of that and discovering what the alternative would be if it is not.

5. CONVERSION AS "PASSAGE" FROM BELIEF TO FAITH

One necessary consequence of what we have said so far is that men and women are natural believers and are religious. Many paths lead to belief, and men and women can only live by belief. Faith, on the other hand, is the encounter with God in truth and charity. God is found through faith — God who is necessarily one and the God of all. He is recognizable as such if one begins from a premise that is human and therefore common to all: reason. Reason guides man along the paths of truth, so that he can ultimately find in God the fullness of truth, and the fullness of being and love. God is this fullness. Only the God who is truth and love is the believable God — the true God — accessible to every person, without distinction of race, culture, or religion. Faith, so to speak, goes beyond the (natural) religion of humanity and leads men and women to accept the supernatural mystery. Faith places men and women before God, teaching them to listen to His Word, to recognize it, and finally to welcome it into their own lives.

Faith, therefore, is a *conversion* which begins with reason, moves the heart, and turns to Being, to the God of love and truth. With the help of grace, anyone who turns to Being, to truth, and embraces it in charity, converts and has faith. Anyone who turns their lives to God and abandons idols, who confirms their beliefs in the light of knowledge and human reason, finally embraces the One who is the Logos and the Reason for everything — Reason which is Love itself.

The Sacred Scriptures present us with models and examples of this conversion. We recall Abraham, father of us all in faith. He received God's invitation to abandon his land, his securities, his human destiny, and to set out toward God's land, which would become a new dwelling for him and his descendants. Called to leave the idols of Canaan and go toward the land of the living God, Abraham was offered a new life.[39] Abraham believed God's Word, and through his perseverance, had an opportunity to experience His presence, to ascertain the truthfulness of that Word of salvation. Abraham believed and became the father in faith, the first of those who, moved by God, will leave their securities and their customs to go toward God and discover His Face. Faith is a journey toward the light, toward the truth. Abraham welcomed the true God, the God who guided him toward the promised land, the land of freedom and truth.

In the New Testament, we encounter the splendid figures of the Holy Magi from the East.[40] Led by the Messiah's star, these great wise men — today we should call them astronomers — came to Jerusalem and then Bethlehem to worship Jesus. The star finally rested above the place where the newborn King, the true King, could be found. He was not what they had imagined finding in Herod's palace, but a different kind of king. They had to learn that God is different from the images of religions and the customs people would normally attribute to him. The Magi went into the house and "saw the child with Mary his mother; and they knelt down and paid him homage" (Matt 2:11). Before the Child of God, lying in the arms of His Mother, they had a true conversion, which immediately led to adoration. Conversion led to worship of God. They learned

---

39   See Gen 12.
40   See Mt 2.

who God really is; how God loves so completely that He even assumes the condition of a slave and ties Himself to a covenant with humanity; why God created the world and the stars; what the meaning of man in the universe is. They came with their ideas about the divine, probably inferred from the traditional religion of Zoroastrianism and they returned with a new heart, a new intelligence. They saw the true Light. The gifts offered signified the homage of those who recognized in the Child the One who is "true God and true man." They found the One whom they were seeking, and their hearts were now filled with joy. Thus, they returned to their country by a different route; they left the previous one, the one which led to Herod, and set out on a new path, that of life. The words of Benedict XVI summarize this rich page of Matthew's Gospel:

> The wise men from the east are a new beginning. They represent the journeying of humanity toward Christ. They initiate a procession that continues throughout history. Not only do they represent the people who have found the way to Christ: they represent the inner aspiration of the human spirit, the dynamism of religions and human reason toward him.[41]

Finally, a model not of conversion or the journey to faith but of perfect and complete faith, albeit always increasing in perfection, is the Virgin Mary. She welcomed God's Word. She obeyed her God and thus became His Mother. In her is the consent of faith which becomes salvific *space* for the whole of humanity.[42] She prepares a place for God

---

[41] Pope Benedict XVI, *Jesus of Nazareth: The Infancy Narratives*, trans. Philip J. Whitmore (London: Bloomsbury Publishing, 2012), 97.
[42] See Lk 1:38.

in our midst, first in her own mind and heart, then in her womb. Without her faith we would never have been saved.

It is always so touching to hear the words of St. Bernard of Clairvaux, who lets fall from the lips of the Virgin the salvation of the world. Mary gives her consent, but it is God Himself, and the whole of creation along with Him, who is waiting for it:

> This answer, O holy Virgin, Adam, with all his race — Adam, a weeping exile from Paradise, implores it of you. Abraham entreats you, David beseeches you. This is the object of the burning desires of the holy fathers, of *your* fathers, who are still dwelling in the region of the shades of death. Behold the entire human race prostrate at your feet in expectation. And rightly, for on your word depend the consolation of the wretched, the redemption of the captive, the freedom of the condemned, the salvation of your entire race, of all the children of Adam. Hasten then, O Lady, to give answer; hasten to speak the word so longed for by all on earth, in limbo, and in heaven. Yea, the King and Lord of all things, Who has greatly desired your beauty, desires as eagerly your word of consent, by which He has purposed to save the world.[43]

The discourse about a proper act of faith leads us to study, in the next chapter, a modern tension that has arisen between the act of faith, as a subjective effort supported by grace, and the object of faith, composed of all revealed truths. We now hope to rightly understand the start of the act of faith.

---

43   St. Bernard, *Homily IV on the 'Missus est.'*

The Tension between Faith and its Proclamation
ACT OF FAITH AND BELIEVED TRUTHS

A YEAR OF FAITH WAS CALLED BY the Supreme Pontiff Benedict XVI, beginning in October 2012, linked to the fiftieth anniversary of the start of the Second Vatican Council and the twientieth anniversary of the promulgation of the Catechism of the Catholic Church. An entire year devoted to the faith was aimed above all at rekindling knowledge of the supreme good that comes from this theological virtue and recalling the ultimate reason for being Christian: "Without faith it is impossible to please God, for whoever would approach him must believe that he exists and that he rewards those who seek him" (Heb 11:6).

Today, faith is suffering an eclipse in human society, for it is often considered an individualistic good that ought to be relegated to a merely private sphere. To reinvigorate faith and its proclamation, especially in the West which owes its glory to the Christian faith, the Holy Father established the Pontifical Council for the New Evangelization. The faith, which is suffering confusion, must be renewed, and its proclamation, which is the victim of some unease, must be relaunched.

Where is the ultimate root of the loss in the rational assent that the Christian gives to God when he or she says with the Church, "I believe"? We will respond to this question with a brief analysis of a new *perception* of faith which has imposed itself today. An increased emphasis on the meaning of Christianity as encounter with Christ, opposed to the loving assent to Christ and His truth, has given rise to this interpretation. It seems there is a division between the assent of faith and a faithful life understood as the experience of faith, the informative and performative aspects of faith, with most people concentrating almost exclusively on the latter. In the end, truth and freedom are divided. Are the two truly incompatible?

1. SEARCHING FOR THE START OF THE ACT OF FAITH

The question can be put another way: has assent to believed and prayed dogma, in itself unchangeable though enriched by an ever greater revealed knowledge, been obscured by a more general approach to faith, beginning at the moment the believer's assents not from obedience to the truth but from the questionability of being and the pluralism of becoming? Assent to revealed truth cannot be opposed to freedom as encounter. Christ is the communication of self in freedom and the definitive revelation of God as unity between the noetic and dynamic aspects of the Word, that is, between the unchangeable *in se* and the realization in time of what that means.

Updating catechesis, which is the preparation and proclamation of faith, has always been at the center of the Church's attention. The mode of updating defined as *post-conciliar*, which has emphasized the simplicity of the believer's assent to God the Revealer, is able to put the truths of faith (the Triune God, Jesus Christ true God and true Man, the Church mystery and body of Christ), into a sort of quarantine, so as to focus on the *way* in which faith should re-emerge, a faith which was believed in at a time of great crisis but had actually caved in long before. While a new impetus given to faith was desirable, problems arose because the impetus itself was a novelty that had to free itself from a now outmoded theological formulation. It was not simply by chance that the new formulation, able to respond to the challenges of the time—that is, challenges of the faith in that moment—soon envisaged new passages of dialogue about matters that were before considered risky, if not in fact heretical, a short time before. K. Rahner, for example, writing his reports for Cardinal König in preparation for the Second Vatican Council without the rigid schema of the Roman theologians, began to call monogenism into question. Are we descended from one person? Was it absolutely clear that the biblical Adam did not serve as a moral representative of a small group fallen into sin at the start of the human generation? For Rahner, the latter view was much more probable from the psychological perspective and more suitable to the discoveries of paleontology.[1] Another burning question was tackled in chapter ten of the preparatory schema *De deposito fidei pure custodiendo*, concerning the destiny of children who died without being baptized, which postulated the reality of limbo. This, too, must be re-examined or at least neglected because it was obscure and not worthy of a definition in the Council. Was such a question, I wonder, a dogmatic statement? But the main emphasis was on another point: how would *men and women of today*

---

[1] See Karl Rahner, *Sehnsucht nach dem geheimnisvollen Gott. Profil-Bilder-Texte*, ed. Herbert Vorgrimler (Austria: Herder, 1990), 101–103.

be able to understand that God's universal salvific activity could be stopped due to the absence of baptism, when God Himself is tied to His universal salvific will?[2] Rahner had something to say about priestly celibacy, too. The Church's duty is to guarantee the Christian community a sufficient number of priests: an obligation certainly of divine right. But since the request for and maintenance of celibacy was not an obligation of the Church — the obligation was not of divine right — it should have the courage (in order to have a sufficient number of priests, especially in South America) to demand celibacy no longer.[3]

We ought to consider another interesting theological and liturgical case, which has come to the attention of the whole Church in recent years because of a letter sent to the Holy Father by the President of the German Bishops' Conference, dated April 14, 2012:[4] the *pro multis* case. The Congregation for Divine Worship, in a letter dated October 17, 2006, had urged the Bishops' Conferences to prepare the faithful, through appropriate catechesis, for a change in the translation of Jesus's words over the chalice, from "for all" to "for many": exactly what the Lord said at the Last Supper. In the letter, the Holy Father reiterated that the translation into the local languages of "for all" had been a theological interpretation, not a true and faithful translation. Here it is not about interpretation but faithfulness to the Lord's words in that solemn and decisive action for our faith and our eternal salvation. In the words pronounced over the chalice, the Lord identifies

---

[2] Rahner, *Sehnsucht nach dem geheimnisvollen Gott. Profil-Bilder-Texte*, ed. Herbert Vorgrimler (Austria: Herder, 1990), 105–106.
[3] See Ibid., 143–146.
[4] See the English text at: http://chiesa.espresso.repubblica.it/articolo/1350236bdc4.html?eng=y.

The Tension between Faith and its Proclamation

Himself with the Servant of Yahweh evoked by Isaiah (53:11), who justifies many while dying for all.[5] The Lord does not exclude anyone from His salvation, but this is not automatic: those saved are those who drink, or at least desire that blood poured out — "for *you* and for *many*." The disciples of Christ, who participate in the Eucharist, bear the responsibility of evangelization for all other people; they are the *you* who sees for others, and for all, so that they may be many in eternity. It is essential to ask God for salvation through Christ's sacrifice, and sadly not everyone will be saved but only those who are well-disposed. Nor can one hope in the salvation of all, but only of many. Otherwise, the Lord's words in relation to the final judgement,[6] inseparably linked to those over the chalice, would be nullified.

Would a theological-liturgical interpretation of salvation for all have fostered in the faithful a broader awareness of the mystery of salvation or would it simply have been in agreement, at the pastoral level, with the natural desire that everyone be brought to salvation and happiness, without an excessive concern about remaining before God in "fear and trembling" (Phil 2:12)? Faith cannot be stated in any language or terminology, even that most suitable to common feelings. A mistaken tradition inevitably ushers in a languidness of faith in the redemptive sacrifice of Christ, to the point of nearly postulating an empty hell or the priority of the universal salvific will against the objective will of the creature. Here we find ourselves faced with the problem of faith and proclamation at its key moment, namely, the liturgical moment, which summarizes and sets out dogma.

---

5 See 2 Cor 5:14; 1 Tim 2:6.
6 See Mt 25:41.

2. FAITH AND PROCLAMATION ON THE THRESHOLD OF VATICAN II

The crux "faith and proclamation" has a moment of particular emphasis in the preparation for the Second Vatican Council. The emerging problem presented itself roughly as a choice: to define faith condemning the errors which were opposed to it, as the Church had always done, or to explain the faith professed with a new language, a new pastoral method, which without undermining faith itself could encourage a perception not too distant from modern sentiment. This *aut aut* was also a sort of clash between the Roman Curia and the theologians of the Council, many of whom manifested almost an allergy to the Curia formulation and therefore to the scholastic formulation of theology. It did not distinguish properly between Curia and Catholic theology. Many concentrated on the renewal of theology, which was largely a renewal of the theological method via a new approach to dogma. In studying the conciliar dynamics, we should ask a series of questions: Up to what point did the clash provoke a change in the Council? What in the epistemological moment ought to have been improved regarding the approach to the dogma believed and prayed? How much did this wind of appropriate modernization of theology, especially of the proclamation of the faith in catechesis, influence the understanding of the Second Vatican Council as spirit of the council?

John XXIII was hoping for a short council to approve the already prepared schema, probably conceiving the incipient Council based on the Roman Synod (1960). The council should be able to conclude in the space of two sessions. However, what was brewing went beyond a simple reproclamation of the faith. Melloni writes:

Nor was there anything surprising about the statements in which the newly elected Paul VI showed his profound veneration for Roncalli's magisterium by announcing his intention to continue the Council. Despite all the limitations put on the Council by the nature of the preparation, by the pressure that the quarrelsome Roman schools exerted on the commissions and their theologians, and by the unnatural supremacy of a Doctrinal Commission that was a faithful mirror of the organizational chart of the Curia, John XXIII's decision to go ahead with the Council had imposed the hopes, insights and expectations of the espiscopate upon the college of cardinals.[7]

There has certainly been a great deal of embellishment about the contentions within the council, likely to accentuate the pentecostal wind which the Council was bringing. Some testimony will help us to better understand what happened. Among many, the figure of H. Jedin (1900-1980), a German historian and expert on the Council of Trent, stands out. He recalls that he was consulted—and would later become a peritus at the Council—especially about the revision of the Conciliar regulations, to simplify the interventions which were too lengthy and to reject potential schema which were not believed to be adequate for conciliar discussions. Frings asked him how the minority could exercise greater influence in the commissions and then impose their opinions on the whole conciliar assembly. Jedin colllaborated with

---

7   Alberto Melloni, "The Beginning of the Second Period: The Great Debate on the Church," in *The History of Vatican II, Vol. 3: The Mature Council, Second Period, and Intersession, September 1963–September 1964* (Orbis: Peeters; Leuven: Maryknoll, 2000), 1.

Dossetti to review the procedure of the conciliar operation.[8] He himself writes:

> In a conversation with Cardinal Frings, there was some discussion about ways and means of bringing to the Council Ratzinger's plan on the sources of Revelation, which in the meantime had been re-worked by Karl Rahner, and possibly the plan on the church, drafted by the Louvain dogmatic, Philips; as well as those mentioned above, the Dominican Yves Congar also took part in this discussion (6 November [1962]).... In the afternoon that same day, Cardinal Döpfner presented me with the text of a petition to the Cardinal Secretary of State, requesting that after every general debate on a schema presented by the commission there should be a vote on whether to hand it on to the competent conciliar commission or not, to be discussed or not; if it were rejected by the majority, there would be a green light for the presentation of a new plan — in our case, therefore, the Ratzinger-Rahner schema. Cardinal Döpfner therefore hoped to mobilize the secretariat, put to one side somewhat in the order of business, for new requests in support of our aim.[9]

Jedin reflected on this after participating in the preparatory work of the commission for studies and seminaries, chaired by Cardinal Pizzardo and secretary, the "extremely decisive," Archbishop Staffa. Jedin noted in his diary:

> I did not become pessimistic in Rome but I was very much afraid that the Curial faction might

---

8 See Hubert Jedin, *Storia della mia vita* (Brescia: Morcelliana, 1987), 297–305.
9 Ibid., 306–307.

interpret the ecumenical council like the Roman diocesan synod [which had taken place shortly before, in January 1961]: a summary of the previous papal and curial directives [but also] repression of new initiatives" (Diary, March 6, 1961).[10]

Jedin also informs us that Vatican II, unlike the last two Councils, did not have a polarized Pope-Council structure, but rather a tripartite one, Pope-Curia-Council[11]:

> This idea could be based on some private statements of John XXIII. He did not at all share the Curia's vision. The curia party, which was usually considered to be led by Cardinal Ottaviani (while the Cardinal Secretary of State Cicognani, at least as influential, kept himself somewhat in the background), was, as a theologian close to the Curia told me, literally in the grip of a "conciliar psychosis"; it had many supporters in the highly-disciplined Italian episcopate, as well as among the Spanish and North American bishops, so at the end of the first period the two German Cardinals were looking to the future with pessimism rather than optimism.[12]

It is appropriate to ask whether the alternative schema prepared by the theologians was definitively better. Ratzinger himself was not convinced of it.[13] Were there openings that were too risky, that often went beyond the aspiration itself for a calm discussion based on a prepared text? There was certainly a strong dominion of theology,

---

10 Jedin, *Storia della mia vita*, 298.
11 Ibid., 310.
12 Ibid., 310.
13 See Joseph Ratzinger, *La mia vita. Autobiografia* (Cinisello Balsamo: San Paolo, 1997), 87–97.

with a primacy of theologians.

D. Chenu testifies to the solidarity of many influential theologians who believed that the *doctrinal* schema was preparing Vatican II to be archaic:

> Letter of Fr. Congar. He has seen Küng. Pessimistic. He wants to oppose the approval of the deliberations starting from the dogmatic schema presented. For this, he is asking that the work begin with pastoral and practical arguments: liturgy, unity. Plan for a collective text from theologians asking the bishops for this: Küng, Rahner, Congar would be the first to sign (September 27, 1962).[14]

Chenu informs us, about a meeting of French and German bishops at the Roman residence of Mgr Volk di Magonza on October 19, 1962, accompanied by various theologians (including Rahner, Grillmeier, Küng, Schillebeeckx, Philips, Congar, Labourdette, de Lubac, Daniélou, Chenu himself, Rondet, and Semmelroth). Volk's report on the schema was very harsh. It was necessary to replace their abstract perspective, which was quite far-removed from the present problems with the Christian perspective on the world. It was necesary to give a positive meaning to the Christian presence in the world.[15] Would this vision, which was more rooted in the practical perspective, beginning from the viewpoint of a Christian in the world to explain the faith, be effective in the post-conciliar period? How would the clergy attempt to update catechesis on faith from this perspective or new method?

---

14   M-D Chenu, *Vatican II Notebook: A Council Journal 1962–1963*, trans. Paul Philibert (Bologna: Il Mulino, 1996), 65.
15   Ibid., 76–77.

3. THE CRISIS OF THE CHURCH IN THE POST-CONCILIAR PERIOD

Meanwhile, in the immediate post-conciliar period the strong emphasis on renewal was accompanied by signs of a defeatist decline. A crisis grew within the Church, accompanied by a crisis of culture and of the world.

It is good to note once more the words of H. Jedin, who, in addition to being a witness of the ecumenical assembly of Vatican II, was also an acute observer of occurences in subsequent years. He himself confessed that

> in the eyes of some theologians and their supporters I had gone from being the "progressive" I was during the Council, to being a "conservative." I am traditonal only in the sense that every Catholic must be traditional; the Catholic Church not only has traditions, it is *traditio*, transmission of the gospel to men and women.[16]

Initially Jedin (upon returning from the United States in 1966) thought he should oppose the idea of a crisis of the Church. Two years later he no longer doubted its existence. In his opinion, the crisis "arose because there was a view that it was no longer enough to have achieved the Council, but it was seen as the initial trigger for radical innovation, which in reality left the conciliar decrees behind them."[17]

Jedin gave a conference on *Kirchengeschichte und Kirchenkrise*.[18] He had a disagreement with Annibale Bugnini,

---

16 Jedin, *Storia della mia vita*, 334.
17 Ibid., 324.
18 Published in *Aachner Kirchenzeitung* (December 29, 1968 and January 5, 1969); translated in *L'Osservatore Romano* on (January 15, 1969). See also Jedin, *Commiato da Trento?*, *L'Osservatore Romano*, December 29–30, 1969. All references are in *Storia della mia vita*, pp. 324–325, footnote 5.

who criticized him for being opposed to liturgical reform. Jedin pointed out that a wider introduction of the vernacular and greater participation of the people had been attempted in Germany much earlier. He listed five points which, in his opinion, were the cause of the crisis:

> What concerned me most of all was the misrepresentation of Catholic dogma — not just those of Trent — by recourse to a suspect hermeneutic, under the guise of a theological "pluralism".... Therefore, together with my friend... on 17 September 1968 I presented to the President of the German Bishops' Conference, which had met a few days previously, a memorandum which illustrated above all the general premises of the life of the Church (the preponderance of left-wing *mass media* and rebellion among the young), and so five individual phenomena of the crisis: 1. Insecurity in the faith continuously on the rise, caused by a liberal diffusion of theologcial errors from university chairs, books and essays; 2. The effort to transfer forms of parliamentary democracy into the Church through the introduction of 'the right to participate' at the three levels of ecclesiastical life: the Universal Church, the dioceses, the parishes; 3. The desacralization of the priesthood; 4. Liberal "structuring" of the liturgical celebration instead of the fulfilment of the *opus Dei*; 5. Ecumenism as "Protestantization."[19]

In my opinion, another point could be added to these five: the separation of obedience from faith due to the loss of truth.

---

19   Jedin, *Storia della mia vita*, 326–327.

K. Rahner, to whom Jedin's memorandum been leaked, radically opposed it. Rahner believed it to be non-democratic — although it was in fact democratic — without considering the facts of Canon Law and parliamentary experiences.[20] With regret, Jedin replied:

> What I felt the lack of for a long time in the current church was the desire of the official representatives to decisively reject deviations in the faith of many theologians (and I am not referring just to political theology and "liberation theology") and slips in Catholic religious conscience (and in liturgy, too), so as not to fear personal consequences. Indirectly they supported the bad interpretation of the exhortation addressed by Pope John to the Council not to brandish the "sword of condemnation." So, the Council argued that it should not condemn but rather expose positively; certainly he did *not* mean to say that the Church did not have the right to reject heresies, as it had done from its origins. The "pluralism" that has always existed in theology cannot be confused with the falsification of the truth of faith.[21]

4. IF FAITH SUBSUMES THE PROBLEMATIC FACT OF EXISTENCE

We must not forget that in July 1966, Cardinal Ottaviani sent a letter to all the Presidents of the Episcopal Conferences, denouncing some errors of interpretation of the decrees of Vatican II. Ottaviani listed ten erroneous opinions or positions which were becoming widespread.[22]

---

20   See Jedin, *Storia della mia vita*, 328.
21   Ibid., 333.
22   Sacred Congregation for the Doctrine of the Faith, *Circular Letter to the Presidents of the Episcopal Conferences regarding some*

We will mention just a few of them: appealing to Sacred Scripture while leaving aside Tradition; restricting the role of biblical inspiration and its inerrancy, and calling into question the historical value of the narrated facts; affirming that dogmatic formulae are subject to historical evolution, so that their objective meaning is susceptible to change; adhering to a certain Christological humanism, in which Christ only gradually became aware of His divinity; legitimizing situational ethics through errors in moral theology; and not least, promoting a false ecumenism, couched more in terms of a pernicious irenicism than based on the truth of the one Church of Christ.

Surprisingly, less than a year after the end of Vatican II a magisterial document denounced the hermeneutical deviations from the Council documents. It is also interesting to note K. Rahner's response to Ottaviani's letter, with the significant title *Magistero e teologia dopo il Concilio*, "Magisterium and theology after the Council." Rahner, reflecting on the condemnations from the Congregation for the Doctrine of the Faith, asked up to what point Ottaviani might be aware of the change brought about by the Council. He attempts a *via media* between a planned monolithism and theological iconoclasm. The monolithism of condemnation and dogmatization was no longer possible. Vatican II had chosen the method of dialogue, "allowing the different theological tendencies to express themselves more freely, etc. It seemed that for some questions formulating a clear and binding teaching was less easy than was thought twenty years ago."[23] The existence

---

sentences and errors arising from the interpretation of the decrees of the Second Vatican Council (July 24, 1966): *AAS* 58 (1966), 659–661.
23   Karl Rahner, "Magistero e teologia dopo il concilio" in Giornale di Teologia, 11 (Brescia: Queriniana, 1967), 25–26.

of the dangers indicated by Ottaviani's letter, especially in German circles, could not be denied. Rather than issuing a general warning, it was appropriate to look at the current situation, at the theological pluralism that now prevented all from speaking just *one* language. Rahner writes:

> Current theology (according to exegesis, philosophy, the contemporary spiritual life) is faced with such a quantity of problems, has such a variety of tools for conceptual enunciation and is so conscious of the ambiguity of all the statements, that it is no longer as easy as it once was to oppose a real or presumed error with a new positive statement immune from any misunderstanding, where all the honest scholars have the impression that not only is something precise being stated, but which also satisfies their own "claim".... This is the situation of a pluralism of methods and systematic terminology, of the immensity of the theological problem, in the face of which an individual theologian, alone, can no longer be a specialist in an adequate manner.[24]

Here, it is clear that Heideggerian memory had entered deeply into Rahner's theological feeling, and so post-conciliar theology had to respond above all to the pluralistic and problematic fact of modernity. This is the problem. It begins not from truth but from the phenomenon, which will prevent the possibility of speaking unequivocally about God and the things of faith. This will allow the act of faith to be subsumed in the moment as an epistemological premise — no longer the certain given of Revelation enlightened by strong reason, but rather the problematic fact of the

---

24 See Rahner, "Magistero e teologia dopo il concilio," 32–33.

various philosophies of existence and of the various conceptions of humanity, ultimately calling into doubt the revealed truths themselves. Faith will not stem from obedience to the Truth, but often from cogency of the newness — that is, the historicity — to be reconciled in some way with faith. Faith ends up being judged and is no longer judge of the life of men and women. Can we have this outcome today in the renewed proclamation of the faith? Here is an exemplary, even if not unique and exhaustive vision.

5. FAITH BETWEEN THE INFORMATIVE AND PERFORMATIVE ASPECTS

As we mentioned, it is essential to renew the proclamation of the faith and Christian catechesis itself, based on the original transmission of Jesus Christ and His Gospel, that is, the living transmission of a Person and His love. The *Lineamenta* for the Synod of Bishops on the new evangelization for the transmission of the Christian faith said:

> referring to the Gospel, we must not think of it only as a book or a set of teachings. The Gospel is much more; it is a living and efficacious Word, which accomplishes what it says. It is not so much a system of articles of faith and moral precepts, much less a political programme, but a person: Jesus Christ, the definitive Word of God, who became man.[25]

This is about transmitting Christ, the divine Person and incarnate, eternal Word. Not uncommonly the focus is exclusively on the experience of Christ and the Gospel, which calls into question the transmission of the *Word* of Christ. The Gospel is the oral and written word:

---

25 Synod of Bishops, *Lineamata* for The New Evangelization for the Transmission of the Christian Faith (May 27, 2012), 11.

proclamation, preaching, catechesis and doctrine, all of which distinguish in the same Word — the Logos of God — the noetic (conceptual-cognitive) and dynamic (experiential-practical) aspects. The two aspects are mutually implicit, so the dynamism would be empty without a content to be realized, and the meaning of the Word realizes by itself what it expresses. For example, there is no catechesis which rejects the truths of faith, or the transmission of concepts and dogma which those truths express, to make room solely for a living encounter with Christ, for an experience of the Risen One. Some time ago a Catholic weekly, *L'Osservatore Toscano*, presenting a new catechetical resource developed by the Diocese of Florence to renew youth catechesis, gave the following title to the initiative: "The old 'teaching'? It's not enough anymore." Although only a newspaper headline, it is telling as far as the *mens* which wishes to express itself is concerned. The aim of catechesis is not that of transmitting notions but of encouraging an encounter with Jesus.[26]

Will there be a living Jesus opposed to the faith which He Himself taught and which the Church has handed on without interruption? In fact, what is posited is a diastasis between two aspects, the noetic and the dynamic, of the same faith. This has been preached now for many years. The notional catechism would be of no use. Room must be made for the encounter, which quickly results in keeping faith itself rather vague and encouraging an approach to the Church that is disembodied and indifferent, because it is devoid of the noetic foundation from which experience begins. It is devoid of the unchanging and suprahistorical presence of the Logos, who only because He is eternal became flesh in time and in every age enlightens our faith. A faith founded solely on the historicity of our

---

26 See *L'Osservatore Toscano,* May 13, 2012, 1.

encounter with Christ, without the priority and epistemic foundation provided by dogma, favors a transmission more in harmony with the times that demand a revision, but in the long run such a faith is increasingly historicized and changing.[27] The change would encourage the perception of faith as a history of salvation. Ultimately, in some theologies, the change itself and historicity come to be regarded as theological places. rendering, in some theologies, the change itself and historicity as theological places. Thus, dogma is falsely subjected to a process of becoming.

But, how can the revealed faith be combined with progress and the new challenges of the time? Christians are faced with a dual longing. On the one hand, they desire to profess the faith of the Church, and to make the effort of being good Christians; and on the other, they are faced with commitment to the world, a belief in humanity and human capacities, and the desire to build a better future. The two aspects should not be in opposition, insofar as the logic of sin is defeated and God Creator and Redeemer separates and triumphs.

But several authors, perhaps neglecting the threat of sin, have noticed a certain intolerance of modernity toward faith and have tried to redeem the opposition between God and world by proposing a renewal of the proclamation of God in the world, beginning with the world as a sort of philosophical *a priori*.

This approach, which is founded on becoming and progress, is particularly promoted by Teilhard de Chardin.

---

27 See the epistemological considerations as indispensable premises of the theological system because it does not expire in a religious philosophy; Antonio Livi, *Vera e falsa teologia. Come distinguere l'autentica "scienza della fede" da un'equivoca filosofia religiosa* in Grande Enciclopedia Epistemologica 8 (Rome: Casa Editrice Leonardo Da Vinci, 2012).

He sees in the Risen Christ the omega point of the evolution of the cosmos (Christ is given as an end, but it is forgotten that He is above all beginning and archetype), "a God of the becoming and of the transcendent. It is in the risen Christ that the apparent opposition between faith in progress and Christian faith, between 'becoming' and the 'transcendent', is resolved."[28]

De Chardin, points everything toward the parousia of Christ as ultimate agent of the evolution of the world, who is capable of combining faith and science, God and the world. He also provides the tools for a new catechesis that is no longer based on the static nature of people or concepts, an abstract or scholastic doctrine, but on the communication of Jesus Himself (the driving point of evolution). The Jesuit Faricy, his interpreter, writes:

> Religious formation can no longer allow itself to focus statically on concepts, but must be dynamically oriented towards progress. It must teach not so much "what", but "how".... The catechetical attempts founded on doctrine or on life are negative because they focus more on content than on development.[29]

So, what happens to doctrinal concepts, and by association to the dogmatic formula which in verbal expressions bear a truth of faith? "Concepts should be used in a pragmatic manner, that is, as a resource to realize a complete Christian vision, in prayer and in life with others."[30]

---

28 Robert Faricy, *All Things in Christ: Teilhard De Chardin's Spirituality or Christian Faith and My Everyday Life: The Spiritual Doctrine of Teilhard de Chardin* (London: Harper Collins Distribution Services, 1981), 71.
29 Ibid., 75–77.
30 Ibid., 79.

Is this an echo of some conciliar experts' idea to speak about the faith in practice? What does it mean to make the concepts pragmatic? In my opinion, the fundamental problem lies in the division which, in this vision from below, is applied to Christ Himself, incarnate Logos, between human and divine nature. How can you communicate Christ without communicating the proclamation of the Logos of God through the human logos? In the final analysis, here is the root of the current division between faith and Christian praxis. Praxis has prevailed over faith and its proclamation from on high, which is before humanity, before history, and comes from God. Is this an effect of the problem that was revealed during preparation for Vatican II, especially during its execution concerning the preparatory schema, that is, the request for a more pastoral method and therefore a more colloquial approach to faith?

Renewal always needs unity between believed dogma, prayed dogma, and Christian life. It is necessary to combine faith and reason, faith and dogma, and therefore faith and proclamation. A catechesis on Christ and on faith cannot simply abandon the formula of faith — the Catechism as dogmatic, moral, and spiritual unity — to make room for a more colloquial approach to faith that is solely experiential with regards to Christ. That path leads us to another Jesus, a lord of our desires, who will teach us a truth more in harmony with the world today and the fashions of our times. If renewal of catechesis only undergoes a reformation in terms of the historical and spatial-temporal approach to Christ that is not based on the perennity of His teaching received in obedience to Sacred Scripture and Tradition through the Church's Magisterium, this renewal will soon end up provoking contempt for the "old teaching." Doctrine itself, and by association the Church, who bears the

The Tension between Faith and its Proclamation

doctrine of faith, is entering a crisis. For this reason, believers are confused about the very perception of faith, which, due to a more historic approach, could also change. This generates a loss of faith or a crisis. A crisis of faith today, coming from the crisis of the Church, has its root in the diastasis between the act of faith (subjective aspect) and the professed faith (objective aspect). The *fides qua* cannot be separated from the *fides quem*, and both demand that the *regula fidei* be respected. It must be received in a fitting manner, by listening to the one and continuous Church, who is the Mother and Teacher of that faith. Faith can be performative, and therefore introduced into life only if its antecedent aspect, the informative — that is, knowledge of the mysteries of faith — is well-founded. God, the Truth, must be obeyed. In this way faith can be listened to once again, and can be taught to others in charity.

Faith and proclamation require a prior unity between reason-love and faith, which is currently missing; a correct approach to the theandric mystery of Christ; a strong, metaphysical, and not phenomenal, merely experiential, or psychological reasoning; a faith rooted in the eternal Word of God, who in Revelation humbled Himself to us and guides our lives. First faith, first the Catechism, and then understanding.

However, there seems to be a perennial threat to the faith: the mystery of evil in relation to the goodness of God. The presence of evil in the world seems to push aside the question about God as superfluous. As we now turn to this new topic, let us be challenged by a question that will guide us throughout the next chapter: does God punish? By approaching this question correctly, we will also offer an answer to the problem of evil.

Does God Punish?
REFLECTIONS ON GOD AND THE PROBLEM OF EVIL

INTRODUCTION

We now tackle the burning question concerning divine punishment or chastisement. This discussion refers to both reason and faith, and the two seem to be excellent allies in offering satisfying arguments. The danger lies in seeking refuge in a certain fideistic sentimentalism which condemns reason to silence and so offers faith no reason to continue to believe in God. Of course, God is not just looking on, nor is He enjoying evil. However, if we deny that God punishes in order to purify men and women from evil — otherwise we would return to the diluvian humanity of the Old Testament — we must admit absurdities of every kind, such as evil has no explanation or the physical and natural causes of catastrophes have nothing to do with God. God is condemned to silence, by prelates and theologians, to avoid alarming people's touchiness, already strained by the trials of life. God says nothing to us. He is forced into silence by us. It is precisely this mutism of theology that condemns men and women to become non-believers or to seek explanations elsewhere. The most widespread experience is a renunciation of faith in God because of evil, often denied (but incorrectly) to be divine punishment, irrationally understood. So, what is the relationship between punishment and the mystery of evil? Does theology offer any solution?

Does God Punish?

Without doubt, this is a thorny issue. "To chastise" means "to make chaste, pure." God's chastisement is a pedagogical action which frees men and women from the evil that dwells within and destroys them, as Sacred Scripture testifies. God punishes sin to correct the sinner and punishes the sinner who has not definitively freed themselves from their sin in hell. Otherwise, He would be participating in their evil, and the evil itself would perpetuate an irredeemable dialectic process. Divine punishment challenges us about physical evil, too, such as sickness or natural disasters. While a correlation cannot be established between physical evil and divine punishment, it always challenges us as regards its most transcendent meaning and demands a clear response about God.

We must clarify who God is to understand divine punishment. If we still wrestle with the problem of evil even when we have found every scientific explanation for natural disasters, it means that a human solution cannot necessarily resolve this universal problem of humanity or that science is not the answer to a problem that is philosophical and, moreover, theological. The mystery of evil, and indirectly of punishment, at least tells us that men and women have limits that only faith and love can overcome.

1. DOES GOD PUNISH?

To introduce this reflection and seek to understand if our God, "Father of our Lord Jesus Christ, the Father of mercies and the God of all consolation" (2 Cor 1:3), is a God who punishes, it is necessary to begin with a fundamental element. We must ask ourselves in a radical way: Who is God? What concept do we have of Him? Of course, if we look around, and above all if we give a quick glance at the culture that daily surrounds us, we immediately note a weak idea of God. God, if He exists — for many people the doubt is now inseparable from their habits of living and thinking — must necessarily be in the image of a thought that has renounced being to focus on desire and then resigned itself to evil, without ever providing an explanation that might be the least bit satisfying.

What began as a critique of metaphysics, which is defined as the study of that being who is subject to all that can be known and loved — being itself, to be exact — led to a choice of desire as infinite desire; the desire, now driven to its greatest level and passing through Nietzsche's will to power, has reached radical pessimism with Schopenhauer, according to whom man is always prey to desires never satisfied, and so the only solution to life is suffering.

God should be the only One who is capable of redeeming our misery, our defeat, and at leat giving us the surety that evil will not destroy us. In this way, God is yielding to our desires for redemption, but He is redeeming us from a life now deplorable without meaning. With this perspective, to speak about God's punishment or chastisement would not only be anachronistic, the stuff of folk tales, but also inhuman. The description "inhuman" is particularly apt, for God is now conceived solely as a means to another end, often for humanity's desires. Absolute existentialism seeks the reason for everything in the world alone, and God must exist in the world, that is, on behalf of the world.

In fact, God is not a work of our hands. He is not the product of our experiments or the One who takes care of our deficiencies, but He is the Creator and the Lord, *the One from whom everything proceeds*. Only when we draw close to Him with a pure heart, free from every preconception, can we pose the question: Does God chastise us? Immediately, we answer "yes" and we seek to understand why.

1.1 What exactly is punishment?

"To punish" derives from the deponent verb *punior* or from the older form *poenio-poenire* which immediately recalls the idea of *paena*. Strictly speaking it means "to inflict a pain, to chastise."[1] It refers to the idea of chastisement, to the composite verb *castigo-are*, which, according to etymologists can present various derivations: 1) from *káston*, in Latin *lignum, fustis*; or 2) from *kástos* pro *kestòs*, in Latin *lorum*, strap or bridle; and, 3) according to recent philologists it could derive from a composite voice, and that is, from *castus* and *agere* like "purgare" from *purus* and *agere*, so with the meaning to "make pure."

So "punishment" means "to compel, to correct" in the sense of calling someone to better behavior, reprimanding, or scolding.[2] "To punish," therefore, is to inflict a punishment, and the act of punishing has a didactic goal, namely, the good of the one who, being punished, is recalled to an upright life.

Twice in the New Testament the Latin Vulgate uses the verb *castigo-are* (with a different Greek term): first of all it can be found in St. Paul (1 Cor 9:27), where the Apostle of the Gentiles speaks about the punishment inflicted on his body (*hupopiázo* in Greek) that reduces him to servitude to prevent him from prevailing over the spirit; secondly, it can be found in Revelation (3:19), where the Lord Jesus Christ speaks the Amen and says: "I reprove and discipline (*paideúo* in Greek) those whom I love." Thus the last book of Sacred Scripture introduces this reflection on God's punishment-chastisement. It is a work of God's love in Christ, to prevent us from falling into spiritual lethargy or

---

[1] Egidio Forcellini, *Lexicon totius latinitatis*, t. III (Padua: 1965), 972.
[2] Ibid., I, 547–548.

the sleep of life like the Angel of the Church in Laodicea, and to urge us to be zealous and repent.[3]

1.2 Cain and Abel

To understand how and why God punishes we must turn to Sacred Scripture. We will choose two examples from the Old Testament before turning to the New Testament and thus discern not an opposition between the two Covenants but a continuity through the fulfilment of all things in Christ.

The first is the example of Cain and Abel (Gen 4:1-16). Abel was a shepherd, and Cain worked the land. Both offered the fruits of their work in sacrifice to the Lord: Abel offered the first born of his flock, and Cain the fruits of the earth. The Lord appreciated Abel and his offering but not Cain or his offering. We do not know why, but the Lord rejected Cain and yet did not interrupt dialogue with him. Because of that, Cain became annoyed and brooded in his heart on one of the most appalling crimes, fratricide. In the countryside, he raised his hand against his brother and killed him. The sin, as the Lord pointed out to Cain, had long been lurking at the door of his heart; he should have mastered it,[4] but he allowed himself to be mastered. The Lord reminded Cain of his freedom in the face of evil before he allowed himself to be dominated by hatred, a freedom which then became the instrument of evil and of death. Death had already entered the world through the devil's trap[5] and the sin of the ancestors,[6] and now it enters again because of Cain. A sin of such

---

3 See Rev 3:14–22.
4 See Gen 4:7.
5 See Gen 3:1, 4–5.
6 See Gen 2:17; 3:17–19.

great severity cannot go unpunished. God intervenes and punishes Cain with a curse, but gives him a salutary and merciful punishment.

Thus, in *Evangelium Vitae* John Paul II comments on this passage about God's punishment inflicted on Cain, which was given according to a logic of compassion, even for a murderer stained by such a serious crime:

> After the crime, *God intervenes to avenge the one killed*.... *God cannot leave the crime unpunished*: from the ground on which it has been spilt, the blood of the one murdered demands that God should render justice (cf. Gen 37:26; Is 26:21; Ez 24:7-8).... *Cain* is cursed by God and also by the earth, which will deny him its fruit (cf. Gen 4:11-12). He *is punished*: he will live in the wilderness and the desert....
>
> And yet God, who is always merciful even when he punishes, '*put a mark on Cain*, lest any who came upon him should kill him' (Gen 4:15). He thus gave him a distinctive sign, not to condemn him to the hatred of others, but to protect and defend him from those wishing to kill him, even out of a desire to avenge Abel's death. Not even a murderer loses his personal dignity, and God himself pledges to guarantee this. And it is precisely here that the paradoxical mystery of the merciful justice of God is shown forth. As Saint Ambrose writes: 'Once the crime is admitted at the very inception of this sinful act of parricide, then the divine law of God's mercy should be immediately extended. If punishment is forthwith inflicted on the accused, then men in the exercise of justice would in no way observe patience and

moderation, but would straightaway condemn the defendant to punishment.... God drove Cain out of his presence and sent him into exile far away from his native land, so that he passed from a life of human kindness to one which was more akin to the rude existence of a wild beast. God, who preferred the correction rather than the death of a sinner, did not desire that a homicide be punished by the exaction of another act of homicide.'[7]

This passage tells us that God punishes the serious sin of Cain but does not repay him with the same evil. He could not do so, being God and not man. Even though Cain is driven away from the land and must always be a wanderer and a fugitive, he is not killed; his lengthy penance will be medicine for his soul. Justice is administered with mercy so that the man might live, repair the evil committed, and return to God with a contrite and renewed spirit.

1.3 Sodom and Gomorrah

Next, we turn to the obvious example of Sodom and Gomorrah (cf. Gen 18:20-19:1-29). While the Lord had promised Abraham to make of him a great and powerful nation blessed by God, there was another nation, that of Sodom and Gomorrah, which had transformed that corner of the earth into a place of perversion. "Then the Lord said, 'How great is the outcry against Sodom and Gomorrah and how very grave their sin! I must go down and see whether they have done altogether according to the outcry that has come to me; and if not, I will know'" (Gen 18:20-21). Abraham repeatedly begs the Lord to save the city on

---

[7] Pope John Paul II, *Evangelium Vitae* (March 25, 1995), 8–9.

account of some just people dwelling within it. Abraham was thinking of his nephew Lot and his family. "Will you indeed sweep away the righteous with the wicked?" asks Abraham (Gen 18:23). If there were at least fifty just people in the city, God would have saved it from disaster. Abraham is forced to lower the number of the just even further, going down to just ten. And yet for those ten the Lord would save the city from destruction. He would even pardon the whole city.[8] However, not even ten just men could be found, and so the city was razed to the ground. However, the biblical text says that God "remembered Abraham, and sent Lot out of the midst of the overthrow, when he overthrew the cities in which Lot had settled" (Gen 19:29).

The just person was not treated like the wicked. The city depraved due to the evil and sin which had become regular and public habits was not saved from punishment. In fact, the real punishment for these cities was the sin itself which dwelt among them, destroyed consciences, and made them numb to evil; through God's intervention the punishment was transformed into sulphur and fire raining down from heaven.[9] In this city, sin had become a social custom. Unlike Cain, it had been transformed into a *chain of sin*.

Benedict XVI, in one of his wednesday general audiences, commented on the significant episode of Sodom and Gomorrah, beginning with the fact that not even ten just people were found in those cities so that the Lord might save them from ruin:

> [It was] a destruction paradoxically deemed necessary by the prayer of Abraham's intercession itself. Because that very prayer revealed the

---

8   See Gen 18:26.
9   See Gen 19:24.

saving will of God: the Lord was prepared to forgive, he wanted to forgive but the cities were locked into a totalizing and paralyzing evil, without even a few innocents from whom to start in order to turn evil into good. This is the very path to salvation that Abraham too was asking for: being saved does not mean merely escaping punishment but being delivered from the evil that dwells within us. It is not punishment that must be eliminated but sin, the rejection of God and of love which already bears the punishment in itself. The Prophet Jeremiah was to say to the rebellious people: 'Your wickedness will chasten you, and your apostasy will reprove you. Know and see that it is evil and bitter for you to forsake the Lord your God' (Jer 2:19).[10]

Sin, because it creates guilt, is already per se a punishment. To be saved by God does not mean, as many would hope, simply eliminating the punishment because God forgives everything, but — to reiterate using Ratzinger's words — it means "being delivered from the evil that dwells within us" and destroying the root of evil which is sin. Otherwise, even an escaped punishment would not lead to the desired salvation, but just another opportunity to return to one's own vices and to the previous behavior.

1.4 Insights from the New Testament

The lack of just men and women and the memory of Abraham, the father of a new multitude of people, leads us to the New Testament and to Jesus Christ, the true just man

---

10   Pope Benedict XVI, "The prayer of Abraham," Catechesis at the General Audience of May 18, 2011, in *L'Osservatore Romano* (Weekly Edition: May 25, 2011), 10.

who takes our sins upon Himself, saving us from eternal death. It is essential to conform ourselves to Him to become truly just and to live without sin, the cause of eternal death.

Clearly, we cannot draw up a mathematical equation or say that every sin is punished by God with its own unique consequence, such as sickness, disaster, a geophysical catastrophe, etc. Yet, we cannot forget God's providential presence.

In addition to Christ's explicit condemnation of the hardness of hearts and lack of belief and his prophetic words about eschatological punishment — such as the words at Chorazin, Bethsaida, or Capernaum, hardhearted cities despite the many signs worked in them by the Lord[11] — the New Testament records two episodes of physical healing, which elevate our reflection from the level of moral evil and sin to the physical level, sickness.

These two healings performed by the Lord seem to point to a different reality about the link between personal sin and sickness as a punishment.

As Jesus passes by the man born blind, His disciples ask Him, "Rabbi, who sinned, this man or his parents, that he was born blind?" (Jn 9:2). In Jewish thought, sickness is linked to personal guilt. Jesus replies saying that neither he nor his parents had sinned; rather, the man was in such a condition so that the works of God might be manifested through him. Blindness here is not a consequence of sin; it is an opportunity for Jesus to give sight to that man and ultimately to reveal Himself to everyone as the "light of the world" and the "light of life."[12]

The case of the paralytic who lay at the pool of Bethzatha and who had been suffering from sickness for thirty-eight

---

11   See Lk 10:13–15; Mt 11:20–23.
12   See Jn 8:12; 9:5.

years is different (Jn 5:5-15). It was the common belief that an angel passed by and stirred up the waters; the first to immerse themselves immediately after the movement of the waters would be healed. Jesus approaches the sick man and asks him if he wants to be healed. He replies that he has no one to help him get into the waters when they are stirred up. By His words, "Stand up, take your mat and walk" (Jn 5:8), the Lord heals him immediately. Later, Jesus meets him in the temple and says to him, "See, you have been made well! Do not sin anymore, so that nothing worse happens to you" (Jn 5:14). Here, then, sickness is immediately linked to personal sin, and consequently seems to be a just divine punishment.

St. Cyril of Alexandria, in commenting on the Gospel of John, unites these two accounts of healing, which seem to give two different responses but ought to be read in a synoptic manner.[13] The greatest difficulty for the Bishop of Alexandria is not the fact that a sickness might be a consequence of sin, but that the sickness of the blind man can be a revelation of the glory of God. What does that mean?

Jesus says that the blind man has no sin and is not suffering from blindness for that reason. St. Cyril clarifies that only the foolish think that the soul is guilty of sin before being united to the body. Thus, Christ's explanation is a response to Platonism in many of its derivations. Then, when the Lord says that the man was not born blind due to his parent's sin, Cyril upsets the mad opinion of the Jews by clarifying that "God does not visit the sins of the parents upon the chilren, as long as they do not share in the parents' transgressions."[14] Jesus's answer — "so that

---

13   See St. Cyril of Alexandria, *Commento al Vangelo di Giovanni*, 9, 3, in *Collana di testi patristici* 9, 3 (Rome: Città nuova, 1994).
14   Ibid., 205.

God's works might be revealed in him" — is not an axiom established with absolute certainty or as a general rule, because, according to the Alexandrian Father, we know from Scripture that some are punished for their sins, like those reprimanded by St. Paul who dare to approach the altar without examining themselves carefully, receiving with wicked hands and profaning the mystical Eucharist.[15] In fact, the healing of the paralytic shows that "for those who are sick or have died, their suffering has sometimes been imposed by divine wrath."[16]

However, it is important to note that there is no principle of cause and effect between sin and physical sickness. Yet, whether the sickness is a just punishment from God in view of repentance and conversion, or not, it is always linked in a broader manner to the will of God who allows it. Physical pain forces us to consider the mystery which envelops it, even when the remote and immediate causes at the scientific and medical levels can be identified accurately. Sickness causes us to look beyond, to a cause that is not merely physical, but moral and spiritual; even if we have the most perfect diagnosis, we will continue to ask ourselves about the cause of suffering. Sickness and physical ailment always refers back to God and so has a mysterious link with Him. There is a bond which eludes us, or annoys us, even leading us to curse God. But suffering is never without a reason if it is sought with a sincere heart

1.5 In summary, why does God punish?

God punishes the sinner to redeem their sin and to reestablish broken justice; and He does so because He has compassion for men and women and bestows His love

---

15 See 1 Cor 11:28–32.
16 St. Cyril, *Commento al Vangelo di Giovanni*, 206.

upon them. If God did not have compassion for men and women, He would never have created them.

From what has been said, we can draw a couple of principles to develop our reflection further:

a.) First of all, *God punishes sin to save the sinner.* It is a punishment which we might call pedagogical. Even with men and women's limitations or sickness due to their finite nature, God turns everything to His good, which is always of a transcendent, spiritual order. The good which God desires when He punishes or when He allows a physical ailment is the greatest good: the salvation of men and women by the redemption of their lives from the evil that seduces them. This salvation begins on earth with the new life which Christ gives, justifying us and freeing us from sin, and is fulfilled in eternity.

b.) *God definitively punishes the sinner who has not freed themselves from their sin.* This is the punishment of hell for men and women who have remained in their sin until the end, who have hardened their hearts and rejected love. If God ignored evil and did not punish in eternal hell those who have become the making of evil by obstinate rejection of the truth, then God would be participating in evil actions. In God Himself there would be good and evil, truth and error. Evil itself would be irredeemable for ever, in an eternal dialectical circle. Unfortunately, this is the Lutheran vision, in which sin is joined to God Himself through a "joyful exchange," so that Christ is now the only true sinner. In this theology, God turns against Himself to forgive Himself with Himself.[17] Finally, Luther's explanation opens the door to Hegel's dialectic philosophy, which

---

17   See Alma von Stockhausen, *Der Geist im Widerspruch: von Luther zu Hegel*, vol. 3 (Weilheim-Bierbronnen: Gustav-Siewrth-Akademie, 2003), 21–36.

has so deeply penetrated Catholic theology. Hegel reduces sin and evil to a good, to the possibility that the spirit lives in an undefined circle of affirmation, negation, and synthesis. In this perspective, the negation of sin would be grace; grace would be the dialectic vindication of sin and not the new life of the children of God.[18]

All these errors encourage us to cultivate the correct vision of the relationship between *justice* and *mercy*. Justice is accomplished in God's mercy, and mercy always presupposes justice. If mercy, as is sometimes hoped, cancelled justice, it would destroy itself; it would have no further raison d'être because there would no longer be any sin to pardon. The actions of men and women would be irrelevant, and God would simply be an empty and useless hope for forgiveness.

St. Irenaeus in his treatise *Adversus Haereses*[19] clearly demonstrates that God's justice cannot exist without His benevolence and vise versa. God is the same in the Old Testament as He is in the New, contrary to the heresy of Marcion, who proclaimed two divinities — a punitive Old Testament God and a good New Testament one. Marcion did not care to truly seek the identity of the Word of God, Christ crucified for us, in whom divine justice and infinite mercy are definitively united.

The profound interconnection between justice and mercy[20] is seen in the fact that the ultimate reason why

---

18   For Hegel the negation of the negation would lead to affirmation, so the negation of sin (negation of negation) would be grace; Christ, taking human nature (which for Luther is nature corrupted by sin) takes upon himself a part of the whole and bears this part on high in a superordinate whole, ultimately God Himself. See von Stockhausen, *Der Geist im Widerspruch*, 35–36.
19   St. Irenaeus, *Adversus Haereses*, III 25, 2–3.
20   See Ludwig Ott, *Fundamentals of Catholic Dogma* (Rockford, IL: 1974), 48–49.

God in Christ justifies us, freeing us from sin, giving us His grace and rewarding our good deeds, is precisely His love and His mercy. In the same way, the reward of the just and the punishment of the wicked is not simply the work of justice, but also the work of divine mercy. For God rewards beyond every merit, even one hundredfold[21] and mercifully punishes sinners in hell, as St. Thomas says,[22] with less than what they should suffer by virtue of their horrible sins.

1.6 God's punishment according to St. Thomas

St. Thomas clearly refers to this doctrine of God's punishment. In the part of the *Summa* concerning the virtue of justice he contemplates just, lawful, and virtuous vengeance enacted through punishment when it aims at restraining evil. St. Thomas Aquinas distinguishes[23] between a chastisement as *punishment for sin* deliberately committed by a person — here the punishment is due only to the sin and is inflicted so that justice might be restored — and punishment *as medicine* to heal from sins committed, preserve from future sins, and encourage the sinner to do good. In this latter case the medicine, which is given even without necessarily having incurred guilt, is never devoid of a greater good, even when it might deprive us of a lesser one. For example, suffering never deprives us of spiritual merits while it can inflict upon us a serious corporal punishment.

More acute but no less important is St. Thomas's chapter concerning the suffering of those who are invincibly ignorant of guilt or truly innocent, such as children. In

---

21 See Mt 19:29.
22 St. Thomas Aquinas, *Summa Theologiae*, I, q.21, a.4, ad 1.
23 Ibid., II–II, q. 108, a.4, co.

Does God Punish?

fact, sometimes the punishment is addressed to those who are in ignorance. St. Thomas argues:

> Thus, the children of the people of Sodom, though they were in invincible ignorance, perished with their parents. Again, for the sin of Dathan and Abiron their children were swallowed up together with them. Moreover, dumb animals, which are devoid of reason, were commanded to be slain on account of the sin of the Amalekites. Therefore, vengeance is sometimes taken on those who have deserved it involuntarily.[24]

And he replies:

> By the judgment of God children are punished in temporal matters together with their parents, both because they are a possession of their parents, so that their parents are punished also in their person, and because this is for their good lest, should they be spared, they might imitate the sins of their parents, and thus deserve to be punished still more severely.[25]

This text encourages careful reflection. Clearly, it is a discourse which we cannot apply as a generalization to all cases of suffering and premature or humanly unjust death, but the fundamental concept is clear. God can punish an innocent being, such as a child, to preserve it from a worse evil—such as imitating the evil conduct of their parents—or from an evil to which it would be enslaved. The evil of sin is worse than physical sickness, whose final expression is bodily death. The question concerns temporal punishments and not spiritual or eternal

---

24 *Summa Theologiae*, II–II, q. 108, a. 4, obj. 3.
25 Ibid., II–II, q. 108, a. 4, ad 3.

ones. St. Thomas relies on the true hierarchy of goods, sadly confused by our common way of thinking; bodily or physical well-being is always subordinate to spiritual and eternal well-being. In preference for the latter, Christian men and women should be ready to lose the former. After all, the Gospel teaches this when it sets out the same hierarchy in simpler terms: human life, the soul, is more than the body or food, and the body is more than clothing.[26]

Thomas' discourse would seem sarcastic to A. Camus[27] or some of his followers. They would say it justifies the existence of God even through the death of the innocent. For the French author, a creation where children are tortured cannot be loved. If God existed and were good — as those who believe in Him say — He should at least avoid pain devoid of guilt.

However, this vision reduces the whole horizon of humanity to earthly human existence. There is no glimmer of the supernatural, of what is beyond. In reality, innocent pain, when there is no rational explanation, more deeply reveals the mystery of the Cross of Jesus and the need to find a response not in earthly life, but beyond, in the mystery of God. The only true answer is faith in Christ.

Innocent suffering, which attacks a life in its first blossoming, is certainly a great mystery. It is worth turning once again to the teaching of St. Cyril of Alexandria on this thorny issue:

> As to those who suffer something terrible from the cradle and their earliest years, or even from the very womb are afflicted with diseases, it is not easy to understand what kind of explanation

---

26 See Lk 12:23.
27 Albert Camus, *The Plague*, trans. Stuart Gilbert (New York: Vintage Books, 1991).

any one can satisfactorily give.... Truly, by our minds we cannot comprehend those things which are far above us, and I should advise the prudent, and myself above all, to abstain from wishing to thoroughly scrutinize them. For we should recall to mind what we have been commanded, and not curiously examine things which are too deep, nor pry into those which are too hard, nor rashly attempt to discover those which are hidden in the Divine and ineffable counsel alone; but rather concerning such matters we should piously acknowledge that God alone knows some things, peculiar to Himself and excellent. At the same time we should maintain and believe that since He is the fountain of all righteousness, He will neither do nor determine anything whatever in human affairs, or in those of the rest of creation, which is unbecoming to Himself, or differs at all from the true rectitude of justice.[28]

2. IF GOD IS GOOD, WHY DOES HE PUNISH?

The question of the section is the same as asking ourselves, "If God is good, why does evil exist?" The problem of pain, and innocent suffering too, introduces another theme: evil. Why does evil exist? The world repeats the same argument again and again: "If God exists, He is omnipotent and, therefore, can prevent evil. Perhaps He does not want to and is therefore an evil God. Or He cannot and therefore is not God!" Such an argument implies that the presence of evil excludes the existence of God.

Again, if God is good and most perfect, why has He created an imperfect world, in which there is evil? Why does

---

28   St. Cyril of Alexandria, *Commentary on the Gospel of John*, 206–207.

God tolerate it, and why does it seem as if He is standing around looking at its ruins, at the moral misery which every day washes over our lives like a turbid tsunami? In hindsight all the questions about the problem of evil are questions about the desired good that we see disappear only to be replaced by evil. In greater depth, the problem of evil is the problem of the goodness that is lacking and is not about evil, which does not exist as such but is just an abstraction. My evil action or my evil behavior exists, that horrific fact and that sickness exists, but evil as a being per se does not exist. The true perspective from which to examine the issue is not evil but goodness. The only response to evil in its forms and manifestations which seem inescapable, is goodness, that is, God. Evil is always the alienation of goodness; it is everything that alienates men and women from God; it forever exiles man to a land where the sun no longer shines, but which makes him feel nostalgic for God and for goodness.

First, it is appropriate to ask, "What is evil?" We are referring to evil in the metaphysical sense, to what is not entirely good, to that good which should exist but does not, and not to absolute evil, which does not exist. All that exists is good, but what exists and what is good — as Genesis 1:18 testifies — can be corrupted and is subject to limitations and the cunning of humanity's will which manipulates it for selfish ends.

Thus, we must distinguish *physical evil* from *moral evil*. The physical is a limitation inscribed in things. The Catechism states that God freely willed to create not the best of possible worlds but a world "in a state of journeying" toward its ultimate perfection. This involves the appearance of certain beings and the disappearance of others, the existence of the more perfect alongside the less perfect.[29]

---

29 See CCC, 310.

Moral evil, on the other hand, depends solely on the free choice of created beings. Angels and human beings, as intelligent and free creatures, are called by God to journey toward their ultimate destinies by a free choice of love. But they can go astray by sinning, that is, rebelling against God and His plan. Moral evil has entered the world through disobedience. God is in no way the cause of it, but, respecting the freedom of creatures, He permits it and in a mysterious way knows how to derive good from it.[30]

The tragedy of evil in the world began with moral evil, with rebellion against God's will, first by the angels in heaven and then by men and women on earth.

In one of his famous homilies on the devil,[31] St. John Chrysostom focuses on the tragedy of humanity, beginning with the fall from heaven. After the wretched fall of Adam and Eve, incited by the devil, humanity was condemned to the pains of this life, but God in His charity brought humanity back to its primitive condition through Christ's salvific work. The fall was like a shipwreck for human life. Even though the ship of humanity had been laden by God with riches and blessings, it was brought to ruin by the bolt of the devil, who accused God in the eyes of men and women. God's goodness and charity did not stop. Once again God welcomed men and women and freed them from the waves of the sea. Evil does not belong to God,

---

30 CCC, 311.
31 There are three homilies by St. John Chrysostom, *De diabolo tentatore* (PG 49, 243–278). An English translation by Bryson Sewell, commissioned by Roger Pearse in 2014, can be read online.

In the first (PG 49, 243–256) — which I summarize in the text — Chrysostom is addressing those who say that the devil governs human affairs and who are dissatisfied at God's punishment, complaining about the prosperity of evil and the misfortune of the just. The other two homilies instead concern the power of men and women to resist the devil.

but it is the free choice of men and women to distance themselves from Him. Despite everything, even in a situation of sin, God does not abandon men and women but bestows His charity upon them. Evil and the devil do not compete for the world, for it remains governed by God's love. Perhaps the most interesting aspect of Chrysostom's thought is that God manifests His philanthropy above all when men and women are in a state of sin, by allowing them to mend their ways but saving them by pulling them out of this abyss of death. Divine charity is also evident when God allows men and women to fail. Through the experience of pain and suffering, men and women perceive more easily the intensity and drama of the loss due to sin and so return to the joy of communion with God. God allows the far-off son to experience hardship and misery so that he might become aware of his inability to live distanced from the gaze of his Father.

God allows the fall of humanity for an objective of love and at the same time punishes sins, acting like a doctor who knows about a sickness and how to cure it with an unpleasant and even disgusting medicine, but one that soothes. God's benevolence does not simply consist of giving earthly paradise to the ancestors but also in expelling them from paradise after their sin. If He had not expelled them they would never have been worthy to return. If God had not immediately punished the sin of presumption on the part of those who built the tower of Babel, mixing up and confusing their languages, would those people have desired to reach the summit of heaven itself? God punished them by confusing their languages so that they might not fall into greater evil. Chrysostom's key teaching is that God is good not only when He shows His kindness but also when He punishes us. His chastisements and punishments are the greatest part of His kindness, the greatest part of His providence.

If the devil ruled the world, men and women would remain prisoners of their misery, and chaos would rule. But despite the chaos brought about by the freedom of humanity order, beauty, and the possibility of ransom from evil rules in the world.

In a world where ruling is not a necessity but freedom is absolute — and not just that degraded or demeaning freedom, but also that true freedom which leads to peace — that which seems truly providential is the punishment of God. For St. John Chrysostom punishment is useful for sinners because it leads to the knowledge of sin and repentance. In addition, it is useful for the just because it keeps them active in the fight and resistant to pride. God is just and gives everyone what they deserve, even if in this world we do not always see that everyone is rewarded according to their merit, in good or evil. For Chrysostom this infinite justice united to God's compassion opens onto the theme of God's providence united with that of the resurrection of the dead. Only in eternal life do men and women see the fulfilment of justice, where everyone will definitively receive what they have deserved.

3. IF GOD WERE NOT TO PUNISH

At the end of our discourse, we must pose some important questions for reflection on the goodness of divine punishment and its providential existence, because if God were to no longer punish us, great evils would ensue for the world and the whole of humanity.

If God did not to punish us, He would not be a caring Father toward His children. Further, due to our weakness and misery, we would live only for ourselves, immersed in our selfishness and interests. If God did not chastise us for love of our good, we would also cease referring to the passive punishments of the spiritual life, such as the night of the senses and the spirit or the mysterious ways of grace, through which the Lord guides us to eradicate vices and encourage virtues by means of contemplative prayer.

If we wished to free ourselves from the concept of the divine and wise punishment, there would also be inauspicious consequences for theology itself, which are already widespread.

a.) The cancellation of God's punishment following sin results sooner or later in ascribing the origin of the wound of human nature not to original sin, which is easily denied as a biblical fable, but to an absurd mystery of the evil that grips us, which is ultimately the responsibility of God alone.

b.) In this human misfortune, where it is no longer possible to identify the start of human weakness and misery because of weak post-metaphysical thought, there is an attempt to make up for the relentless question of suffering and death by trying to involve God in this human misery. God begins to suffer with us, at all the moments when we are suffering. Then, suffering itself, no longer redeemed once and for ever in the passion and death of Jesus Christ, would represent the real snare and nothingness of life. We would no longer respond by showing the Crucifix, because the Cross itself would be without explanation. In fact it would be a sign that we ought to hide and even perhaps to be ashamed of.

If God did not punish us, we would cease to be human. And if we wanted God not to punish us, we would have paved the road to atheism. "Saint Catherine of Siena said to 'those who are scandalized and rebel against what happens to them': "Everything comes from love, all is ordained for the salvation of man, God does nothing without this goal in mind.'"[32]

Humanly speaking it is hard to see that even a divine chastisement comes from love. For this reason, one needs to see love as blooming from the truth, and truth as perfected by love. We now turn to the harmonic complementarity of *veritas* and *caritas*.

---

[32] CCC, 314.

PART TWO

The Circular Nature of the Sources:

REASON AND LOVE,
FAITH AND CHARITY

Veritas *and* Caritas
TWO WINGS OF
THE HUMAN SPIRIT

1. THE TRUTH ABOUT CHARITY FOR A CHARITY OF TRUTH

Paul's Letter to the Ephesians clearly outlines the close link between truth and charity: "But speaking the truth in love, we must grow up in every way into him who is the head, into Christ" (4:15). Charity can never be separated from truth. St. Paul recalls this after having said that Christ constituted the Church in a hierarchical manner for the good of the brothers, to prepare them for their ministry, with a view to "building up the body of Christ" (4:12). To act according to truth in charity (or literally "doing truth in charity"[1]) preserves the Church from being tossed around by any turbulent wind of doctrine, and so enables it to reach the unity of faith and knowledge of the Son of God (See 4:13-14). Truth and charity enable the attainment of the "whole measure of the fullness of Christ" (4:13), a fullness which is faith and knowledge — not just intellectual knowledge but also experiential, which leads to communion, to agape in Christ. Charity *rejoices* in the truth (See 1 Cor 13:6).[2]

---

1 The active present participle *aleteúontes* is used. The Vulgate, in fact, says "veritatem autem facientes in caritate."

2 Literally *sugkaírei*, from *sug-kaíro* (*sug-káris*), rejoice. We recall that *káris* is the New Testament word that indicates grace (See e.g., Lk 1:30). So, charity that rejoices about or in the truth is charity that finds grace in truth.

It is necessary to think about the totality of reality, the totality of being, and therefore about the mystery of God and humanity, starting from two fundamental premises that are open to everything: truth and love. They are like two pillars upon which the edifice of human knowledge is built; it is necessary to start with reason and conclude with love. Reason asks to be completed by love to see all the facets of what can be known, and love needs reason so as not to fall into sentiment or end in a mere voluntary act. Love perfects reason, and reason guides love.

One of the most prolific authors to examine this fundamental pairing was a great disciple of St. Bernard, William of Saint-Thierry. One of his works is devoted to a description of the nature and dignity of love. Love, according to him, has two eyes. "This enlightened love is charity; a love from God, in God, and for God. Charity is God, and 'God is charity.'"[3] William of Saint-Thierry asks what is owed to charity if not charity. A charity *of* truth and a truth *of* charity, the only ones which remove all doubt: "The truth of charity and the charity of truth will do away with all our lack of confidence in the love of God and in the constancy of His truth and unfailing eternity."[4]

Thus, truth and charity are linked because one illuminates the other. They are so linked that charity itself, love in truth and the truth of love, has two eyes: reason and love. Charity is always well-ordered and loves accordingly and in fullness. Fullness and moderation are the most perfect dimensions of love. Let us follow the development of William of Saint-Thierry's thoughts.

He argues that just as there are five senses of the body, through which we approach and know perceptible reality,

---

3 William of Saint-Thierry, *De natura et dignitate amoris*, III, 12.2.
4 Ibid., IV, 32.4.

so there are five spiritual senses of the soul, through which charity gives life to the soul. For this Cistercian monk, charity "is the eye by which God is seen."[5] Love desires to see God whom it loves in faith and in hope; charity already possesses what faith and hope love by desire: it loves God because it sees him. These five spiritual senses of charity are physical love, that love proper to married couples; social or fraternal love; natural love, the love which loves every person by virtue of the similarity of nature; spiritual love, which is love for enemies; and finally, the most noble love, love of God, which is charity. Charity is like sight; it is found within the most noble part of the human person, the head, to govern all the other loves. This supernatural sense that is love of God has two eyes, love and reason, which must not work separately, just as two eyes of natural sight:

> When one of them tries to see without the other it has little success, but when they work together they can achieve great things. Then they are that single eye of which the spouse in the Canticle speaks: 'Thou hast wounded my heart, O beloved, with one of thine eyes.' Each eye has a hard task, since reason cannot see God except in what He is not, while love is not content to rest except in what He is. What, indeed, can the reason grasp, however hard it may try, of which it dare say 'This is my God'? It can discover what He is, only by inferring from what it knows Him not to be.[6]

If reason and love unite, and one remains in the bosom of the other; if reason spreads in love, overcoming the limit of what is known in the desire to possess it, and love

---

5 William of Saint-Thierry, *De natura*, III, 15.2.
6 Ibid., III, 21.3–5.

remains within the limits of reason, of what alone is true and good; then, these two eyes of the soul can really achieve great things together. William of Saint-Thierry continues:

> Reason has its own fixed routes and straight ways by which it progresses. Love, however, advances more by its failures, and understands more by means of its ignorance. Reason appears to advance from what He is not, to what He is. Love leaves behind what God is not, and rejoices to lose itself in what he is. Love came from God and naturally yearns towards its origin. Reason is careful and wise, but love has the greater blessedness. And when I say that these two help each other, I mean that reason instructs love, and love enlightens reason. Reason merges into the affectivity of love, and love consents to be limited by reason. Then it is that they can achieve great things.[7]

What are these great things? William of Saint-Thierry does not tell us in detail but sets out all the prerequisites for them. Systematic reason, grounded in logic, must come to know things step by step and through intermediate objects. Definition lies in distinctions. The more one knows what a thing is not, the closer one gets to its perfect definition. By definition, a created thing is not, while the Creator is the One who is. The creature is not, because its being is received and is not something it has from itself; it is not the reason of its own being. Finally, then, its earthly journey will end when the created thing gives back its being. Reason proceeds through this non-being and comes to know the being precisely, even if not yet perfectly or fully. The fullness of knowledge is love.

---

7 William of Saint-Thierry, *De natura*, III, 21.6–8.

Love helps reason to see things not just as something in existence and other than itself but as capable of more, in it is completeness, just as charity is the fullness of faith.

Love taught by reason goes directly to the heart of things and asks not *what is* but *why* this thing exists. It sees the object known not as a mere object. Rather it is seen as a being whose being-in-relation is not merely of a cognitive but also of an existential nature. It is an object or reality that is part of life and can enter into my life. Love grasps the reason precisely because that thing exists and can be in relation to me. Reason is knowledge of things; love is being-in-relation with things. Truth is known in a participatory relationship: the knowing subject surrenders to the known object because it is seen no longer and only as object, but as other than itself, even potentially as a person. Reason sees God and determines His necessary existence, but it is only love that begins to penetrate His mystery, going beyond the concept of cause and effect, and sees that God, the reason of everything, must have a heart. Otherwise, He would not have created everything. Speaking in absolute terms, God, the cause of everything, would also be able to create things for a rigid manifestation of His glory. Yet human love does not rest until it discovers the reason for that love which it sees inside itself. First faith, and then charity, reveals this mystery to reason and to love.

Kant is mistaken when, criticizing metaphysics, he discerns an aporia between the God-cause of pure reason and the God of religion.[8] There would be "a vast abyss"[9]

---

8 See Immanuel Kant, "Of the Impossibility of Physico-Theological Proof" in *Critique of Pure Reason*, ed. Marcus Weigelt, (London: Penguin Classics, 2007), 518–524.
9 *Eine so weite Kluft*. Kant, "Of the Impossibility of Physico-Theological Proof," 520–521.

between Cause and God if that were true. This is because metaphysics cannot provide us with a decisive concept of the supreme cause of the world, and therefore it would be insufficient as a theological principle which is foundational to religion. For Kant—and this is his truly unforgivable *a priori*—"the step leading to absolute totality is entirely impossible on the empirical road."[10] In other words, God can only be reached through moral effort, not by reason. In reality, the uncaused Cause, reason of everything including my own being, is a Person with an intellect and a will, with a heart. The God-cause is Reason and Love. A morality without reason is pure voluntarism and the cause of contemporary barbarity. Today we have cultivated a love without morality, an empty love.

2. REASON AND LOVE AS RATIONAL PRESUPPOSITION

The pairing of reason-love is a cognitive paradigm and, as we will see, is the foundation on which another pairing rests: the union of faith and charity. Reason and love form a virtuous circularity, within which reason informs love, and love perfects and completes reason. Reason brings me to love, and love reveals the need for reason. Reason, initially moved by will—by which I decide to know something instead of remaining inactive—acts as a beginning, while love acts as perfection and completion. I must approach things I want to know and see reality as other than me through being—something that is—and so I decide to know what that thing is. Reason moves me to grasp the truth of something, to know precisely what it is, and to name things. A name corresponds to

---

[10] *Der Schritt zu der absoluten Totalität ist durch den empirischen Weg ganz und gar unmöglich.* Kant, "Of the Impossibility of Physico-Theological Proof," 520–521.

and indicates an essence, not simply the sound of a voice, contrary to the claims of nominalism.

Reality is other than me and therefore is knowable. The substantial difference between the knowing subject and the known object must be preserved. Otherwise, there is no cognitive encounter, and I myself would shape the object. Such is the error of idealism, which ultimately concludes in the gloomiest pragmatism, stating that reality is the source of power and is shaped through action. It would not be knowable as other than me, but as an *I* which works and in working does things, establishes laws, determines what is good and what is evil. True reason, on the other hand, is objective; it drives toward reality and gently contains it within itself as known object (known because it is other than the subject). The two spheres, the objective and subjective plane, cannot be confused. Ideological systems, especially Communist dictatorships, unite subject and object to transform things into a source of domination, trampling freedom and the otherness of reality underfoot.

While reason moves me toward what is other than me, it does not tell me that what is other than me is something more than a mere object. To see the entity toward which I stretch as *res* to be respected and to leave in its otherness, reason must be accompanied by will so that love may proceed from it. The will understands the object known by the intellect under the species of good, that is, as an entity which is not just true but also morally important because it exists. Precisely because it is morally good that object is more than a mere intellectual fact. It is always a good according to its nature, but that good could also be a person with whom a relationship can be initiated. The will guides love to discover in the known object first its goodness and finally its relationality, which I know and love. I know because I love — otherwise I would not even know — and I love because at last I have known. Here love is not to be confused with falling in love, which involves affectivity, but is rather the rationality of freedom, which drives us to become one with the object known, if indeed that *res* is not just necessary for my knowledge but is also a source of interrelation. So, love guides reason in the settling of an interpersonality, that is, in moral responsibility. Love establishes a personal bond with reality.

What's more, desire drives me toward that good known as truth and guides me in faithfulness to that good. Love is faithfulness to the known good. It is devotion to the good which is truth par excellence. Truth is a good, and goodness is the supreme truth. Reason gives me truth, and love reveals to me that truth is a good; it is a good per se, without selfishness. So, I move to embrace it and make it my own in freedom and in giving. Love drives me even to give my life for that truth. Think of Socrates who chose to renounce his earthly life rather than betray the truth. The truth of Socrates, since it is embraced by love, does not die with the great philosopher but survives in Plato and the other great pre-Christian philosophers, thus preparing the path for Christianity. In Socrates's own life, it is the *logos* which encourages *diá-logos*; truth initiates dialogue, and dialogue is possible in respect of the other — we would add in love for the other. Benedict XVI writes: "Truth, in fact, is *lógos* which creates *diá-logos* and hence communication and communion."[11]

Without truth I would have a non-good. In other words, I would not have good because truth would be transformed into mere interest. Without love of the good I would have non-truth, because truth would be pure

---

11   Pope Benedict XVI, *Caritas in Veritate*, 4.

evaluation or a selfish possession. Reason and love must go together and thus discover that reality is greater than the knowing subject. Reality precedes men and women and surpasses them in their effort to know and love. It is also true that humanity embraces the whole of reality, visible and invisible, if it remains steadfast in its aim to link intellect and will, reason and love. This embrace is not possession but the revelation of the paradigmatic harmony of reality. To overlook it and always encounter it with a sense of wonder, one must understand and love. One must understand to love and love to understand.

3. FAITH AND CHARITY AS REVELATORY FULFILMENT

Reason and love guide us by the hand to the fullness of reality, and thus to faith, hope, and charity. Faith and charity are closely united, so that one recalls the other and relies on the other. Together they offer us the totality of what it means to be Christian. The circular process that characterizes reason and love is also presented again in the revealed sphere. Faith is the truthful measure, while charity is the fullness that satisfies it; faith reveals the truth of God, and charity His life communicated to humanity in grace. Faith purifies in order to 'see' God, charity is the possession of God, namely, being in Him. Faith and charity find their unity in the mystery of God believed and loved. Indirectly, reason and love enable us to see the totality of being and so draw close to God, contemplating Him as Logos-Love. There can be no faith without charity, nor charity without faith. Faith is the measure for charity, the truth of love. Charity is the fullness of truth for faith; it is fulfilment, revelation of the intimate longing to see God, passing from knowledge to love. Faith is adherence to God; charity is His loving possession.

3.1 *From faith to charity*

Charity that renounces faith would be tantamount to a divine sentiment, and a faith which renounced charity would be a calculation aimed at guaranteeing one's own salvation, which, however, could not be secured without charity. Thus, Benedict XVI explains the circular link of faith and charity, which has its starting point in truth:

> *Only in truth does charity shine forth*, only in truth can charity be authentically lived. Truth is the light that gives meaning and value to charity. That light is both the light of reason and the light of faith, through which the intellect attains to the natural and supernatural truth of charity: it grasps its meaning as gift, acceptance, and communion. Without truth, charity degenerates into sentimentality. Love becomes an empty shell, to be filled in an arbitrary way. In a culture without truth, this is the fatal risk facing love. It falls prey to contingent subjective emotions and opinions, the word "love" is abused and distorted, to the point where it comes to mean the opposite. Truth frees charity from the constraints of an emotionalism that deprives it of relational and social content, and of a fideism that deprives it of human and universal breathing-space. In the truth, charity reflects the personal yet public dimension of faith in the God of the Bible, who is both *Agápe* and *Lógos*: Charity and Truth, Love and Word.[12]

Faith acts as generative principle and charity as perfective form. We find this link in St. Thomas Aquinas when he says: "*Caritas dicitur forma fidei, in quantum per*

---

12   Benedict XVI, *Caritas in Veritate*, 3.

caritatem actus fidei perficitur et formatur."[13] Therefore, in the logic of circularity, faith is at the start in that it is first in the *ordo generationis,* while charity is first in the *ordo perfectionis.*[14] The latter comes second because it is generated, but it retains primacy since it is the only thing that remains into eternity. A central idea emerges in the New Testament: faith only exists pursuant to charity.[15] Faith *works* through charity (cf. Gal 5:6). So, there can be no faith which is not per se directed toward love, that is toward union with God and service of one's neighbor; faith, when it is the act of a believing subject, but is not also assent to supernatural truths that are embraced and put into practice, is a non-faith; it simply does not exist as such. A *fides qua creditur* that is not simultaneously *fides quae creditur* is not faith. The drastic separation between these two dimensions of the same theological faith has caused enormous and ruinous consequences for Lutheran and Catholic theology. One of the many is the justification of doubts about faith raised to the same level as the act of faith, so that within the same believing person the non-believer and the atheist could co-exist.[16]

Man enters into the way of God by faith, which is the start of new life. Faith reveals God to humanity, and by

---

13   *Summa Theologiae,* II–II, q. 4, a. 3.
14   Ibid., I–II, q. 62, a. 4 and I–II, q. 66, a. 6.
15   See Andrea Bellandi, *L'amore pienezza della fede. Solo la carità conosce* (Milan: Paoline, 2004), 9. See also, inter alia: 1 Cor 13:2; 2 Cor 8:7; Eph 3:17; Col 1:4; 1 Thess 5:8; Rev 2:19. In his monograph on the faith-charity relationship, Bellandi takes his lead from the reflections of Rino Fisichella, "Fides quaerens caritatem: ovvero l'amore come presupposto della fede" in Rino Fisichella, ed., *Noi crediamo. Per una teologia dell'atto di fede* (Rome: Edizioni dehoniane, 1993), 177–193.
16   See Antonio Livi, *La deriva irrazionalistica nella teologia cattolica e le sue radici luterane,* 89–121.

faith men and women respond to God, recognizing Him as Creator and Lord. Now, the One who *reveals* Himself in faith is in Himself love and gift. He *is* Love. He is at the intimate door of men and women and knocks so that He may be given complete access. Here, charity completes faith, giving it, in the inspiration of relatedness, the true joy of being and living in God. Thus, friendship with the Lord is nourished, and from His being-with the Christian grows in his or her charity toward neighbor.

The stronger the faith is, the richer is the charity, which, filling men and women with God's presence, pours out, as if overflowing, over others. We cannot give what we are not. We give to others in effective and generous charity that which we have drawn from diligent faith. Otherwise, we would be giving only ourselves; we would be giving from what St. Bernard defined as *amor carnalis*.

Without faith, charity as such does not exist. While action could certainly be beautiful social work, all things considered, it is limping along between the total desire for good and the ability to offer solely what we consider to be such — a good which we have not drawn from God. Insofar as we believe in *Deus-Caritas* we recognize true good, and we always give to others what is true and good. Again, Benedict XVI highlights this intimate connection: "Faith is knowing the truth and adhering to it (cf. *1 Tim* 2:4); charity is "walking" in the truth (cf. *Eph* 4:15). Through faith we enter into friendship with the Lord, through charity this friendship is lived and cultivated (cf. *Jn* 15:14ff)."[17]

Faith should never be alone or against charity. Then, one will begin to despise good works, thus isolating oneself in a sort of self-redemption. This is the risk of fidesim.

---

17 Pope Benedict XVI, Message for Lent 2013: "Believing in charity calls forth charity."

Nor should charity stand alone without faith, for then Christianity is reduced to a mere organization that does many things but lacks a clear identity. This is the risk of moral activism. Both risks have been denounced by Benedict XVI.

However, the most harmful of the two is lack of faith because it affects the Christian *incipit* itself. Where faith is struggling and vague, the apparent charity is prone to a relativistic moralism; faith becomes moralism. Notable and deferential agreements for co-operation can be reached, but the truth will no longer be clearly proclaimed.

Recently, the debate about non-negotiable values (surprisingly for Pope Francis they should not even be called non-negotiable, because all values should be such) exchanged for questionable ethical substitutes, has its basis in a mistaken idea of charity without faith and truth. The Church should be ready to take a step back to understand the real needs of humanity and distinguish what is most compelling from what is not. In the name of the "common good," it is necessary to come to an agreement. Where there is no clear starting point — which is truth, because *all* truth is always first — for which there is a precedence, charity is susceptible to the most varied interpretations.

3.2 From charity to faith

Faith cannot stop at the noetic element, satisfied at a superficial knowledge or formal adherence to Christ. It is necessary to live by Him, to contemplate Him, and so carry Him by the works of one's own hands. Contemplation and action must always co-exist and be integrated. If they were to split apart it would be easy to go from a faith without charity to a charity without faith. Several authors have tried to identify the essence of Christianity — that indispensable nucleus which would mean everything else could be put to one side — and have often recognized it in the Gospel's "ethical message." An *ethos* would rule over *worship*, contemplation, and adoration. In this case, it would not matter if Jesus was really the Son of God — which according to A. Von Harnack, for example, is improbable — for the only necessary thing would be His teaching on goodness, whose only foundation is love.

In our culture, which is beset by weak thought, the great temptation to reduce Christianity to a religion of goodness without truth remains, because the latter would not be knowable. Only subjective and partial truths, not the whole truth, would exist. According to some, it is difficult to affirm the salvific uniqueness of Christ compared to other religions without the claim degrading into intransigence and intolerance, and therefore becoming foreign to the Christian life. The path of goodness could then be wider and would allow us to resolve the dilemma *in nuce*. In charity we encounter the other without pointing to a truth that could divide us. The Gospel itself would invite us to realize the moment of truth in the experiential and relational moment, because, after all, the universal judgment itself will be based on charity.[18] One forgets that at the same judgment the Lord will demand profession of faith in Him and recognition of Him before humanity.[19] The charity on which the judgment will focus does not exclude faith but presupposes it. So, if there is faith in the Son of God there will also be the truth of charity, which is to do to Christ that which will be done to one of the least of *His* brothers or sisters in need. How will we be able to see the face of Christ in the least of His brothers

---

18   See Mt 25:31–46,
19   See Mt 10:32–33; Lk 12:8.

and sisters, and therefore be charitable, without first having seen Christ with faith? It is simplifying, if not banal, to base a sort of salvific ecumenism on the charity of the final judgment. Charity without truth is pure sentiment.

In addition, an impossible division in God between omnipotence and goodness is postulated. Faith and charity are not opposed, just as reason and love are not divided. Rather, they imply each other. Without reason love is empty, and without love reason is cold necessity. Without the truth of the Gospel, charity dies out. Therefore, the greatest charity is precisely the gift of faith — the proclamation of the Gospel to all men and women. The greatest charity is to work for the conversion of everyone to Christ in His Church. Our evangelization must be firmly based on this indissoluble pairing, which enlightens the being of God in Himself. Otherwise, one is self-condemned to good intentions or moralisms, which the world applauds.

Finally, we can ask ourselves: Would charity ever be given without sanctifying grace and therefore without faith? No, charity begins in faith and perfects it. Just as in God omnipotence and love, logos and agape, are one, so in the believer faith and charity form a unity with hope in sanctifying grace. There is never charity without faith, even though it is possible for faith to remain without charity. A parallel can be drawn with the sacrament of faith, Baptism, and the sacrament of charity, the Eucharist. Faith is the entry into God's inner dwelling. The Eucharist is the heart. Without faith the Eucharist cannot be understood; the former, in fact, is pulling toward the latter. Without charity the gift of baptism does not develop; it risks remaining frozen at its beginning, until it becomes dry.

It is a great challenge for the new evangelization to position faith and charity in unity. We are called to give the Truth, Christ, to everyone through love, and to reveal Him not by word but by deed, through works of truth. Faith reveals to us the truth about Christ, incarnate Love. Charity makes us enjoy this Love. Everything converges in love and is rooted in God forever.

4. DOCTRINE AND PASTORAL CARE IN A CIRCULAR RELATIONSHIP

To deepen the relationship between reason and love, faith and charity, we must now consider another relationship that is at the foundation of Christian life and based precisely on the fundamental circularity of truth and charity: the relationship between doctrine and pastoral care. Doctrine is the faith of the Church, the truth believed and understood — or even better understood and believed — while pastoral care is charity which sees and realizes the believed doctrinal principles, tranfoming them into food for the faithful. Thus, faith becomes operational. This is the origin of pastoral actions and choices.

4.1 *The doctrine of the Logos*

Let us begin with the question: what is doctrine? It is the teaching (*didaké*) of Jesus, coming ultimately from the Father who is in heaven (cf. Jn 7:16). It is a new teaching, astonishing because it is accompanied by the authority of the one teaching (cf. Mk 1:27); and therefore, it is a definitive teaching (cf. also 2 Jn 1:10). The didaké of Jesus is the only oral testimony we have of the Son, reported in the Gospels, and it is His definitive revelation of the mystery of God and our salvation. Jesus did not write the Gospel, as we well know, but He proclaimed it by teaching His *doctrine*. We already see an intimate relationship between doctrine and life, teaching and salvation: the (oral) teaching of the Lord is aimed essentially at the conversion of men and women through the proclamation of the truth; vice versa, eternal salvation is achieved by listening to this proclamation — *"fides ex auditu"* (Rom 10:17) — from which the faith, and therefore charity, originates. The divine Tradition, therefore, as a progression from oral proclamation to oral and written transmission of faith, is the compendium of doctrine and Christian life, faith and charity. Without the teaching of Jesus there is no Christian life. Thus, fruitful and up-to-date pastoral care always starts from the pure teaching of the Lord, handed on continuously by the Church; in return, doctrine is necessary for our salvation, so that faith might be aroused.

Doctrine and pastoral care, therefore, are tied to truth and love in a circular manner; doctrine serves pastoral action and pastoral care emanates from doctrine. While we can begin with one of the two, we can never exclude one from the other. For pastoral reasons, we might prefer to emphasize missionary work and creativity, but we would not renounce the doctrine by geting rid of it or leaving it to one side, as if it were a threat to creativity; that would be mere pragmatism. Likewise, we could begin with the doctrine of the faith, in a more speculative or catechetical context and thus provide the correct principles for action and evangelization. However, we would not exclude pastoral care, believing it to be counter-productive, and refuse to make a choice while awaiting the most auspicious historical moment; in this case, faith would become mere intellectualism. Doctrine, like faith, has a commencement reason, while pastoral care, like charity, has a reason of implementation and therefore perfection. Only when praxis is rooted in doctrine does it resist falling into mere Christian activism, a praxis which from time to time tries to change the world through our own actions and abilities. Only when doctrine is understood with a view toward evangelization, the winning over of all people to the Gospel and to the Truth, does it resist becoming reduced to a mere intellectual exercise, which nourishes the mind but does not reach the heart and easily disposes itself to the accusation of Pharisaism.

In reality, wouldn't it be more compelling to try to replace the word *pastoral* — so full of unfortunate conontations, and even contradictory meanings — that has become like a password in the current Church, which willingly describes itself as post-conciliar, along with the word *evangelization* or *new evangelization*? Pastoral should mean nothing other than supporting the Christian zeal to bring all men and women to the Gospel. On the other hand, if pastoral is conceived as a practical alternative to dodge the narrow doctrinal bottlenecks and favors a softer approach to faith, then, it would not only turn into ideological praxis, but we would also have eliminated its meaning of love, which begins from truth and bestows truth. Truth ought to be given, and the gift is only truly a blessing if it carries the truth with it; otherwise, it is a deception.

4.2 Knowledge of the Good Shepherd

We can look in-depth at the intimate circularity between doctrine and pastoral care by reflecting on the Johannine teaching of the Good Shepherd. Pastoral care must always be inspired by Jesus, who is the unique pastor who guides us. All pastors, made such by priestly ordination, must imitate Him. In fact, we can say that in the Church there is one pastor, Jesus, and that all other pastors are such only in Jesus because they represent Him. The Petrine ministry, too, is a *munus* of the Good Shepherd.[20] Jesus is the Good Shepherd who gives His life for His sheep.[21] The Good Shepherd knows His sheep and His sheep know Him, just as the Father knows the Son and the Son knows the Father and gives His life for the sheep.[22] The Greek expresses this relationship between Jesus and His sheep in a more profound manner,[23] rooted in *knowledge*, which establishes a familial relationship and therefore an experience. The sheep are indicated only with the possessive pronoun *tà emà*, meaning "my own," which places an even stronger emphasis on (cognitive) possession of them by the Good Shepherd and vice versa. The Shepherd knows *His* and *His* know Him.

This knowledge is therefore an intimate, intellectual, and affective relationship between the Shepherd and His sheep — a reflection of the Father's love toward the Son and vice versa. At the center of this life-giving relationship between the Good Shepherd, the sheep, and the Father (the Father, the mediator of salvation, and the faithful)

---

20 Jesus institutes Peter as "rock" to confirm his brothers in the faith (See Lk 22:32), and this *munus* of the truth and of doctrine must be exercised with the aim of feeding the Lord's sheep and lambs (See Jn 21:15–18). In the office of the Supreme Pontiff the necessary circularity of faith and charity, faith and pastoral guidance is highlighted. Peter must learn to equate the love of Christ: his *filial*-love will become *agápe*-love and only thus will he be able to guide all the sheep in this *communion* with the Lord, remaining firm in His Word and so confirming in the one Word. Peter will learn this fully in the offering of his own life.

21 See Jn 10:11.

22 See Jn 10:14–15.

23 See Jn 10:14. The verb used is *ginósko*, which in this context means "to get acquainted," "to become familiar," in the knowledge of God and of Christ and in things about them. See also Jn 17:3; 1 Cor 1:21. Cf. Joseph Henry Thayer, *Thayer's Greek-English Lexicon of the New Testament* (1995), 1097, II.

is the eternal Logos become the Good Shepherd in His incarnation, which has its salvific fulfilment in redemption through His death on the Cross. By dying, giving His life for His sheep, the Good Shepherd has become ransom for them and the food of life. Christ gives His life to His own, because He Himself is Spirit, Giver of Life. The Logos is the Bread of Life. Contained in the Eucharist is the food for the sheep, which is doctrine and life, truth and love, tied together for ever in the unique person of the Savior Word.

At the center of this cognitive and experiential relationship is the Son, the incarnate Logos. The doctrine and teaching of the Son, the reflection of His mystery of *Word* made flesh, is the relationship between Christ, the Father, and His sheep. The doctrine of the Son who feeds the sheep with the Father's truth is at the center; the sheep, remaining united to the Good Shepherd, in the truth of His salvific doctrine, remain united to the Father. Only if the sheep remain in the knowledge of Christ do they experience His love. His love is true freedom. It is the freedom of the ninety-nine who do not wander off while the Shepherd goes in search of the one who is lost.[24] Knowledge of the Good Shepherd is the source of life. It connects with God and joins us in Christ; it invites us into this relationship in which Christ is the door, through whom there is access as Logos, measure, truth, and therefore love.

Through salvific knowledge of the Good Shepherd, we can better understand what Jesus means when He states that His teaching is not His own but that of the One who sent Him: "*Mea doctrina non est mea sed eis qui misit me*" (Jn 7:16). Commenting on this Johannine passage, St, Augustine, in rhetorical fashion, asks himself: "What

---

24   See Mt 18:12–14.

then is the doctrine of the Father, but the Father's Word? Therefore, Christ Himself is the doctrine of the Father, if He is the Word of the Father."[25] So, if we speak of the doctrine of Christ, we speak of the Word of God. St. Augustine adds: "The Word then is God; and it is also the Word of a stable, unchangeable doctrine, not such as can be surrounded by syllables and fleeting, but abiding with the Father, to which abiding doctrine let us be converted, being admonished by the transitory sounds of the voice."[26]

So, rejection of Christian doctrine is rejection of Christ, the very Word of God, and not of fleeting syllables. To set aside doctrine to make room for pastoral care is not only contradictory, but hides an explicit rejection of Christ. To shelve doctrine, with the hope that it might be preserved intact, but thus isolating it from life and from the flow of existence, is to distance Christ from the life of humanity. In the end, rejection of the doctrine of faith is a new but ancient Christological heresy; it is a modern version of Arianism, in which Christ is not just a mere creature and not God, but also a mere praxiologist and not the truth to be contemplated. Christ's teaching, far from being a cold and dark system of concepts distant from life, from the daily and frenetic rush of things, is in reality the heart of the Christian life, because it transmits the life of the eternal Logos, which without any division or confusion is Truth and Charity. In Christ, doctrine and pastoral care are joined together and acquire mutual meaning.

As we now turn to the next chapter, we try to discover a paradigmatic circularity of truth and love offered by the Encyclical letter *Deus Caritas Est*.

---

25 St. Augustine, *Tractates on the Gospel of John*, Homily 29, no. 3.
26 Ibid., no. 4.

The Truth about Love for Love in Truth
THE PARADIGM OF *DEUS CARITAS EST*

INTRODUCTION

"God is love, and he who abides in love abides in God, and God abides in him" (1 Jn 4:16). Thus begins Benedict XVI's first encyclical letter, a reflection on God and humanity in the third millennium. Love is the key to the Christian mystery because it is the essence of God and the first element of humanity. To understand love in its true essence one must formulate a correct judgment about God and humanity. The defense of love, the restoration of its true face in a time and culture which speak only of love when there is no love, is a fundamental requirement to speak about God to modern men and women. Love in truth is a path which leads us to God, which is hidden in the intimate primordial whisper of humanity, that is, in love. God becomes close to men and women as the truth of His loving being. In true love one can see the true God and, in return, true humanity. God and humanity are combined by the truth of love. The true God, the true *religio*, and the true theology create the only melody of the truth of love, in other words of the manifold unity of the being of love. To be and to love are one in God and can become one in us, to the extent that, giving back our truth to love, we truly begin to love, to love truth, and to see the truth in love.

The Truth about Love for Love in Truth

In this section we will highlight the main aspects of Benedict XVI's first encyclical, clarifying a manner of theological progress somewhat attributable to an apologetic progress, an apologia of love from which a defence of God and humanity arises. The theological-magisterial passages of the encyclical will thus introduce us to the discourse concerning the circularity of truth and love, which could be defined, in a certain sense, as the totality of reality. Thus, we would like to insert once again and widely in the theological-fundamental semantics the meaning of *apologetics* or *apologetic discourse*, which moving from its unity with fundamental dogmatics, is characterized precisely as *defence* and *proposal* of the truth of love, for a love *in* truth and a love *of* the Truth. For this purpose, we will begin with metaphysics, an essential prerequisite for theological work, the agapic feature that enlivens a cold analysis of being as being by opening theological doors to a being that certainly is what it is and cannot not be otherwise. This being is known to be love through Revelation and faith; love is true being because God is love. The agapic circularity of being, that is, the logic-ontological pairing of truth-love, would thus become a sort of apologetic-fundamental union, which would enable us to identify mode of proceeding in both theology and philosophy that never departs from the totality of reality in fidelity to the agapic truth. Truth-love stands in contrast to those who have either not yet accepted the faith of Christ or have squandered it; additionally, this mode of proceeding is opposed to a theological preparation that, often dissolving truth in love, ultimately raises serious difficulties about the mystery of God, consequently promoting a distorted image of humanity and its affairs. Finally, the symphonic pairing of truth and love could become a fundamental theological tool for an apologetic deconstruction of the non-truth that presents itself as barely persuasive goodness, which makes an appearance in nearly every theoretical system; by eliminating this falsehood, truth-love could prepare a fertile ground for the supernatural circularity of faith and charity.

Therefore, we are humble upholders of a firm theology, rooted in the truth of the God who does not change according to the times and seasons — a theology that becomes a "ministry of the Spirit" (2 Cor 3:8), of the "Spirit of truth" which "guides into all the truth" (Jn 16:13), of the Spirit who is Love alone, who is agapic communion alone.[1]

1. DEUS CARITAS EST, AN APOLOGIA OF LOVE

Benedict XVI's first encyclical, with a majestic touch, reaches out to God. *Deus* is the first word of Benedict's document; the God who is love combines at the same time a metaphysical fact of the divine being realizing itself in *agape* and His eternal complicity in the gift of self. *Deus Caritas Est* is not a programmatic papal encyclical, but rather a theological response to the human imperative that is love, so widespread today with many new and often erroneous meanings. Love is on everyone's lips. Everything is love. In this way it is disincarnated from its true soil so that it is reduced to nothing, a simple thing, an item, something sold or produced. Surrounded by a culture in which even offences against love pass for love, it was necessary to point out to Christians, and to all men and women of goodwill, that love "is greater than our heart" (1 Jn 3:20), that love is greater than us, because it comes from God and that God is love. So, Benedict SVI's first document on God's love is presented as a synergy of two well-composed parts. The first is aimed at defining love

---

[1] See Phil 2:1

as stemming from a unique source, namely, God who is love in a dialectic of eros and agape. The latter dimension of love purifies and elevates the former in a circularity of the truth of love and love in truth. The second part places the emphasis on the caritas of the Church and on the Church that is caritas. Caritas-agape manifests the mystery of the *Ecclesia de Trinitate*, that is, of the Church, which originated from the embrace of the three eternal Co-Lovers. From here the emphasis is on the Church's structures of charity—the Church's expression of the mystery of love—with a final call to those responsible for the Church's charitable works.

The historic and ecclesial time in which Providence has placed us is certainly not the happiest of times. The panorama which presents itself is that of a strongly secularized society, whose most pronounced need is the absence of the concept of truth as "*adequatio intellectum ad rem,*" as the objective reality which is outside the subject and other than the subject. Humanity is weak, incapable of definitive and satisfying judgements. A secularization of the concept of God as the living God has opened the doors to the sacred sought in a disorderly way, which gives life more often than not to a do-it-yourself religion. With the loss of the concept of truth and the good consequent to it, and therefore the loss of a moral life capable of enlightening the subject about decisive choices, men and women find themselves closed within their exasperated individualism. Within themselves they choose, create, and plan. While the concept of truth is overturned in the sea of relativism, the life-giving strength of men and women, which is love, has not fallen, but has in fact grown disproportionately. The only longing left to humanity is that of love; this original and fundamental longing, now deprived of its ontological foundation, falls one minute into vulgar passion, the next minute into a feeling pursued like pure lust. Love in some way is the only *chance* given to post-modern humanity to continue to be; everyone clings to love to continue to be themselves, as a last reaction to that bleak subjectivism which reigns supreme.

1.1 *Agape as truth of eros*

So why not tell today's men and women the truth about love, which is so glorified but at the same time so misunderstood? Why not begin with love to tell men and women, who only want to hear about love, that the truth about themselves, about reality, about God, is realized precisely in love? "God's love for us," the Pope writes, "is fundamental for our lives, and it raises important questions about who God is and who we are."[2] In the truth of love, love for truth will be reached. In fact, the encyclical starts with the truth of love, rewriting a difficult but true harmony of the pairing that many thought was diametrically opposed: the eros-agape relationship. In the dialectic of these two components of the one unique love the truth of love comes into play, ultimately guiding today's men and women down a path which, beginning with love — that phenomenon so fundamental for their lives — leads them to God through a path of ascesis, purification, and sacrifice. Eros, Benedict XVI tells us, needs agape to be itself, so that it does not fall into mere sensual pleasure and contribute to the commercialization of love. Men and women need God. Eros becomes a path to agape, a path to God.

In this way love is redeemed, in its human element, from that subjectivist and selfish sphere of intoxicating transcience, which, left at the mercy of itself, arrives at

---

2 Pope Benedict XVI, *Deus Caritas Est* (December, 25, 2005), 2.

an erroneous conception of love. After all, this is what gave rise to Friedrich Nietzsche's criticism of Christianity: Christianity corrupts eros, poisons it with its prohibitions, and degenerates love into vice.[3] When eros becomes a norm in itself, it seeks degeneration in the poison of its truth. The German philosopher responds with an initial philosophical analysis of eros in the post-Christian world, the climate of natural creation common to all, to demonstrate that Christianity did not poison eros, but that eros per se needs to be redeemed, raised, and purified. The Pope's analysis of Greek philosophy shows that, first and foremost, eros is bound in some way to the Divine and is a kind of communion with the Divine: "love promises infinity, eternity — a reality far greater and totally other than our everyday existence."[4] Love therefore always remains at a higher level because it truly is elevated and not blind instinct; it needs to follow the "path of renunciation."[5]

Men and women discover a path of redemption for selfish eros by examining their constitution: they are not just body, that is, matter, but they are soul and body, spirit and matter. These two dimensions interpenetrate each other. One needs the other and is the truth of the other. "Only when both dimensions are truly united, does man attain his full stature. Only thus is love, eros, able to mature and attain its authentic grandeur."[6] In fact, euphoric and undisciplined eros leads to the debasement of humanity. Men and women need to regain their true identity. Eros is fascination that goes beyond the finite, seeking the beautiful through the finite. The spirituality of

---

3 See Pope Benedict XVI, *Deus Caritas Est*, 3.
4 Ibid., 5.
5 Ibid., 5.
6 Ibid., 5.

men and women — their intelligence and will — is the natural path for the discovery of a beauty that surpasses the natural. Thus, eros is taught, through a path of ascesis, to transcend pure covetousness and open itself to love as gift.

Turning to the Bible — which at this time is in the background of salvation history and therefore supernatural Revelation — to further support the eros-agape pairing, the Pope examines a book of the Old Testament very dear to the mystics, the Song of Songs (In the first part of the document Benedict XVI explains the unity of love in creation and in salvation history). Here one sees a sort of gradual perfection of the concept of love. Initially love is rather possessive and selfish; it is *dodim.* Then this word is replaced by *ahabà* (in the LXX *agape*), a characteristic expression for the Biblical idea of love. This word will be essential to the New Testament to indicate its full scope. Love-agape becomes a love that cares for the other, that desires the other for the reason of the other and not to rediscover oneself in the other, a love that wants to move out of one's own self toward the other. Love-agape "is [not] self-seeking, a sinking in the intoxication of happiness; instead, it seeks the good of the beloved: it becomes renunciation, and it is ready, and even willing, for sacrifice."[7]

Together, eros and agape carve out the true face of love. Their intrinsic bond testifies that love is one despite its dual dimension: the ascending (eros) and the descending (agape). They intersect and are required like body and spirit, reason and faith. The love of humanity seeks perpetuity; it needs to renounce the selfish 'I' to find in the other the fullness of self, and, in the final analysis, to rediscover true identity in God. The word of the Lord looms on the horizon: "Anyone who tries to preserve his life will lose it;

---

7 Pope Benedict XVI, *Deus Caritas Est*, 6.

and anyone who loses it will keep it safe" (Lk 17:33). Love has its fullness only in God. The love of men and women is purified by the love of God, by the agape which is God. So agape becomes the truth of eros, that is, agape makes eros capable of perpetuity and raises it to an eternal condition.

In this regard, Sacred Scripture provides us with an extraordinary image of God and humanity. There is a magnificent harmony between creation and redemption, the key pairing of the possible unity of eros and agape. The God of Israel is the one God, Creator of all things, and therefore the God of all men and women. He is a God who loves and chooses His people. Nevertheless "God loves, and his love may certainly be called *eros*, yet it is also totally *agape*."[8] He is a God who loves His people passionately, even when He is betrayed. His is a love which pardons, a love that pursues the lost sheep even to the Cross, where Love lets Himself be crucified. God becomes man and allows Himself to be condemned and killed for love. In Christ eros and agape touch. God's love is "so great that it turns God against himself, his love against his justice."[9] In the Bible, Love becomes the metaphysical essence of God.

With great theological prowess, the Pope sees in this God's loving turning against Himself a dual meaning of the concept of God, a metaphysical image of God which is outlined in an agapic vision. The idea of God presented to us by Sacred Scripture is a metaphysical concept that is realized in love. The Pope says: "The philosophical dimension to be noted in this biblical vision, and its importance from the standpoint of the history of religions, lies in the fact that on the one hand we find ourselves before a strictly metaphysical image of God: God is the absolute

---

8   Pope Benedict XVI, *Deus Caritas Est*, 9.
9   Ibid., 10.

and ultimate source of all being; but this universal principle of creation — the *Logos*, primordial reason — is at the same time a lover with all the passion of a true love. *Eros* is thus supremely ennobled, yet at the same time it is so purified as to become one with *agape*."[10] The unity of eros and agape resides in the Logos, in the Word who is the fullness of creation and the Lord glorified in redemption.

The Love of God in Christ becomes Love which is made flesh. The Lucan parables of mercy,[11] in fact, are not just a simple description of the compassionate, loving God who seeks the lost sheep, the lost drachma, or the son who had died and has now come back to life; rather, it is the very journey of Christ, the fate of the grain of wheat[12] fallen to the earth to let Himself be ground in His passion and buried in His death to then rise again in the resurrection. The Eucharist, "God's own *agape*"[13] becomes the sacramental expression of this paschal mystery, the everlasting seal of Christ's love "to the end" (Jn 13:1), to the last drop of His blood pouring from His side pierced on the cross.[14] The Eucharist is God's agapic love in Christ forever. The bread that is Christ makes us His and in Him makes us one.[15] In the Eucharist, then, we discover in a tangible way that the commandment of love of God and love of neighbor are one commandment, because it is one love. In the Eucharist, "Love of God and love of neighbour are now truly united: God incarnate draws us all to himself."[16]

---

10 Pope Benedict XVI, *Deus Caritas Est*, 10.
11 See Lk 15:1–32.
12 See Jn 12:24.
13 *Deus Caritas Est*, 14.
14 See Jn 19:34.
15 See 1 Cor 10:17.
16 *Deus Caritas Est*, 14.

The Truth about Love for Love in Truth

In the Eucharist love of God and neighbor, eros and agape, inter-penetrate; they merge in a greater lover, that love which is God and which comes from God.[17] In the agapic sacrament faith, worship, and *ethos* also inter-penetrate, without any need to separate worship from ethics. This union creates an irreconcilable opposition between prayer and help to the person in need. It is the Eucharist, supreme thanksgiving, that brings us to the person in need, that brings us out of our selfishness and opens us to the needs of others, to *caritas*. Intrinsic unity with others is born from participation in the one bread, that is, from forming one body. Christ, who is praise and thanksgiving[18] to the Father, the Amen which rises to God,[19] becomes the strength and courage of our charity by uniting us to Himself in the Eucharistic gift. Thus, the second part of the Pope's document is already clear.

1.2 Caritas-Agape as truth of the Church

In the second part of the encyclical Pope Benedict moves from agape as truth of love to caritas as truth of the Church. Here the Pope sets out a discourse that defines truth as the agape of God. The choice of referring immediately to the pairing caritas-agape[20] highlights that the great New Testament texts praising charity use the Greek term agape. For example, 1 Cor 13:3 says, "If I give away all my possessions, and if I hand over my body to be burned, but do not have love, I gain nothing," which is described as "the *Magna Carta* of all ecclesial service,"[21] and 2 Cor 5:14, "The love of Christ urges us on." Clearly, Christian charity is always

---

17 See Pope Benedict XVI, *Deus Caritas Est*, 18.
18 See Eph 1:6.
19 See Rev 3:14.
20 *Deus Caritas Est*, 25/b.
21 Ibid., 34.

caritas Christi, a Trinitarian reflection of the love which finds in Christ all its human-divine reason. Charity is a manifestation of the Trinity,[22] as the Pope tells us at the start of the second part. One can thus see a thread which again binds love into a unity, precisely in the consideration of caritas-agape as service to others, driven by Christ, by the God agape of 1 Jn 4:16, which is the *incipit* of the whole magisterial document.[23] That God who is love and in Christ has revealed His Face makes our charity practical. There is no Church without charity, which is a reflection in time of the mystery of the divine One-Trinity, and there is no charity without the agape of God. So, love of neighbor rooted in love of God becomes a task for each of the faithful, but especially for the Church as a community.[24]

The exercise of charity is an essential task of the Church. This reality is proclaimed in the election and consecration of seven men of good standing, "full of the Spirit and of wisdom" (Acts 6:1-6), who are set aside for this task. They are the foundation of the *diaconia* of the Church dedicated to service of love of neighbor, an office that would remain inscribed in the "fundamental structure of the Church,"[25] "as one of her essential activities, along with the administration of the sacraments and the proclamation of the word."[26] In such a way, the intimate structure of the Church — and with the passage of the centuries it was confirmed — became tripartite: kerygmatic-martyrological (proclamation of the Word of God), liturgical (celebration of the sacraments), and diaconal (service of charity).[27]

---

22   See Pope Benedict XVI, *Deus Caritas Est*, 19.
23   Ibid., 1.
24   Ibid., 20.
25   Ibid., 21.
26   Ibid., 22.
27   Ibid., 25.

So, caritas-agape is an essential part of ecclesial structure. It is not something added as an external work. The Church's charity should never be considered an activity foreign to the Church, as if it should be left to others because it is a kind of welfare activity. On the contrary, it is "an indispensable expression of her very being" (cf. Ibid.); it is that agapic characteristic, that love of God in Christ, which colors our charity, that is, the charity of the Church, with divine truth. For that reason, charity is of the Church and can never be relegated to third parties. Here then is a new defence of love. While the first part of the encyclical offers a brilliant defence against Nietzschean accusations, here there is a defence against Marxist attacks. The poor — the argument has been repeated to the point of boredom — need justice more than charity. The Church's charitable work for the poor and the needy would only endorse a state of injustice. In such a way, charity would encourge the preservation of the status quo, and therefore of injustice. In fact, according to Marx's ideology, rather than the good and practical here and now we should prefer a justice that is not here but on its way — a utopia of justice. In truth, the Pope says, it is "an inhuman philosophy. People of the present are sacrificed to the *moloch* of the future — a future whose effective realization is at best doubtful" (n. 31/b). Doing good here and now cannot be rejected in anticipation of some potential justice in a future that is always unpredictable. In truth, "Love — *caritas* — will always prove necessary, even in the most just society. There is no ordering of the State so just that it can eliminate the need for a service of love. Whoever wants to eliminate love is preparing to eliminate man as such."[28]

---

28   Pope Benedict XVI, *Deus Caritas Est*, 28/b.

From the consideration of caritas-agape another essential element for Christian charity arises: it cannot become "just another form of social assistance."[29] The Church's caritas is not mere social welfare; we cannot get rid of it by consigning it to other state bodies deputed for the task nor let it fall into a work that *does* many things, perhaps organizing humanitarian assistance, but losing its center and heart: Christ. This would lead to charity driven by social ideologies rather than by the truth of the Gospel. Agape is once again the truth of the *caritas Ecclesiae*. God's love which fills the love of neighbor with self cannot allow our charity to become anonymous love. Of course, charity is not proselytism,[30] but it is still a witness of God's love in Christ, even when before a Muslim, for example, we let facts, works, or a smile speak for us. Through those facts, those works, that smile, is the proclamation that God is love, a love which has a face in Christ. "It is the responsibility of the Church's charitable organizations," writes Benedict XVI, "to reinforce this awareness in their members, so that by their activity — as well as their words, their silence, their example — they may be credible witnesses to Christ."[31]

From this, then, stems the need for prayer, so that the breadth of need does not lead us into the temptation of full-blown activism to the detriment of the constant and daily encounter with the One who is our strength[32] and gives strength to our tired hands. Here is the example of the saints and among them the the all holy Immaculate Virgin Mary, whose union with God is a hymn to charity in truth, to charity in the truth of that God who communicated

---

29   Pope Benedict XVI, *Deus Caritas Est*, 31.
30   Ibid., 31/c.
31   Ibid.
32   Ibid., 37.

Himself to her, of that Logos who is her Son.[33] The Virgin Mary and all the saints tell us that "those who draw near to God do not withdraw from men, but rather become truly close to them."[34] The saints teach us that the true measure of our love is God alone, that the truth of ecclesial charity is always and solely the agape of God in Christ. Therefore, as always, contemplation will be given primacy over action, and prayer over activity, as a theological synthesis of the primacy of God over humanity, of agape over charity, and of agape-caritas over love of neighbor.

2. LOVE IN TRUTH FOR A LOVE OF TRUTH

The theological message which the Pope gives us in his first encyclical is of great importance. It starts from that aspect of the life of men and women, from that feeling so common and so close to humanity which is love, and travels a path of ascesis and purification to arrive at men and women's integral truth. Of course, love is true initially, from its first whisper, because it is the whisper of men and women, of their being. If it is not led along the paths of integrity, it soon leaves men and women in a vortex where love itself becomes blind and rejects its truth, rejects God from whom it emanates. Men and women often experience difficulties identifying the good to follow fully. They are more easily satisfied by the immediate good which can be transformed into evil. It is easier to do evil than good. It is easier to choose a good which is not ultimately the good but an evil. It is easier, more comfortable, and more tempting to follow the paths of eros alone than an eros purified by agape. Men and women realize that only good is the truth of non-good, in other words evil. Truth

---

33 See Pope Benedict XVI, *Deus Caritas Est*, 41.
34 Ibid., 42.

illuminates the good and routs all those shadows which grip them and that we define as evil.

Therefore, agape is the truth of eros. Agape is the truth of the good which loves itself and therefore desires itself. If "love is the desire to possess the good for ever,"[35] then men and women, in loving, choose what is good for them. In truth, men and women want what is good for them, the whole good, and only in a more noble dimension — that of agape which descends to eros to take it on its own shoulders and raise it from the earth toward heaven, toward God-Love, where there is fulfilment of humanity's love. Its love finds fulfilment in the love of God, good in Goodness. God and humanity reach each other and touch each other in the goodness of love, in the truth of love. Here one begins to see the essence of God who raises humanity: His agapic Truth.

God in His agapic essence is the foundation of the love of humanity, and only God's love — in other words He Himself who is love — can bestow truth on the love of humanity and in the end on men and women themselves. God and humanity are united by love. So, the redemption of love from all human wrinkles becomes the necessary condition to reaffirm the truth of God and humanity. Love in truth leads us to the truth of God and humanity. To give truth to love, by that circular process of truth and love, would therefore mean rediscovering love for truth. Love will be the path for truth, and truth will be the foundation of love.

Truth without love would be arid, cold, distant from humanity. Love without truth would be vague sentimentalism. For example, we would love men and women and their mistakes, justifying their mistakes by virtue of a religious liberalism, as J. H. Newman said. Today, tolerance of everyone and everything is found everywhere, even in those who

---

35 Plato, *Symposium*, 206a.

do not believe in God. Also widespread is a strange love of tolerance. There is a need to be increasingly tolerant; otherwise, one can be accused of fundamentalism. On the other hand, it is more difficult to practice steadfastness in principles and condemnation, our love for one's brothers and sisters, and their mistakes. The apostle John shines as an example of an indispensable pairing for our faith: respectful love for humanity and zeal for the truth. John loved his own in truth[36] (cf. 3 Jn 1). So, Newman would say that it is essential "to proclaim the 'truth in love' . . . 'loving in truth' . . . . Only then will Christians be successful in the fight when [. . .] they will be loving in firmness, in rigor, in holiness."[37] It is necessary to denounce error to love the errant, without pretending to love them by keeping silent about the truth and thus choosing falsehood. Silence is kept in the belief that one is loving, but instead the other person is offended because they are being offered falsehood. The first and greatest charity is to give the truth.

The irrepressible circularity of truth and of love — of the truth of eros in agape — becomes in theological circles the relation and *koinonia* of faith and love, theological knowledge and charity. Faith precedes charity in the order of generation, while charity has precedence by reason of perfection, in perfecting and shaping the act of faith. This is the beginning of a harmonious circularity of faith and caritas-agape: faith illuminates charity, while charity bestows fullness and perfection on faith.[38] R. Fisichella

---

36 See 3 Jn 1.
37 Quoted by Herman Geissler, "John H. Newman: 'Charity, the only thing truly needed'," *L'Osservatore Romano* English weekly edition 9, August 16, 2006, 4.
38 See *Summa Theologiae*, I–II, q. 62, a. 4; I–II, q. 66, a. 6; as a theological development of these statements, see Bellandi, *L'amore pienezza della fede. Solo la carità conosce*, 7–12.

writes in this regard: "Love and faith live, therefore, in a circularity which allows a clarification starting from each other, but both constitute being Christian in a foundational manner. The salvific event which Jesus of Nazareth represents can be recognized only on the basis of the two, because together they form the authentic and coherent response which can be made to revelation."[39]

3. THE APOLOGETIC DISCOURSE: GIVING TRUTH TO LOVE IN LOVE OF TRUTH

Having reached this point, I want to link the apologetic theme which concerns us closely with the analysis of the circularity of truth and love — the natural indispensable foundation of the circularity between faith and charity. Love in truth leads us to the truth of love. There is a need to speak the truth to love. Love wants truth by its intrinsic constitution. Love loves truth first, and by the truth of the object loved, the person loved is open to their love. We are made to love truth by loving in truth. Christian apologetics is nothing other than telling the truth in love, speaking the truth to love, defending the truth in love, to reach, in a philosophical-theological framework, the defence of the truth of God and humanity by rendering His eternal love credible. From the start of Christianity, the apologetic discourse has been seen as a requirement of the truth of love — the need, that is, to make credible that God-agape who has spoken, revealing Himself in history; to say to everyone, defending the genuine proclamation of it rationally, that that God Who has spoken is the "Father of our Lord Jesus Christ" (Rom 15:6), who "in these last days... has spoken to us by a Son" (Heb 1:2). The apologists,

---

[39] Fisichella, *La Rivelazione evento e credibilità* (Bologna: Dehoniane, 2002), 201.

moved by the infallible certainty of God's revelation in the Logos made flesh, have, throughout the centuries, taken on this great charity, first toward non-believers, then also toward those who believe but are mistaken. They proclaim the truth to them, the incarnate Logos, fullness of a Love which makes God's truth visible. Apologetics has reformulated the cry of truth in 1 Pet 3:25, which is addressed to everyone, in a theological manner: to give to everyone an account of our hope; to guide everyone along the path so suited to humanity — that is, reason — to our Logos, our Christ, the one Savior.

Apologetics has characterized Christianity since its inception. One thinks, for example, of St. Justin in his two *Apologia*, of St. Irenaeus in his treatise of dogmatic theology, *Adversus Haereses*; then of the eloquence of Tertullian, especially in the *Apologeticum*, and finally an Augustinian treatise, *De vera religione*, which prepared the path for the religion of truth. And so, from era to era: from the luminous centuries of the Middle Ages to the controversial treatises of the post-Tridentine era. One thinks especially of St. Robert Bellarmine. With the founder of the Catholic theological school of Tübingen, Johann Sebastian von Drey (1777–1853), the apologetic treatise assumes a more theological connotation. It becomes a discourse integrated into the dogmatic-fundamental framework, able to rationalize divine Revelation in its historical unravelling. Thus, fundamental theology was born as the study of Revelation in historical-theological terms, which created space for understanding the entire Word of God addressed to humanity, of which Christ is the center and fullness; apologetics were no longer simply presented in argumentative and apologetic terms but with a broader direction — precisely that of the faith which seeks to understand its very own dogmatic foundations. The apologetic treatise becomes a theological-fundamental discourse which embraces the foundations of theology: from the historic revelation of God, to faith as the human response to God, to Tradition and its theological settings as channels of the Church's *paradosis*, and finally to the Church as mystery of faith.

If the Tübingen School of Theology has made great progress in the furrows of speculative theology, we cannot, however, but complain about some loss, matured during the course of theological seasons: the insertion, with good reason, of apologetics into fundamental dogmatics has, in some renewed theological treatises, cast classical apologetics, into oblivion. The culture in which one lives has not softened its anti-evangelical clutches, and theology, inside such a culture, is not always so gentle in proclaiming itself as the gift of truth for the Church. Only someone, with good cause, takes on within a theological-fundamental framework the apologetic task of providing credibility to faith, a task so necessary for culture and for the Church of the third millennium.[40] I want to offer my own modest contribution to the rediscovery of apologetics as emanating from fundamental dogmatics, which is capable of revealing to men and women mostly drowned in nameless eros, that outside the agape of God not even eros would have any raison d'être. Then I would like to say to the one theology that love of truth in the truth of love, in docile obedience to the Magisterium, comes before our convenience and does not get caught up in the fashions of the time.

---

40 We must consider the manuals of fundamental theology that open the discourse on the credibility of faith: Rino Fisichella, *La Rivelazione evento e credibilità*, in *Teologia fondamentale*, ed. Giuseppe Lorizio (Rome: Città Nuova, 2004–2005), vols. 1–4; Fernando Ocariz and Arturo Blanco, *Rivelazione, fede e credibilità. Corso di teologia fondamentale*, (Rome: EDUSC, 2001).

3.1 A metaphysical-agapic apologetic

Above all it is necessary to give back a metaphysical inspiration to our theology. There is a need for a metaphysics propaedeutic to theology, which through its discussion on being—essential for really doing philosophy—carefully guides theological reason in study of Revelation and therefore of knowledge of the faith, in which the harmony between faith and reason, between faith and love, shines out. It is essential that our theology, primarily fundamental theology, establishes the relationship between faith and reason in a metaphysical context informed by love, to generate an agapic metaphysics. There is a need for a metaphysics that unites thought concerning being to the gospel fact, that harmonizes truth and charity. "The 'agapic metaphysics,'" writes G. Lorizio, "does not intend to establish any alternative with regard to the classical 'metaphysics of being,' but enables the *lumen Revelationis* to re-clothe it in the new light which emanates from the Gospel; ... In the end ... it enables the unmasking of the false dilemma which tends to put truth and charity as alternatives."[41]

In *Deus Caritas Est*[42] the Pope asserts that a dual reality concerning the divine image can be found in the Bible: a strictly metaphysical concept of God, "absolute and ultimate source of all being"—although not simply like a "motor that moves and is not moved"—alongside His love; God is "a lover with all the passion of a true love." This magisterial statement contains an important fact for theology, which could repair the rift that is often posited between the God of metaphysics and the God of

---

41 Giuseppe Lorizio, "'Pensiero rivelativo' e 'metafisica agapica.' Una prospettiva di teologia fondamentale," in *Rivista Teologica di Lugano*, 2 (2005), 178.
42 Pope Benedict XVI, *Deus Caritas Est*, 10.

the Bible, almost as if the Bible, in order to make room for a condescending and loving God, wanted to cast into oblivion that same God who is and who cannot not be. If such were the case, in identity between being and acting, He would not be condescending; if it were not, even His Word pronounced for us would have no raison d'être. If God is not the One who is, He is not even love.[43]

A theological testimony about Christ can be preserved only if it is reformulated within the categories of our understanding of reality, so that in the debate with modern thought theology is not dissolved into philosophy, but from theology—especially the Trinitarian perspective—arises a new category of relationship, understood as being in-relation. The category of relationality which has its archetype in the Father-Son relationship, the heart of the biblical testimony, should be an alternative to the Christological perspective provoked by Chalcedon. Having focused interest almost exclusively on the intrinsic constitution of Christ so that the person-nature relationship—in a metaphysical catalysis causing only the arousal of Luther's anger—would have replaced that more fundamental existential Trinitarian relationship.[44]

---

[43] In this regard see the new attempt to repair the aforesaid rift in Benedict XVI's *Address at Regensburg* (September, 12 2006). To consult the annotated version see the Benedict XVI-Discourses section of the Vatican website www.vatican.va. However, the common background is John Paul II's Encyclical, *Fides et Ratio*, especially chapters II and IV. The then Cardinal Ratzinger already had an opportunity to comment on its philosophical-theological significance in a conference given in Madrid on February 16, 2000, and published in Italian in *MicroMega* 3 (2000) 207–224, with the title *Quid est veritas?*

[44] See Bernd Jochen Hilberath and Theodor Schneider, "Gesù Cristo/Cristologia," in *Enciclopedia Teologica*, ed. P. Eicher (Brescia: Queriniana, 1989), 423.

The alternative Bible or ontology would work out the Trinitarion relationality between Father and son in a new category that is "existentially" ontological and biblically central.

To posit this alternative, at first glance more understandable of the mystery, in fact introduces a division in the very being of God. God *is* love. Either God is the being of love and the love of being, or, in terms of the intra-Trinitarian hypostatic relations, the relation of being-love and the love of being-relation. The relation of love implies the being of God, and being is realized in love which is relation. Relation without being, like saying love without truth, implies a multiplicity without unity: God without being one and consequently humanity without being human. It is not by chance that the anthropology which originates from such a vision — from a merely existential and no longer metaphysical vision — leaves men and women alone in their love, in the labyrinth of multiplicity without showing them how to come to terms with it or find the way toward the unity which is the truth. Men and women are always more alone, alone in their love.

Love is manifold, while truth is unity. God is one and three in the unity of the Trinity and in the trinity of Unity. In God there is the inter-twining of truth and love. Truth, being One, is the foundation of the love of the being Three, and being Three is the perfection of being One. In God love remains in truth, and His truth is love: the Trinity in Unity and Unity in the Trinity. Every multiple needs to become one, and every unity is fulfilled in multiplicity. Therefore, you cannot simply get rid of metaphysics without getting rid of God, of His being in love, and in the end getting rid of humanity, of being man.

Unfortunately, metaphysics has been deliberately abandoned in discussions about God because it is no longer comprehensible to post-modern humanity. In effect, Hegel reproached the theology of his time for this fatal loss, that is, no longer being "guardian of the speculative mysteries and of metaphysics," and for preferring to move in different but misleading spheres: that of feelings, what was popularly matter-of-fact, and erudite historicism.[45] Isn't there perhaps at the origin of this metaphysical-biblical dilemma a split between truth and charity?

Truth and charity are not competing for primacy and are not opposed, as is often said. They are not doomed to fall either into a syncretistic relativisim or an integralist fundamentalism. The then Cardinal Ratzinger, in the homily at the Mass *Pro eligendo Romano Pontifice*, tracing the outline of his future Petrine ministry, said: "And it is this faith — only faith — that creates unity and is fulfilled by love. On this theme, St. Paul offers us as a fundamental formula for Christian existence some beautiful words, in contrast to the continual vicissitudes of those who, like children, are tossed about by the waves: make truth in love. Truth and love coincide in Christ. To the extent that we draw close to Christ, in our own lives too, truth and love are blended. Love without truth would be blind; truth without love would be like 'a clanging cymbal' (1 Cor 13:1)."[46]

---

45   See George Wilhelm Hegel, *Science of Logic* (Rome: Bari, 1974), vol. 1, 26.
46   Joseph Ratzinger, *L'Osservatore Romano*, April 19, 2005, 7. In this homily, Cardinal Ratzinger said that today a new metaphysical paradigm, namely relativism, tends to assert itself, which becomes the post-modern counter to fundamentalism: "Today, having a clear faith based on the Creed of the Church is often labeled as fundamentalism. Whereas relativism, that is, letting oneself be

So, rather than separating truth and love, we must find the way for their indissoluble union. A metaphysical-agapic vision is needed to enlighten our discussion about the credibility of Revelation and therefore our apologetics offered as the logos of hope. The credibility of love in a theological-metapysical context will reveal to the theologian first, and then to all the interlocutors, the ability of Christianity to dialogue with the various areas of human knowledge. In such a way the credibility of Revelation will coincide with the credibility of love.[47] In short, it could all be traced back to this axiom: to render Revelation credible by making love credible — according to *Deus Caritas Est* — and to render love credible by affirming the fullness of the truth of the Christian Revelation, in a bond of reason and love, religious philosophy and existence. So, it is possible to overcome that "extrinsic and historical approach of recent apologetics" which "seems at first . . . must be the only other way. For at least it is not completely denied room beside philosophy and existence since it only seeks support from these in a secondary and supplementary manner: faith completes and elevates metaphysics and ethics when it is faith expressed in an historical kerygma."[48]

"tossed here and there, carried about by every wind of doctrine", seems the only attitude that can cope with modern times. We are building a dictatorship of relativism that does not recognize anything as definitive and whose ultimate goal consists solely of one's own ego and desires" (6–7). Is not the "dictatorship of relativism" perhaps generated more often than not by pitting truth against charity as if they were diametrically opposed? Truth comes off worse and is diluted in charity.

47   See Lorizio, "*'Pensiero rivelativo' e 'metafisica agapica,'*" 179.
48   Balthasar, *Love Alone*, 43.

3.2 A fundamental apologetic: to offer everyone the Logos of hope

The metaphysical-agapic theological discourse, rooted in the truth of being and informed by the love of *Deus-Caritas*, sheds light on a problem we dare to call fundamental for apologetics: the theological discourse about religion, or, in other words, the conversation about *religio vera*, which is intimately linked to that about *Deum verum*.[49] Theological reason and love can help us to respond to the invitation of the First Letter of Peter (3:15), uniting the logos of hope to the unity of reason and love, which are one in God and in return enlighten the truth of humanity. Reason and love, truth and love, are the way to the truth of God and His Word, who becomes the Logos of hope for humanity and the *religio* of certain hope through an encounter with the Logos-Love, the fulfilment of every multiplicity in unity.

3.2.1 *"Always have your answer ready for people who ask you the reason for the hope . . . " (1 Pet 3:15)*. The apologetic syntagma of the First Letter of Peter is enlightening. To understand its full significance, one must refer more widely to the Peter's message. Now the rock of the Church (cf. Matt 16:16), Peter invites Christians to set themselves close

---

49 I will not enter into the debate about the theological dimension of religion and the theological method in the context of religious pluralism, which would divert us from our purpose. On such an issue see the recent essay *Teologia delle religioni. La questione del metodo*, ed. Mariano Crociata (Rome: Città Nuova, 2006). In any case, I dissent from the approach that ends with a mere description of the religious phenomenon, characterizing it with theological labels without even asking the crucial question about the religion of truth or *religio vera*. If it does not end up putting Christ alongside other "saviors," it certainly dilutes His person in the ethical fabric — however just and worthy — of the great religious traditions. Religion is more than just ethics.

to Christ, the "living stone" (1 Pet 2:4) and, amid the pagans, to be beyond reproach in doing good, so that they may come to glorify God.[50] Setting their soul in this way to see truth through goodness, through love — "It is God's will that by your good deeds you should silence the ignorant talk of fools" (1 Pet 2:15) — Christians take on a great mission to offer apologetically the Logos of hope, adored first in hearts. St. Peter writes: "Simply proclaim the Lord Christ holy in your hearts, and always have your answer ready for people who ask you the reason for the hope that you have" (1 Pet 3:15) (the most important parts of the text in Greek say: "étoimoi *aeì logo apologían pantì tô aitoûnti umâs logos perì tês en umîn elpídos*," that is, to be always ready to do apologetics, to offer a discourse in favour (*apo-lógos*) of one's own faith to those who ask the reason (*Logos*) for the hope that is in us, disciples of Christ.) Peter, therefore, invites the Christian faithful to offer the logos of hope in Christ, the reason, or reasons (which will become the so-called *signa rationis* or motives for credibility) of one's own faith, not a blind faith but a rational faith, enlightened by the Logos. Humankind is essentially logos, reason that investigates and seeks to understand, that needs signs to help it believe. The Christian must offer to humanity the logos of hope, without which men and women would not be able to believe completely on their own strength, aided only by reason and the heart. Desire moves intelligence in the sphere of faith, insofar as it has been previously moved by grace.

Further, St. Peter asks that the logos be offered to pagans[51] who delighted in the desires of the flesh, putting aside reason and so despising holy works. Through

---

50   See 1 Pet 2:12.
51   Ibid.

goodness, the Christian wins over the goodwill of the pagans and prepares them for the proclamation of the Logos with the help of the logos of hope. Again, Peter exhorts Christians, the people of God,[52] to be witnesses to the wounded Savior,[53] sharing His sufferings,[54] among the pagans who are still the non-people[55] and for the most part unaware of their conscience. In this way, Christians testify to their belonging to Christ. Offering the logos for their hope, they become witnesses of the Logos in whom they believe and hope. Christians believe in Christ, whom God raised from the dead, so that their faith and their hope are now fixed in God,[56] and they can yearn for the goal, the salvation of souls.[57]

When Christ is believed, He then becomes the Logos of hope offered to those who are still immersed in the shadows, as long as this gift is received with gentleness, respect, and upright conscience (See 1 Pet 3:15–16).[58] Christ is the Logos who shines in the logos given to men and women (the logos which asks for the reason for the hope). Every person yearns for this Logos since every person is looking for hope. Goodness is then a path to the true. One arrives at the truth of hope — and also love — by offering reason which issues from Reason, from the wounded Logos believed and loved.

At this point we can answer the question: who can offer to men and women, who are themselves logos seeking to

---

52   See 1 Pet 2:10.
53   Ibid., 2:21–25.
54   Ibid., 2:20–21.
55   Ibid., 2:10.
56   Ibid., 1:21.
57   Ibid., 1:9.
58   See Ceslause Spicq, *La prima lettera di Pietro* (Rome: Città Nuova, 1971), 176–180. For a more in-depth exegetical comment, see Rinaldo Fabris, *Lettera di Giacomo e prima lettera di Pietro: commento pastorale e attualizzazione"* (Bologna: Dehoniane, 1980).

understand, the logos of hope? Obviously, the person who has logos. One cannot give to men and women something one does not have. Only Christianity can offer the logos for hope, because, rooted in the existence of the creator Logos, it believes in the incarnate Logos. A religion which cannot rationally offer the logos for its own hope is a natural religion in search of hope and, if it pretends to offer hope, it must move toward the unity of truth and goodness; otherwise, it is forced to necessarily struggle along outside the orbit of reason. Reason aims at truth in unity, while love aims at goodness in multiplicity. The setting aside of reason — the most widespread temptation as well as the hastiest practice — causes religion to fall into irrationality, that is, it pretends to give what it does not have; it would multiply the truth and unite the multiplicity, relativism in the case of the former, and fundamentalism in the latter. This is precisely the panorama of our times. Only Judaism is an exception, as a true supernatural revelation and preparation for the new and definitive Covenant of God with us.

From its origins, Christianity has claimed to be the religion of truth precisely because it places itself in the orbit of reason, of philosophy, in marked contrast to the pagan myth which favors sentiment and emotions,[59] ultimately accumulating as many idols as possible rather than risk spiting any. The strength with which the Christian religion imposed itself is precisely that of the logos, the force of truth which has led to the non-truth of idols, "made by human hands" (Ps 115:4), falling into oblivion. In fact, with the setting aside of the logos, the trap of polytheism lurks in the logic of cultures and humanity. In

---

59 Pope See Benedict XVI, *St Justin*, Catechesis at the General Audience March 21, 2007, *L'Osservatore Romano*, (March 22, 2007), 4.

the end, we no longer privilege a *fact* that can really unite people, which is the truth, but rather pluralism, adding details that have a purely decorative purpose to make the images more colorful. It is no coincidence that we speak, often good-naturedly, of a god with many faces, for he is the implication of a multiplicity without unity, without God. If, however, an individual among many pretends to highlight his or her color while lacking the strength of truth, the fundamentalist superstructure that easily leads to violence comes into play. The only true alternative to any manipulation of religion and any oppression of humanity by a true and proper "dictatorship of the casual" is the strength of reason, and Christianity is the religion of the Logos.[60]

This will certainly horrify those who, precluding humanity's access to the truth, admit, as a logical consequence, the soteriological good of the plurality of religions, not realizing that in so doing they are not solving the real religious problem, summarized by the question *who is God and who is man*. Nor does it help religion to redeem itself from those doldrums of fear and suspicion in which it seems to have run aground due to the rash of violence in the name of God. In Christianity, religion becomes love of wisdom, love of the believed Logos. "So it is taught and believed as a chief point in man's salvation that philosophy, i.e. the pursuit of wisdom, cannot be quite divorced from religion."[61]

---

60 See Joseph Ratzinger, "Quid est Veritas?," *MicroMega* 3 (2000): 208–212.

61 St. Augustine, *De vera religione*, V.8 (PL 34), 126. In the introduction to an Italian edition of this work (Mursia 1987) which the Holy Bishop of Hippo did not change as his thought matured, M. Vannini, commenting on the extraordinary significance of these words, which mark the truly central link between Augustine and

3.2.2 *Christianity, the one* religio vera. Religion must necessarily respond to the question *who is God and who is man*. Humanity cannot ignore God, nor simply try to imagine Him, but must draw close to Him, through both His imprints in creation and what humanity is in itself. This is humanity's path to God. Man can travel the path of creation back to God because it was first God's path to humanity. We are participants in what God is, otherwise the God problem could never be posed, either in terms of affirmation or denial. Humanity has always posed this problem, one which can be summarized in two vital, yet central, thoughts. So, humanity must draw close to God by the very path God has trod, the way of being, of His being; humanity must experience the living God. Otherwise, humanity would believe in a non-living God, and religion would detriorate into praying to a God it does not know. Natural religion follows the path of the God whom we do not yet know completely, but who is in some way perceived through desire, by a rational or instinctive deduction, or perhaps — erroneously — by self-projection.[62] If we pretend to know Him without

---

Plato, writes: "It must be emphasised that Augustine takes from the Platonic philosophers, and passes into the Christian world, the fervour and the primacy of reason above and against every other faculty — above the changeable sensitivity and the capricious and vain representations that it produces, and which we call 'thought'; but also above every 'revealed' content, which is placed uncritically as true and to be believed in an authoritative manner: which places any religion at the same level as superstition. Therefore Augustine underlines that religion and philosophy are in agreement — one needs the other in the common effort towards the common objective which is truth; reason and faith ... are the same thing, just like intelligence and love: once again the profound meaning of Plato's Symposium continues to work" (7).
62   Would critics of the Christian religion who threaten to oust humanity perhaps not turn towards natural religion?

knowledge, that indicates a great limitation in humanity and promotes an irrational religion. Here, then, knowledge must necessarily progress to purify our images of God and finally to meet the God who *is*. This knowledge, however, is not separated from love. Humanity is ontologically knowledge and love, reason and eros, which always exist together.

Religion purifies itself and becomes evermore what it is as it becomes sapiential love; it must lead humanity to God through a love of wisdom, a love of the logos, to finally find the logos of love. So, can God and humanity meet? Yes, insofar as humanity comes out of itself—even comes out of its religion—and places itself in God's footsteps to find Him living in the rationality of creation, in the reason for humanity itself, which can only be the Reason from which everything issues rationally (even scientific reasoning); He is in the rationality of the order of love, in the rationality of goodness. In the end, the encounter happens in truth and goodness, beginning—as the First Letter of St. Peter suggests—from right conscience and progressing from being good to seeing the being of goodness in the goodness of being, the truth of love in love of truth. God is Truth and Love and can only be such; otherwise, nothing would be such. Humanity would not be true or lovable. God and humanity meet in reason and in love. God gives truth to humanity's reason and love. Healing its love in His Love, He enlightens its reason in His Reason. So, the *religio vera* will be the religion of sapiential love, the one in which God is encountered, is known through what He is (where the being of humanity must necessarily agree) and is loved; it will be the religion of fullness, of every fullness; the religion in which the truth of creation (natural truth and goodness) exists alongside the truth of sanctification (supernatural truth and goodness); the religion that unites humanity to God in the unity of nature with grace, of reason-love with faith, of multiplicity in unity, of truth and goodness in the beauty which shines in the holiness of the Kingdom of Heaven with the active commitment to the world here below, of the saints with the great people of the world who are benefactors of humanity. It is this world which must be transfigured, this humanity which must be saved. Salvation begins here and is possible only where there is a God who is the fullness of humanity and of everything—that is, who presupposes and elevates what humanity is in what He is, in the most sublime harmony. A God who ignores humanity and does not respect what it is or what the world is, is not God, because then He is neither Creator nor Savior. The *religio vera* is the religion of reality in its totality, of reason in its fullness, of love in its eternal charm: in a word, the religion that is the decisive encounter with God.[63]

Finally, the time has come to say who our God is, the One who is unique, recognizable by everyone through His grace and whom we proclaim to everyone because He is the one living God. God, says John, is love.[64] He is the being of love and the love of being. God and humanity come together in the truth of love.[65] So only in God-Love does humanity finds its fulfilment and its fullness. Only in the truth of life does humanity find its realization; only in the God-Love does humanity truly know itself, give fullness to its being, and encounter the living God who puts to flight

---

63 See Ratzinger, "Quid est Veritas?," 222. On the distinctiveness of Christianity see also "Il pluralismo religioso una sfida al cristianesimo," *La Civiltà Cattolica* II (2006): 209–218.
64 See 1 Jn 4:8, 16.
65 See Pope Benedict XVI, *Deus Caritas Est*, 1–2.17.31/c

the shadows of superstition, myth, irrationality. The *religio vera* corresponds to the truth of *Deus Caritas*.

God is love, a love which does not have the limitations of humanity, which loves to an end which has no *terminus*, because love is eternal.[66] In the madness of His love, *Deus Caritas* took a face, our face, the face of humanity made in His image. He became flesh in our flesh to raise it to God. God-Love raises humanity to the heart of God in the pierced heart of Christ. God's love is always and only gift: gift of self, gift of the Son. The incarnate Word is the face of God-Love. In Him, forever united and joined together, are Reason and Love, Logos and Agape. The words of the First Letter of John about God-Love are echoed in those of his prologue: the Logos became flesh.[67] Jesus is our Logos-Love, our Logos of hope in a love that gives fullness to humanity and its history. Logos is the purpose of every history.

So, who is God? He is the agapic Logos made flesh, made man. Humanity, every man and woman, in and through Him touch the summit of incarnated Love and Reason. God let Himself be touched in the flesh of the Son, the Logos incarnate. In Him humanity knows and loves God. That, then, is who man is: the one who reaches his fullness in Christ — love of truth in truth of love, multiplicity in unity for a unity of multiplicity. Only Christ can give to humanity what it seeks and desires. Men and women who are reason and eros — which is often unruly and greedy when separated from reason — need to be enlightened precisely where they are, in their intimate vitality. The person taught to recognize the logos through goodness and love can finally, with the aid of grace, grasp

---

66   See Jn 13:1.
67   Ibid., 1:14.

the Savior, the Logos, Christ, who raises the person wholly, infusing light to their reason, giving them the truth of His love. God and humanity are reunited forever in Christ; only in Him, agapic Logos, can they encounter each other definitively and fully. Christ alone is our Logos of hope, our agapic metaphysics.

In the end, if men and women remain themselves, open to truth in the freedom of their love, they can meet Christ on their path, and only when they encounter Him — the reason of love, the God whose truth is love — do they find themselves. Only by violating the freedom of love for truth in the truth of love can men and women be diverted from Christ; they are left with images, with vague reflections, in other words, with what God is not. Such a denial leads to contradiction, for example, attempting to understand what it means to be human through a violation of humanity's freedom of thought, of seeking, of religious expression. A collective freedom is no longer humanity's freedom: it is the masking of a collective oppression. If men and women are reason and love, they can only desire that God who is Logos and Love. Men and women desire to be fully what they are. The true God and the religion of truth reveal to humanity what God wants it to be. Our reflections are well-summarized in an enlightening work by a theologian and pope who always sought to ensure that the truth of God and humanity, traceable to the truth of love, shone out:

> We have seen that, in the conception of early Christianity, the notions of nature, man, God, *ethos* and religion were indissolubly linked one with the other and that it was this bond that helped Christianity to see its way clearly through the crisis of the gods and the crisis of rationality in antiquity. Religion's orientation towards

a rational vision of reality, the *ethos* as part of this vision and its concrete application under the primacy of love, are all associated one with the other. The primacy of the *Logos* and the primacy of love proved to be identical. The *Logos* no longer appeared as mere mathematical reason at the basis of all things but as creating love to the point of compassion for the creature. The cosmic dimension of religion that venerates the Creator in the power of Being and existential dimension, the question of redemption penetrated each other and became one. In practice, any explanation of reality that cannot in any sensible and comprehensive way establish an *ethos* must always be insufficient.... The attempt in this crisis of humanity to restore a comprehensible meaning to the notion of Christianity as *religio vera* must, so to speak, look equally to orthopraxis and orthodoxy. At the deeper level its content must consist in the fact — today as always in the final analysis — that love and reason coincide in that they are fundamental pillars proper of reality: true reason is love and love is true reason. In their unity they are the authentic foundation and purpose of reality.[68]

4. A SKETCH OF THE CONTEMPORARY PHILOSOPHICAL PANORAMA: TWO NIHILISMS COMPARED

The circularity of reason and love, following the path of *Deus Caritas Est*, suggests an interesting union, a symbol of reality in its true being, that could recover the instrument of the metaphysical inquiry of thought, for it is nourished not by the cold mathematical numerability

---

68 Joseph Ratzinger, "Verità del cristianesimo?," *MicroMega* 2 (2000): 52-53.

of truth, but by the warm passion for it. This union is nourished by a true love which becomes love of truth by a truth of love. It is a return to the logos through love, to the eros recovered in the truth of agape, so as to love the logos, which is love-thought, love-truth; it is a return to truth in love. Then, a fruitful and indispensable dialogue between philosophy and theology could be of interest once more. We need a philosophy capable of the being of love in love for being, which prepares the ground for God whose being is love and whose love to the end is the *Logos sarx*; it must be a philosophy, therefore, which does not renounce being out of fear of remaining trapped in the prison of cold and schematic truth, a truth which in the final analysis is impossible (post-modern culture has known the twilight of the God of the great moral truths and humanity trudging solely among *tout court* values). This culture, which for various reasons should mark the start of a post-Christianity, now weakened, experiences its moments of strength in love alone. However, the more being weakens due to the fatal loss of truth, the more love becomes strong and intoxicated, to the point that, through an intolerant relativisim, there is no truth which stands before love alone. So, we find ourselves faced with a major contradiction: we have the truth of a love without truth, so therefore we have a love alone. On the other hand, precisely in love, insofar as it becomes true and does not fear the truth, being can shake off weakness to save itself without losing itself.

Post-modern culture, from Nietzsche to our time, can be described as the playing out of nihilism, strongly defended by its apologists. However, a nihilism that has dismissed God from the sphere of humanity does not make men and women greater, but smaller and more needy.

While there was a desire to get away from the prison of absolute, rigid, and uniform truth, what is being provoked more and more is a return to the life of the jungle, where everyone, left alone in their being, decides on their own what is good and what is evil. Everyone chooses their own truth and anyone who opposes their arbitrary choice is accused of fundamentalism, and ultimately condemned as an oppressor, since it stifles an individualist conscience which becomes evermore the supreme judge of reality. Unfortunately, there will be as many judges as consciences, as many truths as individuals, as many whims as desires. In this chaos of do-it-yourself choices, everyone chooses; there will inevitably be someone who chooses the opposite of what someone else desires, and so denies the other's choice. So how can one defend one's own arbitrary and individual choice, which is so linked to one's desire to be? The only weapon is strength. The splendor of truth gives way to the oppression of strength, to the law of the strongest. Relativism — whether it is strong or weak — is, in truth, as we shall see, the origin of violence and oppression. A relativistic philosopy necessarily generates an intransigent position toward truth and toward those who do not wish to amalgamate so as to challenge truth with strong action. A world that privileges the individual freedoms which easily degenerate into a conflict of mere personal interests is a world of the alone. There is no communication or relationship between people. There can be no relationship in relativism, although the word appears to imply it. The only possibility of being in relation, of truly communicating, is in agreeing on what is common to all, because it is a good for all: the truth. Only freedom in truth does not fall into fundamentalism, because it alone is capable of gathering together freedoms in the communion of what can be shared by all as objective, universal goodness. On the other hand, one is alone in the world of force, alone in the world of violence. The isolated subject also easily loses the possibility of simply being there. Abandoned to themselves, they are exposed to every whim, to every slavery, however obvious or subtle it may be. Today we live in a world of subversive, enslaving dictatorships. They are the dictatorships of the subject's nothingness: a subject who is nothing, although he wants to be, but who is easily extinguished in his nothingness; precisely the way in which he has the dignity of being is removed from him. Weak or relativist thought generates a strong action, in other words, a "struggle without compromise."[69]

So, relativism is the true origin of fundamentalism:

---

[69] Giulio Giorello and Bruno Forte *Dove fede e ragione si incontrano?*, (Cinisello Balsamo: San Paolo, 2006), 54. Relativism as seen by Giorello can be summed up using his own words: "[...] there is no need to use one's head and decide rationally in our lives to possess absolute certainties" (35). From here we arrive at the fundamentalism of relativism we are talking about, while for Giorello and others the opposite is true: fundamentalism would be generated by non-relativism. Here is what he says: *"Freedom cannot be restricted except for the benefit of freedom.* Not for the sake of some other basis, but simply for the purpose of playing the game. If someone then comes to tell us that fredom is only licence because it violates this or that absolute, and the followers of some fundmentalism complain that they are not willing to bear it, our answer is simply one: not weak thought, but strong action. In other words, a struggle without compromise" (54). See also Giorello, *Di nessuna Chiesa: la libertà del laico* (Milan: Cortina, 2005).

Which freedom cannot be restricted, that of those who pose it or that of those who must be respected in their freedom? Evidently, that of the person who poses it, otherwise there would be a restriction to the disadvantage of freedom and to the advantage of another basis. And is not this the fundamentalism of relativism? It is not about *imposing* individual freedom on someone else and perhaps even on a collective level?

When humanity is excluded from the truth, only chance, arbitrariness can still dominate it. This is why it is not "fundamentalist" but a duty of humanity to protect humanity against the dictatorship of the accidental becoming absolute and to restore its dignity, which consists precisely in the fact that no human instance can ultimately dominate it, since humanity is open to truth itself. The Encyclical (*Fides et ratio*), precisely due to its insistence on the capacity of truth, is a truly necessary apologia for the greatness of humanity against what is passed off as "culture tout court."[70]

So, it is right to question a stance fashionable today, a stance which, by dispelling the truth, has in effect caused a significant emancipation of individual liberties, of the lustful and satisfied eros of self which clouds reason and pretends to be a measure of all things, even the truth of God. An eros of pure longing simply dilutes life, and life itself no longer has any meaning, so that you no longer know what to prefer, an embryo or a cat which meows.[71] If there is only this life — or, in existential terms only being present without being — does life still have any meaning? In this world of the erotic without reason, it becomes more difficult to live; it is increasingly difficult to enter this world despite the preaching of life alone; it is difficult

---

70   Joseph Ratzinger, "Quid est Veritas?," 212.
71   "What type of rights to allow the embryo? Of course, I may not want to exterminate the embryos, as I do not want to exterminate the cats because I hurt the old men who go to feed them. If anything, the cat has much more rights than the embryo because when I step on its paw it pulls it back meowing, but this does not happen with the embryo." Gianni Vattimo, Frederico Orlando, and Santiago Zabala, *Nichilismo e religione* (Rome: Valter Casini, 2005), 16.

to be born — we must now be selected — while it is always easier to die, to be kicked out when we are elderly and useless to the community of loneliness. Why? The world of nihilism is not a people-oriented world, even if it pretends to be. When there is just humanity, humanity soon is left alone. When reason is abandoned in the name of eros, men and women lose themselves, lose their freedom as children, and become slaves. Men and women are either children or nothing. But if, along with life, we also lose the dignity of childhood — that is, being oriented to the truth — what remains for us? What could ever bridge the abyss of solitude into which we sink if our lives are no longer lively? Nothingness is not the everything of humanity. We see the effects of nihilism in progress. Nothingness has a limit: man, his reason, his love, his ability to encounter God in reason and in love, his being for Christ.

Here, then, is the apologia of reason and of love — of reason in love — to speak to today's men and women, who are harnessed in the reins of a meaningless nothingness. Our apologia wishes to be also an apologia of Christian charity in truth. Just as one does not give eros without agape, so one does not give charity without faith and faith without reason. It is easy to free oneself from reason in a weak culture to build systems of a fideistic creed and so continue to be there in the mere sensual which desires what God does not want. To free oneself from reason, however, means freeing oneself from love, from faith, from God — to remain *alone* with *one self*.

After this succinct introductory analysis, let us examine two philosophical stances which are strongly opposed despite their nihilistic commonality. As will be seen, the reason for the contrast centers on an erroneous interpretation of Nietzsche, the father of post-modern culture and the two philosophical systems to which I will refer. It is good to emphasize the contrast which is generated between the two philosophical assumptions I have chosen for their uniqueness. Certainly different (the first accepting only charity, and the second only eros), they share a denial of God and truth, and — dare we say it — both choose an eros without reason which becomes non-charity.

4.1 The weak nihilism of Gianni Vattimo

The first philosophical system we want to analyze — albeit briefly, taking into account its considerable breadth and progress over time — is that of G. Vattimo, who, in the wake of his preferred masters, Nietzsche and Heidegger, summarizes and develops them into what is defined as weak nihilism. In defining his system, I will refer briefly to an hypothesis of one of Vattimo's favorite disciples, S. Zabala, according to whom weak thought brings about not only the end of metaphysics, but also the end of the deconstruction of metaphysics: thus one gets to the point where it is no longer possible to easily state if one believes in God or not. The end of metaphysics is the end of objectivity. We can no longer speak of religion, of God, or of science as facts which stand before us.[72]

So, in what terms will we have to speak? In terms of *tout court* values, in other words, values no longer cogent and decisive. Here, in the arena of weak culture, the work of the Turin philosopher comes in as a real apologia for nihilism, the latter resulting from the nullification of being in the mere talk of being there. For Vattimo, nihilism is on-going: you cannot do an evaluation of it, you can only try to understand at what stage it stands. The only position that can be taken to deal with nihilism is that

---

72 See Gianni Vattimo, *Nichilismo e religione*, 13.

of Nietzsche, that is, fulfilled nihilism: he understood that nihilism was his only *chance*. Nihilism is essentially what Nietzsche defined it to be: the situation in which humanity rolls away from its center toward X. Heidegger argues along the same line, and according to him, nihilism is that process in which, at the end, "being as such is nothing more." Vattimo, in fact, demonstrates that Heidegger' Citation?s position is complementary and definitive to Nietzsche's nihilism. Humanity rolls toward the unknown X precisely because "being as such is nothing more." Nihilism concerns precisely being as such.

Nietzsche summarizes the whole process of nihilism in his thesis concerning the death of God, that is to say, the "devaluation of supreme values." Not all *tout court* values have disappeared, but the supreme values summarized in the value par excellence which is God have vanished. They have disappeared because humanity no longer needs them, does not care about them, and no longer raises the problem: knowledge no longer needs to reach the ultimate causes; men and women no longer need to believe they are immortal souls.

According to Heidegger, being is wiped out as it is transformed into value and becomes above all an exchange with the subject. The subject takes possession of being as a value, not in the sense of privileging the object in the subject-object relationship but solely in the sense that an *exchange value* is attributed to being. For Heidegger, nihilism is precisely the reduction of being to exchange value. So, the link with Nietzsche is confirmed precisely in that eliminating God, the supreme value, that is the *terminal instance*, then *interruptive* and *obstructive* values can unfold in their true nature, which is controvertibility, the indefinite transformability process.

Both for Nietzsche and for Heidegger, values exist but in an autonomous fashion. For both, nihilism is the consummation of the value of use (a value in itself) into the value of exchange. Being is completely dissolved in the non-spreading of value, in the indefinite transformations of universal equivalence.

4.1.1 Consequences. For the fulfilled nihilism the liquidation of the supreme values is neither the establishment or re-establishment of a situation of values in a strong sense; nor is it a repossession because every "own" has become superfluous. That is why in the *Twilight of the Idols* Nietzsche writes that "the real world has become a fairy tale": not the alleged true world but the *tout court* world. For Nietzsche, then, it is no longer truly a fairy tale because there is no truth that reveals it as appearance or illusion. Fairy tale is the reality, and the reality is the fairy tale. However, the fairy tale does not completely lose its meaning; it forbids attributing to the appearances that comprise it the cogent force which belonged to the metaphysical *ontos on*.[73] Precisely because everything is appearance there is no longer truth. Every claim of truth becomes an absurdity if not a violence against reality (understood in a fantastic way).. On the other hand, as Vattimo says, one must also beware the traps which Nietzsche's thought can hide. One trap, which is highly topical in M. Onfray as we shall see, is when one,

> recognising the characteristic of fairy tale attributed to the real world, attributes to fairy tale the ancient metaphysical dignity (the "glory") of the real world. The experience which opens out for the fulfilled nihilist is not, instead, an experience of fullness,

---

73 See Gianni Vattimo, *La fine della modernità* (Milan: Garzanti, 1991), 27–33.

of glory, of *ontos on*, but only untied from claimed values and referred instead, in an emancipated fashion, to the values which metaphysical tradition has always considered base and ignoble, and which are thus redeemed to their true dignity.[74]

In this system of nihilism — which we define as weak precisely to avoid succumbing to Nietzsche's distorted interpretations — being is a Being-there, and "Being-there is founded as a hermeneutical totality only insofar as it continually lives the possibility of no-longer-being-there."[75] Reflecting on Heidegger, Vattimo concludes:

> not only has the hermeneutical constitution of Being-there a nihilistic character because man rolls away from the centre towards X; but also because the being whose meaning is being recovered is a being who tends to identify himself with nothingness, with the ephemeral characters of existence, as if locked up between the terms of birth and death.[76]

So, *Dasein* is hermeneutic totality. Doesn't hermeneutics then become the true metaphysical measure of the nihilism of being? The aesthetic perception, too, is nihilistic. The aesthetic conscience in its punctuality, ahistoricity, and discontinuity presents itself as an experience of mortality.

> And even if in this momentary experience Being-there does not meet the ontological transcendence of nature present in the work of genius, as the Romantics thought, it is not even true that he only encounters himself as a subject: on

---

74 Gianni Vattimo, *La fine della modernità*, 33.
75 Ibid., 125.
76 Ibid., 129.

the contrary, he meets as an existing being, as a mortal, who in its capacity to die experiences being in a manner radically different from that familiar to the metaphysical tradition.[77]

4.1.2 Christianity against metaphysics. In the development of his thought, Vattimo goes further. The end of metaphysics is foreshadowed in Christianity itself, or rather in Christ and in the values preached by Him, among which is charity-solidarity. Vattimo reads the figure of Christ through the prism of Dostoevsky, who creates a paradoxical case with respect to Christianity: in his work *Demons*, he prefers Christ to truth.[78] There Vattimo sees his weak Christianity. Here is the abandonment of the truth — understood in the classic sense of correspondence to a state of things — and above all the abandonment of the Christian claim of identification of Christ with the truth, consequently rejecting the possibility of an alternative between the two terms. According to Vattimo, the traditional idea that eternal life consists in contemplation of God face-to-face has been interpreted in the Spinozian sense, which ends up identifying bliss with perfect knowledge of geometry. Did Jesus become flesh and sacrifice Himself on the Cross for this?[79] The classical metaphysics, resulting in the theology of the adaptation of Christ to the truth interpreted by Spinoza, would be belittled to a mathematical idea of God, thus departing from the essential message of the Gospel.[80]

---

77   Gianni Vattimo, *La fine della modernità*, 136.
78   Part II, ch. VII
79   See Gianni Vattimo, "Cristianesimo contro metafisica," *MicroMega* 2 (2000): 132–133.
80   The rejection of the truth *sic et simpliciter* is rooted here: the claim to provide a geometrical-mathematical vision of existence, with a binding morality. See Joseph Ratzinger, *Quid est veritas?*, 212.

The Truth about Love for Love in Truth

For Vattimo, Dostoevsky is the most faithful to the Gospel, with the choice of Christ set against the truth. More than Dostoevsky, Nietzsche represents this paradoxical faithfulness to the Gospel, in his proclamation of the death of God:

> Not only does this announcement, in its literal sense, simply repeat the evangelical history of the crucifixion, but most of all it means that since God who is dead, killed by his faithful, is justly, and only, the moral God—the supreme guarantor of this order of the (geometric) world who made the dying Socrates say that a righteous man has nothing to fear, either in this life or in life after death—it is primarily in Nietzsche himself that the most radical expression of Dostoyevsky's paradox is to be found.... The death of the "moral" God marks the end of the possibility of preferring truth to friendship, because this death means that there is no "objective" or ontological truth, etc., which can claim to be anything other than simply the expression of a friendship, or of a wish for power, or of a subjective relationship... Even those who believe "magis amica veritas" do it in the name of love of another or of themselves, of the tradition which is expressed in them, or for the "human, too human" motives which Nietzsche so meticulously analysed in the wake

---

However, the truth does not ensnare freedom but liberates it from irrationalistic conditioning, illustrating a path of self-determination in goodness and in love, not in geometry. God, who is said to be dead, is not the moral God but the living God. A morality without truth is irrational. Nietzsche and his followers do nothing but shake off the burden of this morality. We, on the other hand, follow the living God, the God *who is Love*.

of the French moralists. Friendship, Will or even, to use Paschal's words, "reasons of the heart."[81]

Therefore,

> Christianity, to summarise somewhat hurriedly but faithfully, is the condition which prepares the dissolution of metaphysics and its replacement with gnoseology — that is to say, in Dilthyian terms, Kantism; the emphasis on the subject, the foundation of knowledge on the basis of self-confidence are the principles which would inspire Descartes and Kant and would dominate modern philosophy. For some time this remained a metaphysics dominated by an objective vision of interiority itself, due to the fact that the new principle of the objectivity introduced by Christianity does not succeed in asserting itself immediately.... [82]

The conflict between the Christian inner reality and the visual or aesthetical objectivism preached by the Greeks is represented by St. Augustine, as Dilthey shows: the inner reality emphasizes will to the detriment of intellect. European thought can be seen through Vattimo as the history of a struggle between the principle of dissolution of metaphysics — inner reality, will, certainty of the *cogito* — introduced into the world by Christianity and the visual or aesthetic objectivism of Greek culture. In such a way the Christian proclamation is a historic event and not a revelation by Christ of an eternal truth, and Christianity is the struggle between two historical possibilities or between two friendships.[83]

---

81 Gianni Vattimo, "Cristianesimo contro metafisica," 133.
82 Ibid., 135.
83 Ibid., 136. In truth, it is an erroneous reading of St. Augustine

It is sufficient to acknowledge—and this is the sense of Heidegger's existentialism in *Sein und Zeit*—that Kantism is still a sort of Augustinism, namely it is a claim that spiritual certainty can be traced back to a non-historical, "natural" structure, which in this sense is an objective structure (the transcendental of Kant, which had already been criticized by Dilthey in these terms), in order to see that the most radical inheritors of the anti-metaphysical principle introduced into the world by Christ, are Nietzsche in his Death of God and Heidegger in his doctrine of *Ereignis*.[84]

Vattimo, therefore, promotes friendship in place of truth, surpassing his teachers Nietzsche and Heidegger. Contrary to the saying attritubuted to Aristotle, "*Amicus Plato, sed magis amica veritas*," Vattimo chooses to be a friend of Plato to overcome the final "objectivist residue" of Greek metaphysics and the force of Christian newness. To a different extent, Nietzsche and Heidegger, for reasons broadly analogous to those of St. Augustine, "remained imprisoned by Greek objectivism and fundamentally refused to develop all the implications of the anti-metaphysical Christian revolution."[85]

> These implications cannot be fully developed without recourse to charity. To express this again in a very schematic way: it is only friendship which is explicitly acknowledged as a decisive factor of truth which prevents us from thinking

---

and of the origins of Christianity. See Joseph Ratzinger, "La verità cattolica e Il cristianesimo oltre la tradizione," *MicroMega* 2 (2000): 41–64.
84   Gianni Vattimo, "Cristianesimo contro metafisica," 137.
85   Ibid., 138.

of the end of metaphysics as bringing to a head what we would call, with Nietzsche, reactive (and even reactionary) nihilism. I will confine myself to an outline which seems to me to be at least an indicative one but which is in need of further clarification. It is impossible for me not to see, in the central role assumed by the other (the Other? Here we encounter the problem of the theological objectivism of Levinas himself), in theories as diverse as the thinking of Levinas and Habermas's philosophy of communication, or in the use of the term "charity" by Davidson, a confirmation of my own hypothesis on the central role of charity.[86]

Vattimo argues further:

> Friendship can only become the principle, the factor of truth, if thought has abandoned any claim to an objective, universal, and apodictic foundation. Without a genuine opening to Being as an event, the other of Levinas always risks being seen as deposed by the Other (with a capital O) — which this time is a truth which "justifies" friendship for Plato only by eliminating the other as a historic individual.[87]

Again, he says:

> The Christian preaching of charity is not only, or is not by any means, an ethical, or rather an edifying consequence of the revelation of "objective" truth regarding our very nature as children of God. Rather, it is an appeal which arises from the historical fact of the Incarnation (which is

---

86   Gianni Vattimo, "Cristianesimo contro metafisica," 138.
87   Ibid., 138–139.

historical not only in the sense that it is a "real" fact but in the sense that in its *Wirkungsgeschichte* it constitutes our existence) and which speaks to us of a nihilistic purpose of Being, a teleology of the enfeeblement of any "ontic" rigidity in favor of an ontological being, namely of *Verbum*, *Logos*, words which are interchanged in the *Gespraech*, which we are inasmuch as we are historical beings. Truth as charity and Being as *Ereignis*, or as an event, are two aspects which are closely associated with each other. The central role of the Other in many contemporary philosophical theories acquires the whole of its significance if we put it in the context of the dissolution of metaphysics, and it is only this condition which avoids the risk of what is purely and simply an edifying moralism[88], or of what is purely a "pragmatic" moralism.... With all the inaccuracies which a conclusion such as this (even a provisional one) allows to exist, it seems to me that it is from this point that reflection has to commence on what remains not only to be remembered but also to be done, two thousand years after the event of Christianity.[89]

4.1.3 An irrational charity. Obviously, here the word charity serves only as *flatus vocis*: it is impoverished of the rich biblical content we previously recalled, underlining the Latin translation of the original agape, present in the

---

[88] Here he is reflecting *his* religious education. See Gianni Vattimo, Pierangelo Sequeri, and Giovanni Ruggeri, *Interrogazioni sul cristianesimo. Cosa possiamo ancora attenderci dal Vangelo?* (Rome: Esperienze, 2000), 119–120.

[89] Gianni Vattimo, et al., *Interrogazioni sul cristianesimo*, 139. See also Santiago Zabalo, ed., *Il futuro della religione: solidarietà, carità, ironia* (Milan: Garzanti, 2005).

two fundamental texts of St. Paul on charity (1 Cor 13 and 2 Cor 5:14). So, a charity without God is watered down into the mere relationship to others which is, however, only a conflict with the will of others. It becomes a *caritas* that justifies even abortion and euthanasia — that is, the death of the other — a relativist caritas in which God is nothing. Men and women themselves become nothing. Again, Vattimo says:

> God! But I can only speak about God from a mythological point of view. What does that mean? I am not certain that the Christian God is the God of everyone. In this perhaps Israel had its own truth of modesty: this is our God, the one with whom we have made an agreement. The God in whom I believe is the God of the Bible because that is the one I have had in my hands from childhood. If I pretend to know God beyond his images, I would feel just like someone who wants to identify with him, so there is always a tension. I know full well that God is not a father, that Jesus is not sat at his right-hand — really, we're not mad — but I also know that I cannot speak of it except in these terms. If I met a Buddhist I would start again discussing these things with him, certain that I would not want to convert him. The problem is this: are missions really fundamental? Today, fortunately, missionaries go around the world building hospitals and not forcing people to accept that God is one and three. Besides, Christianity, perhaps, will save itself only if it becomes mystic, if it stops from pretending that everyone really believes that Jesus was born on a specific day at a specific time. We were saying yesterday with Santiago, speaking

with the priests at dinner: "The Church must be saved from itself!"[90]

It is impossible to remain passive in the face of a hermeneutic-nihilistic framework like that of Vattimo. A Christianity reduced to an apparent charity derived from a hermeneutic without truth is no longer recognizable. Here lies the danger: we become everything, tolerant of everything and everyone, except the truth, except Christ. Isn't this perhaps the current political implication of an irrational Christian faith? Europe, by now old and decrepit in its eternal values, would be willing to be anything — preferably Islamized — except for returning to what it was. The truth scares, while relativism kills.

Where is the weak side of this weak vision? We can clarify it through the shrewd thought of Francesco Botturi. In Vattimo, pre-categorical or trans-categorical access to being is not possible and therefore access to truth as such is not possible. In the end, common sense as preparatory to every word and to every philosophy, as well-explained by the philosopher of common sense, Antonio Livi, is

---

90 Gianni Vattimo, Frederico Orlando, and Santiago Zabala, *Nichilismo e religione*, 26. I have quoted this excerpt for those who are easily impressed by the Christianity of Vattimo. We see how that ancient idealistic temptation to deplete Christianity with philosophy and then for it to materialize in the moment of absolute synthesis is always so strong in philosophers. Hermeneutics is the science that tells us that there are no facts, only interpretations. After metaphysics one has to deal with history, with one's own historicity. The "I cannot but call myself a Christian" of the Cross becomes, then, "I cannot but accept" Christianity *also* to bring it out into discussion along with many other different problems (See 13–14). It is necessary to incorporate Christianity by diluting it, to control it by sweetening it with good feelings, otherwise it is always imposes itself and nullifies other ideas with its claim to truth. It is like wanting to win a battle on horseback by turning it into a horse race. You play but you don't win. When will you finally stop playing?

rejected.⁹¹ However, this also means overcoming the principle of non-contradiction, which must be respected to say something that makes sense. So, what is the meaning of what is said? "We cannot think of something that does not have a *unity*: multiplicity, too, can be thought of as a whole. Everything thought or said must be *intelligible*, otherwise we would not be able to think it; we always hypothesise a meaning of what we think, its truth."⁹² Logical truth, then, presupposes ontologcial truth, whose cornerstone is God. So, "self-confutation is real: the assertion about the *end of truth* is simply false. This is the real paradox which we must have the courage to proclaim; this is the *outdated consideration* that the market derides just as the *madman* derided in the well-known Nietzschean text...."⁹³

4.2 The strong nihilism of Michel Onfray

At this point, let us turn to a philosophical position opposed if not hostile to Vattimo's, although united to it in the historicist vision of humanity: the militant hedonism of M. Onfray. Onfray's thought is more polyhedral: in wanting to rationally end theism and religion, he uses all knowledge, even atheistic militarism, to reach his goal. Yet, on several occasions he confesses that religion and God fall with reason alone. Onfray fights against relativism, having

---

91 See Antonio Livi, *Senso comune e logica aletica*, Sensus communis, Annuario di logica aletica, 1 (Rome: Leonardo da Vinci, S. Marinella, 2005), with a wide-ranging final bibliography.
92 Francesco Botturi, *Testo di una conferenza del 1992*, cited in Antonio Livi, *La filosofia e la sua storia*, vol. III/2 (Rome: Società Editrice Dante Alighieri, 1997), 942.
93 Aldo Vendemiati, *Povera e nuda. Saggio di filosofia della filosofia*, Euntes Docete 3 (2006): 217. I refer the reader to the whole article for a summary vision of contemporary philosophies and for a shrewd humanistic-metaphysical proposal aimed at determining nihilism.

truly recognized it as the cause of the proliferation of one truth into multiple truths, particularly in the area of religion. So, it is necessary to fight the monotheistic religions where the truth of God, and His unity, resides. Religious relativism is, in his opinion, the greatest disaster, because it ends up allowing religion to impoverish humanity in its true being, which is matter, pleasure, pure *eros*.

Onfray's atheism aims primarily at combatting relativism. Interestingly, his philosophy condemns relativism as deadly affliction for the true freedom of humanity, which is freedom from God and from His precepts. In Onfray's opinion, the greatest danger to the advancement of secularism is relativism, which puts everything on the same level and brings it into strong contradiction, endorsing error and truth, good and evil, humanity and its negation. Post-Christian secularism, according to Onfray, must set itself against relativism with the strong truth of atheism: God is simply not there, so every hypothesis of inter-religious dialogue is impractical and threatens the truth of humanity. Thus, he denounces the true mortal post-modern sin:

> ...by matching all religions and their negation, as secularity suggests today, one endorses relativism: equality between magical thought and rational thought, between fable, myth and reasoned discourse, between thaumaturgical discourse and scientific thought, between the Torah and the *Discourse on the Method*, the New Testament and the *Critique of Pure Reason*, the Koran and *The Genealogy of Morals*. Moses is worth the the same as Descartes, Jesus, Kant and Mohammed, Nietzsche...[94]

---

[94] Michel Onfray, *The Atheist Manifesto. The Case against Christianity, Judaism and Islam* (New York: Arcade Publishing, 2007), 260.

And so, he continues highlighting the truthful contradictions that emerge from the comparison between Judaism, Islam, and Christianity, saying that if the opposite is true — as it is true — we should stop thinking.[95] Onfray is even more decisive:

> This relativism is harmful. From now on, under the pretext of secularism, all discourse is the same: error and truth, the false and the true, the fanciful and the serious.... At this hour when the final battle — already lost — looms for the defence of the Enlightenment's values against magical propositions, we must fight for a post-Christian secularism, that is to say, atheistic, militant and radically opposed to choosing between Western Judeo-Christianity and its Islamic adversary — neither Bible nor Koran. I persist in preferring philosophers to rabbis, priests, imams, ayatollahs and mullahs. Rather than trust their theological hocus-pocus, I prefer to draw on alternatives to the dominant philosophical historiography: the laughers, materialists, radicals, cynics, hedonists, atheists, sensualists, voluptuaries. They know that there is only one world, and that promotion of an afterlife deprives us of the enjoyment and benefit of the only one there is. A genuinely mortal sin...[96]

---

95 See Onfray, *The Atheist Manifesto*, 261. Even if one gets rid of religion by a depletion of religions, one is not freed from worry that the logical contradiction might emerge from the various hypotheses, whether philosophical or scientific. Even in the worldly truths there are those who returns to what someone else removes.

96 Ibid., 261–262. Onfray is pitiless in the rejection of monotheistic religions and consequently religion — here is the unfortunate leap which logic does not allow without cutting the very history of humanity: "Religion, this creation of fiction" (64). In truth,

Essentially, then, Onfray advocates for a *post-Christianity*. In opposition to Vattimo (whose weak thought gives rise to a justification of nihilist-theist relativism that is in some way truthful), for Onfray the real obstacle to strong materialism against weak relativist thought is Christianity (along the same lines as the Pythagorean, Jewish, and Platonic ascetic ideal), particularly Christian ethics. His hedonism is built according to a post-Christianity. "How do we stay free in a loving relationship?" asks Onfray. The only way is the de-Christianization of ethics: the realization of a licentious feminism and the promotion of a mild, frivolous eros, that is recreational and without norms.[97]

For Onfray, God is neither dead nor dying. This is the reason for his combative atheism. A fiction does not die, an illusion does not pass away. "Wouldn't the killer of God be a superior God?" Onfray asks. Unlike Nietzsche, who kills God through his knowledge, or others, who kill God through books with ideological impulses, Onfray believes that God cannot be killed, because a breath, a smell, an aspiration cannot be killed. A God made by men and women in their image exists only to make daily life possible, despite the tragedy that everyone is headed toward nothingness. The last god will disappear along with the last of humanity and with him dread, fear, anguish, and machines that are only suitable

---

it is a significant cultural factor—after the events of September 11, when clearly a religious war was taking shape: Islam against Judeo-Christianity (See Onfray, *The Atheist Manifesto*, 61–65). In truth, one cannot simply get rid of religion because one disagrees with some religions. It is necessary to decide on the *religio vera*. Perhaps Onfray is asking for clarity between religions?

97 See Onfray's fundamental work, *Théorie du corps amoureux. Pour une érotique solaire* (Paris: Grasset, 2000). His recent work *La puissance d'exister. Manifeste hédoniste* (Paris: Grasset, 2006), is a summary of post-Christian atheology and clear hedonism.

for creating deities. The dead God will presume tamed nothingness.[98]

Onfray proposes an atheism that is post-modern, in other words, post-Christian. The atheism preached up to some time ago was simply the denial of the affirmation of God, the denial that God came in some way, no matter what. But real atheism must get rid of God and the transcendent with an enterprising spirit. One must not only deny, but also affirm; therefore he does not promote a nihilistic atheism, but rather a sort of doctrine without God which renounces a theological and scientific reference in order to build a new, flattened morality: neither God nor science, but philosophy, reason, usefulness, pragmatism, and individual hedonism used to overcome all the values preached by Christianity. For Onfray it is necessary to go beyond the religious and geometric model — perhaps the very model generated by Spinoza and to which Vattimo also reacts (this is the common point between the two philosophies and the trick of both) — as Jeremy Bentham and his disciple John Stuart Mill had already done with utilitarianism, toward the thought of the immediate certainty, although sometimes a little restricted, restricted but certain. Thus, good and evil exist no longer as the notions of faithful and unfaithful, of sin and grace, of perdition and salvation, but now exist in relation to the useful and the good of the greatest possible number of individuals; good and bad are therefore linked to a hedonistic contract.[99]

---

98   See Onfray, *Traité d'athéologie*, 38–40.
99   Ibid., 83–87. I will not go into the arguments which Onfray cites to deconstruct Christianity. In summary: the crystallization of a hysteria in an era made foolish by a strange catalyzing idea of the marvellous, namely, Jesus of Nazareth. St. Paul would be responsible for the promotion of this fable (Onfray, *Traité d'athéologie*,

Post-Christian Atheism must establish itself worlds apart from the values preached by Christianity. One must free himself from all the feelings of guilt set in motion by faith to create a new ethical project to create in the West conditions for a true post-Christian morality where the body is not a punishment, nor the earth a valley of tears or life a disaster, pleasure a sin, women a curse, intelligence a presumption, desire a damnation, grief a redemption.[100]

What about suffering? It must be suppressed. Euthanasia is touted as a remedy to suffering, to life. Suppressed pleasure in voluntary death is preached, instead of gazing at the Crucified One. Life is the power to continue in a dull and inherent existence which removes every right of citizenship to the transcendent.

An initial response to Onfray can only move along the same lines as the Holy Father's response to Nietzsche in *Deus Caritas Est*.[101] The mild, frivolous eros is not the real 'yes' to the body, but rather its demotion. To go no further than dull eros is to remove from eros itself the desire for which it was born: that of already seeing in some way the intelligible in the perceptible, the rationality of desire, its possibility. If the eros is not already grasped in some way as intelligible, it does not move, but it becomes irrational,

---

88–89, 147–174). I will outline a response: perhaps in the face of the many executioners in the history of every age, wouldn't many men and women who preferred Christ to their lives have come to their senses? Rather, they offered their lives out of love for Christ and their neighbor's salvation, not allowing themselves to be killed by martyrdom out of love for their ideas and in hatred of others.
100   See Onfray, *Traité d'athéologie*, 90.
101   See Pope Benedict XVI, *Deus Caritas Est*, 3. A reference to Nietzsche, whose philosophy, however, Onfray did not understand well, as noted, somewhat ironically, by Vattimo in a concise review of his treatise on atheology, www.fazieditore.it/f2/default.asp?p=RecensioneStampa&id=637&id_rec=4058.

it falls, deameaning humanity rather than raising it. The death of eros becomes the medicine of the lonely life.

Why did Onfray's atheism have to be colored with military tones while the strength of reason was sufficient? Is it perhaps the demonstration of the fact that a theoretical atheism is simply a logical contradiciton? Rather, Michel Onfray, floundering in the dark meanders of lonely eros, of its truth about humanity (a half-truth, in fact), is still seaking, "What is truth? Which is the true religion?" It is not possible to suppress the desire for truth in the debauchery of the solitude of eros.

What is more problematic and sensitive to self-refutal is, as has been said, the trap into which one falls assuming the nihilism of Nietzsche — as rightly pointed out by Vattimo, who knew well the thought of the father of nihilism — and coloring it with strong, powerful values, which give back vigor to truth. The true face of Nietzschean nihilism is simply this: "If the purpose is missing, the answer to the 'Why' is missing." Onfray pretends to base a metaphysical nihilism, a strong nihilism, on values which, precisely since they are *tout court*, have lost their metaphysical cogency and are destined to be simply exchange values with the now weak being.

We respond to Onfray with Vattimo's witty remark, while Vattimo must rely on reason and logic. To both, with the "defenceless, poor and *pure* character of the true,"[102] with love in truth for a truth of love.

5. A CONTEMPORARY RISK FOR THEOLOGY

The apologetic circularity of truth and love, or of reason and love, now leads us to glance at theology, to attempt a

---

102   Gaspare Mura, *Intervista a Vittorio Possenti su nichilismo e metafisica, Euntes Docete* 3 (2006): 224.

response of the truth of love to a theological spirit which is in vogue but which, in my opinion, is in clear contrast to this circularity and so to the fundamental question of who God is and who man is. Is it possible to think of a deconstruction of the systems of theological thought different from the truth of love, the being of love in the love of being?

Reflecting on the theological panorama in the third millennium, a number of perplexities appear. The repeated rejection of God and His exclusion from public life, thus relegating Him to the subjective sphere of conscience, has contributed greatly to the placement of men and women, their conscience, and therefore the subject, at the forefront. Now, there is only humanity without God. For its part, theology seems to want to remedy this deficiency by restating God in some way but at times to the detriment of humanity. In some cases, there is the risk of theologically assimilating humanity into God, to transform Him almost into a machine. It seems as if the response to the weak post-modern entreaties reaffirming God is to replace Him with humanity. Weak men and women, incapable of strong, lasting judgements, need One who replaces them but is strong. God should provide for the evermore acute deficiencies of humanity, should shoulder its miseries, especially those miseries which men and women are no longer able to recognize as such.

A sort of post-modern grief, which torments theology concerning God and humanity, and humanity in God, agitates us from various quarters. God once again becomes man. He suffers the pain which men and women are no longer capable of seeing with the eyes of God, and which falls like a boulder on their shoulders. On the other hand, only God would be capable of raising up both humanity and the boulder, taking both on His shoulders. God suffers the suffering of humanity. Jesus suffers the ignorance of humanity. So, one comes back to God but in a distorted way. God would enter into the world of human weakness, becoming weak Himself. By so doing, however, humanity disappears and is completely replaced, also putting an end to everything that is linked specifically to its finiteness, such as sin and, in the end, the soteriological value of redemption is diluted.

I would like to distance myself from a theology which wrongfully affirms the suffering of God, and which seems to be an implication of the weak philosopohical thought I was just speaking about. Christologies that are set specifically on a staurological vision see in the Cross of Christ the favorable moment of God's entry into the mystery of suffering. Freeing Christology from the exclusive character of the Chalcedonian language of substance and nature, and opening a relational Christology, one can also easily integrate God into the contradiction of suffering and death, so that a more correct divine dignity and explanation can be given to suffering. In this way the title "Son of God" assumes great importance, since at the most painful moment of the passion, the Cross, He also involves the Father in His suffering. The passion and death of the Son, by the understanding of being as being-in-relation and of person as a being him/herself in relation and of subsistence in self-realization,[103] become the suffering of the Father, and therefore the suffering of God the Trinity in a sort of historico-salvific perichoresis experienced by God as God. The drama of the suffering and death of Christ is not fulfilled beyond an impassive and elusive Trinity but rather "determines for ever the eternal being of God.... In the cross of the Son, the God of glory

---

103   See Bernd Jochen Hilberath and T. Schneider, "Gesù Cristo/Cristologia," in *Manual de teología dogmática* (Barcelona: Herder Editorial, 1996).

participates in the suffering of humanity and the pain of humanity becomes destiny proper to God, too."[104] Only thus can one think of the "life of God and the death of humanity radically joined together in the cross of Christ."[105] Thus, making room for a God closer to humanity by bringing the mystery of suffering into the Trinitarian mystery, one ends up transferring the problem of evil in God and eliminating the responsibility of humanity, while suffering becomes a blind necessity which structures the very being of God: God replaces humanity and humanity's suffering becomes banal. In truth, it is necessary to

> re-think the "primacy of Being" in the metaphysical vision of God, impoverishing it, of course, by the superficial deposit of an interepretation which has deduced from it an apathy and immutability hardly compatible with the Living God of revelation; but at the same time not falling into the trap of introducing into God — in order to make his life dynamic and render Him in some way more compassionate towards humanity — a freedom of choice which no longer allows the mysterious identification in Him of freedom and being.[106]

In a vision that unites ontology and Scripture — a God who is always Himself and always alongside humanity — it

---

104 D. Wiederkehr, "Croce/Sofferenza" in *Enciclopedia Teologica* (Rome: Queriniana, 1990), 175.
105 Ibid., 175.
106 Piero Coda, *Il Logos e il nulla. Trinità religioni mistica*, (Rome: Città Nuova, 2003), 272–273. However, Coda's spirituality of the "abandoned Jesus" does leave us somewhat perplexed: the metaphysical formulae of the Trinitarian dogma are replaced by the *dialectic* formulae of idealistic religious philosophy (Hegel, Schelling), so that the Word, instead of *assuming* human nature *becomes* man and in that sense would then be "abandoned by the Father."

will not be necessary to add to God as God the mystery of suffering. God has said everything in His Word made flesh. God suffers in the Son who undergoes suffering and dies. If it were only the Son to undergo suffering, as made capable of so doing by a human nature identical to ours, human suffering would not be redeemed and evil would always have the ultimate and decisive say about humanity. There is no apathy or indifference in the Father although He is not suffering the Son's pain. His greatest mercy for sinful and suffering humanity is precisely the gift of the Son. "God so loved the world that He gave his only begotten Son" (Jn 3:16). The Father gives Himself in the Son, and the Son, in the gift of self to the point of death on the cross, is the total loving compassion of the Father. In fact, "how was He, the Father, truly able to make his, in the Son, the world's pain, if not by enabling the Son to drink to the full the chalice of the passion? Precisely in that way showing and realising, even as man, a great love like that of the Father?"[107] The Son is the total gift of the Father. To involve the Father, too, in the suffering of the Son is to devalue the gift, to permeate the Father with a fundamental weakness in His being Eternal Parent, and therefore a weakness in His commencing the inexpressible life of the Three Eternal Co-Lovers, an indifference and

---

107   Piero Coda, *Il Logos e il nulla*, 277–288. I completely agree with the theological vision of the author who confesses: "Personally, I do not find convincing, in fact, they leave me puzzled, those suggestions which, playing on the *pathos* of the fellowship of God with humanity, speak shamelessly and without distinction of God's pain, attributing it to the Father, too, both in a poetic and indirect way" (280–281). See also Piero Coda, "Quando a soffrire è il Figlio di Dio, volto nascosto dell'uomo," *Camillianum* 16 (2006): 5–16, where the author talks about the suffering of the Son of God and only of the Son who, in his humanity, opens to humanity the possibility of experiencing suffering, always as son.

scepticism in the *ad extra* missions of the Son and the Holy Spirit. The only response to suffering is the one which God gave in Christ crucified and risen once and for ever, even if it is always impregnated with a mystery which transcends us. It transcends us precisely because it is mystery. Even with all our good intentions to explain it, we cannot make of God a non-God, that is, ultimately resolve the mystery; we must bow dumbfounded and with wonder let it speak to us.

In truth, there is mortal suffering due to a metaphysical void, filled for the most part by a love which knows more of eros than agape. Instead, there is a need to return to the truth, to go back to the true capacity of humanity to love in truth and so to love the truth, rediscovering the true God — that God who is always Himself, always infinite love. In Him there is no opposition between being and freedom, being and love, nor could there be. It is necessary to return to the true Christ, the incarnate Logos, with the help of strong reason and through the mediation of the Virgin Mary, handmaid of the Logos, disciple of the Truth, mother of the incarnate Word. Is it not perhaps because we have got rid of the Madonna — minimizing, redefining, whittling away here and there at her unique presence in the mystery of Christ and the Church — that faith has got rid of an important ally such as reason? The Virgin is a sign of the truth which opens itself to faith, of the reason which seeks to understand with the Logos of God, His Son. The incarnate Logos, God-Love, becomes flesh through her and comes to us through her. The Virgin gives us Christ, the Logos of incarnate love which gives to humanity the true face of God: the face of Being always identical in an infinite love. Christ is that God who knows how to sympathize, how to pardon, because He is a God who *is*, because He *is* God. In this way humanity's true face is given back to it. Humanity will be capable of looking at reality with real eyes, with the truth of love, *with* the Logos of Love, *through* Mary, the handmaid of the Lord.

CONCLUDING REMARKS

At the end of this first attempt to present the circularity of truth and love through the profound careful examination of *Deus Caritas Est*, I hope at least to renewed apologetic discourse, demonstrating its necessity at a time of great weakness in being and fortitude of love. It is necessary to reestablish the alethic value of knowledge, restoring full rights to the passion for the truth about God and humanity; a truth which does not become the enemy of humanity, threatening its future but which is the spring of hope, that is still able to be in an agapic tension which warms the heart and gives wings to love. Theology, often forgetful of metaphysics because it is closed in an historicist hermeneutic, has largely abandoned the theological-alethic discourse about God to expand into concepts more in tune with humanity, more comprehensible to humanity. God has been forgotten to make room for humanity so that interest in humanity has even replaced the first theological inspiration about God as its beginning. There is often an anchoring in theological anthropology, more anthropo-centric than theo-centric. Yet the hermeneutical approach is the theo-logical one.

> The advent of nihislim leading back to the *death of God* is an invitation to take up again the theological theme, always consubstantial with philosophising, and perhaps to adopting the following posture: enough has been said about humanity, it is time to think about God. Not for one moment

does that remove the current centrality of the anthropological question, but integrated into its natural place which is that as long as humanity exists, God must also be thought about.[108]

God must be thought of first and foremost; the true God who is reason and love, Logos and Agape. God cannot be what humanity is not, and humanity cannot be what God is not. A God who is not reason and love is a monolithic and lonely God who easily becomes a totalitarian, arbitrary God: what God is not and humanity is not. God is Reason, Meaning, Love, and this is reflected in humanity, which is reason and love, rationality and eros called to grow along with men and women. God comes to meet men and women and educates them to His truth which is agape. Men and women are made for God, and only in Him do they find their meaning, their fulfilment. Men and women find in God the reason for their love and love of reason — in a word, the truth of love. One cannot go beyond the being of love and the love of being. Men and women, in fact, are no more than that. God is the being of love and the love of being, because "God *is* love." The man who is logos and love can find only in God the love he seeks in his being. God became man.

Christ is for humanity, and humanity is for Christ. For, in God, Love is incarnated in the Reason of everything[109]; the face of *Deus Caritas* is the *Logos sarx*. The agape of God in Christ became flesh in the Logos. Only the incarnate Logos is the face of the sempiternal Love. Therefore, to remain in Christ means to remain in love.[110]

---

108   Gaspare Mura, *Intervista a Vittorio Possenti su nichilismo e metafisica*, 224.
109   See Col 1:16.
110   See Jn 15:1–9.

Consequently, only in the true God, in the Christ, can we build the Church with that perfect sharing of the Gospel and adherence to the message about which St. Paul speaks in writing to the Philippians: "communion ... in the gospel" («*koinonía ... eis tò euangélion*»).[111] The proclamation of the Gospel as "word of truth" (2 Tim 2:15) is the ever new and ever current proclamation of that Logos who is life, who is truth, who is love. By listening to Him in us with our prayer, to then give Him to others, we will build up that *koinonía* in the Gospel in the truth — a spiritual *koinonía* which then becomes consolation in Christ, comfort in the charity-agape which generates sentiments of compassion and of love.[112] This constituted the joy of St. Paul when he wrote to the community of Philippi: the union of the spirits, the same *caritas*-agape, the same sentiments.[113] *Koinonía* in the Gospel, faithfulness to the truth, generates the agape of the Church and in the Church, to think with the same thoughts and sentiments ("*súmpsuxoi, tò èn fronoûntes*").[114] So, St. Paul would say again to the Philippians: "Make your own the mind of Christ Jesus," ("*Toûto froneîte en umîn ò kaì en Xristô Iesou*", 2:5), that is, think like Christ, think Christ, think in Christ.[115] In Christ — in the Logos-Love — truth and love, eros and agape are united. Only thus is generated true *koinonía*, the Church of the living God, so as not

---

[111] Phil 1:5.
[112] Ibid., 2:1.
[113] Ibid., 2:2.
[114] Ibid.
[115] See Pope Benedict XVI, *Cooperare e collaborare con il Dio della pace che è con noi*. Meditation during the first General Congregation of the Eleventh Ordinary General Assembly of the Synod of Bishops (October 3, 2005), *L'Osservatore Romano*, October 3–4, 2005, 4.

to love with "just words or mere talk, but [our love must be] something active and genuine" (1 Jn 3:18).

In love there is eternal truth; because love is eternal, it surpasses all limitations. The Church is animated by a love which surpasses the limitations of human poverty. True love, which is infinite, is limited through atheistic thought, through weak thought, both philosophical and theological. Humanity is afraid of limitations, and so removes or avoids them. Only love can go beyond limitations, not ignoring them or eliminating them, but overcoming them in an infinite dimension already present in the non-limitation of love. Love is truth. Truth is love.

The very good news about truth and love is that they are close to uniting in one single mystery: the Word incarnate, the Logos that has become the Good Shepherd. This will be the topic of our next analysis of the mutual (and personal) circularity of truth and love.

The Good Shepherd

WHEN LOGOS AND LOVE ARE *ONE* PERSON

IN CHRISTIAN ART, THE FIGURE OF the good shepherd constitutes one of the two ideograms of salvation history, along with the praying figure. The good sheperd, almost as in a compendium, recounts to the admirer the long story of God's salvific love. The image of the good shepherd has its origins in the late antiquity figurative tradition, where the bucolic material was assumed as a representation of the afterlife, imagined as a calm and ideal place of rural *otium*. In this place of beyond-earthly peace, the image of the good shepherd with the sheep on his shoulders was an idyllic-pastoral formulation of *philantropia* and *humanitas* (according to the tradition of the psychopompos Hermes), virtues which led to the totality of peace. In fact, one of the representations of Hermes depicted a shepherd carrying a ram (an animal sacred to him) on his shoulders; it was a symbol of his mission to accompany the souls of the dead to Avernus.

Christianity, as with other pagan representations, assumed the figure of the good shepherd, and the image soon appeared in catacomb portrayals to express the Christian faith in Christ the Savior who, as Good Shepherd, leads His sheep to the pastures of eternal life.[1] In this way

---

1   Fabrizio Bisconti, ed., "Buon Pastore," in *Temi di iconografia paleocristiana, Sussidi allo studio delle antichità cristiane*, vol. 13 (Città del Vaticano: Pontificio Istituto di Archeologia Cristiana,

the Christian faith was testifying to the expressive fullness of a symbol, which in Christ finally acquired its full and definitive salvific meaning. From here the Greek Fathers developed the concept of divine philanthropy.

1. THE "GOOD SHEPHERD" IN SACRED SCRIPTURE

The theme of the shepherd has a strong biblical resonance. The image of the shepherd understood as guide and leader has its fertile breeding ground in the Old Testament.[2] In particular, Ezekiel prepares the eschatological coming of the Shepherd who will go in search of the lost sheep of His flock, lead them to pasture, and make them rest; He Himself will bind up the wounded and heal the sick.[3] It is within the unity of revelation and as its total accomplishment, that the Johannine discourse on the Good Shepherd should be read. Jesus, recalling the Old Covenant, says: "I am the good shepherd: the good shepherd lays down his life for his sheep" (Jn 10:11). Jesus is the messianic Shepherd to whom is given the throne of David and whose kingdom will have no end[4]; the Shepherd who, offering Himself as ransom, carries the lost sheep on His shoulders to the Father's sheepfold.[5] Every sheep is personally known and loved by the Good Shepherd, and for each the Shepherd has poured out His blood: that is why He cares about the ninety-nine left in the desert. Christ is the true philanthropist, the One who out of love for humanity became man and saves humanity by bringing it, through His human nature, into the divine life of the One-in-Three God. Here is the full realization of the late antiquity figure of the Good Shepherd. Christ is the true

---

2000), 138.
2   See Ez 34; Jer 31:10; Is 40:11; Ps 22:1–5, 79:2.
3   See Ez 34:11, 15–16.
4   See Ex 34:23 in light of Lk 1:32–33.
5   See Lk 15:4–7.

Cyrenian who through His Cross establishes a sempiternal bridge between us and God. In Him one goes to the Father. Only in Him, who is the "gate of the sheepfold" (Jn 10:7), does one go to God, is one led to eternal salvation. The New Testament, reflecting on the salvific role of the Good Shepherd-Redeemer, would continue to refer to Christ as the "wounded Shepherd" to express its faith in salvation brought by Him,[6] Christ the lamb offered in sacrifice who, now glorious, leads to the fount of living water.[7]

2. THE "GOOD SHEPHERD" IN THE REFLECTION OF BENEDICT XVI

The image of the Good Shepherd is dear to the theological reflection of Benedict XVI. In his homily at the start of his Petrine ministry, the Pope referred to Christ the Good Shepherd. On that occasion, so unique for a new Peter preparing for the mission of universal Pastor of the Church, the Pope, recalling the significance of the pallium (woven from lamb's wool, which alludes to the sheep which the Shepherd carries on His shoulders), said:

> For the Fathers of the Church, the parable of the lost sheep, which the shepherd seeks in the desert, was an image of the mystery of Christ and the Church. The human race—every one of us—is the sheep lost in the desert which no longer knows the way. The Son of God will not let this happen; he cannot abandon humanity in so wretched a condition. He leaps to his feet and abandons the glory of heaven, in order to go in search of the sheep and pursue it, all the way to the Cross. He takes it upon his shoulders

---

6 See 1 Pt 2:25.
7 See Rev 7:17.

The Good Shepherd

and carries our humanity; he carries us all — he is the good shepherd who lays down his life for the sheep.[8]

The Good Shepherd then returns in the encyclical *Deus Caritas Est* among the New Testament figures who give flesh and blood to biblical concepts, expressing that already unpredictable and, in some sense, unprecedented activity of God: "This divine activity now takes on dramatic form when, in Jesus Christ, it is God himself who goes in search of the 'stray sheep', a suffering and lost humanity."[9]

The image of the Good Shepherd becomes the symbol of the convergence in the God incarnate of what is proper to man, eros, with what is of God, agape. God assumes what is of man to purify it in what He is, namely, love. "Christ the incarnate love of God" is the Good Shepherd who carries eros on His shoulders to ransom it from every empty seduction, to redeem it from concupiscence soaked in drunkenness and indiscipline. The incarnate agape of God in Christ gives truth to the eros of humanity, and humanity in Christ can truly reach the threshold of a love which no longer ends, participating as sons and daughters in the agape of God.

Christ, the Good Shepherd, is the One who gives back truth to love, enabling us to discover love in truth. From love in truth, one reaches the truth of love, and therefore the truth of God and of humanity. God and humanity meet in the truth of love and are one in Christ who is the incarnate Logos-Agape. The Johannine phrase in the Prologue echoes the Johannine truth of *Deus Caritas Est* (1 Jn 4:8): "The Word became flesh, he lived among us"

---

8 Pope Benidict XVI, Homily (April 24, 2005), *L'Osservatore Romano*, April 25–26, 2005, 6.
9 Pope Benedict XVI, *Deus Caritas Est*, 12.

(Jn 1:14). Deus-Caritas has shown His face of love in the *Logos sarx*. Love can be touched in the Logos who becomes close to us. In God reason and love are one. In Christ reason and love become flesh. In Him, the Good Shepherd, as in a magnificent canvas, the Logos and Agape, reason and charity, harmonize in the perceptibility of the flesh. The Eucharist we eat is this perceptibility par excellence. In Him, man, who was made in His image and likeness, is reborn in the truth of the unity of reason and love, a reason which is the foundation of love and a love which is the fullness of reason.

What is more, in the incarnate God, Logos and Agape are united in a harmony which unifies everything: beauty. Christ is the Beautiful Shepherd—*o poimène o kalòs* in the original Greek acceptation[10]—who summarizes Logos and Agape in the truth of His beauty, like a scorching arrow which burns the mind and the heart. Beauty has an objective value and is not simply an effect on our heart as Hume believes.[11] Christ is the Beautiful One who enchants and translates into aesthetic content the truth of love in the love for truth. The face of the Good Shepherd is the face

---

10   See Jn 10:11.
11   See the reflections on this by Dietrich von Hildebrand, *Estetica*, ed. V. Cicero (Milan: Bompiani, 2006), 22–25. Hume's famous thesis is formulated in this way: "If we take in our hand any volume ... let us ask: "Does it contain any abstract reasoning concerning quantity or number?" No. "Does it contain any experimental reasoning concerning matter of fact and existence?" No. "Commit it then to the flames: for it can contain nothing but sophistry and illusion" (*An Enquiry Concerning Human Understanding*, in von Hildebrand, 24–25, footnote 6). So this thesis, in effect, is nothing but a *petitio principii*, that is, it falls into the simple contradiction of believing a thing to be obvious (the non-evidence of beauty) that is not obvious. The value of beauty interpreted badly is opposed to fact: to what is unfounded and a fortiori not evident. See von Hildebrand, *Estetica*, 25.

of beauty, which is summary and compendium; in it truth and love, logos and agape, are harmonized. Drawing close to Christ, in the beauty of His gaze, we are enchanted by the goodness of truth and by the truth of goodness, to be reborn according to His figure in which the many becomes unity: truth, love, beauty are one, are Him, the Good Shepherd.

3. A THEOLOGY BETWEEN THE LINES

The image of the Good Shepherd, then, expresses a rich theology that can be read between the lines. The Shepherd who takes the sheep on His shoulders — a ram in relation to Hermes — is the Agape of God incarnate, Christ, who in the unity of His divine person assumes our humanity and redeems it by carrying it on His shoulders. On Him the sheep is calm; it returns to the sheepfold.

Reason and eros, drawn into a unity at times disorganized and impulsive — mostly in the oblivion of reason and the accentuation of eros as a mere selfish craving — rediscover their unity in Christ. They are assumed by Christ, redeemed in Him, so they are again able to live in an organic whole that is now the participation of both in a more noble paradigm, that of the Logos-Agape, which gives light to reason and truth to eros. Giving truth to *eros* by making it partner of agape moves us in the truth of love; we learn to discover truth in love. Humanity, walking on the paths of love that are so appropriate, discovers in Christ the foundation of its being, the truth of its love, the possibility of its thought of love (agape) and of its love of thought (logos). This must be drawn today when there is insistence on love; starting from love, humanity is led to discover the truth and fullness of self in God-love. Love is fullness.

To men and women today, who are tangled in the reins of post-modern thought incapable of truth, which forces them to content themselves with mere illusions—everything is illusion if there is no truth—it is necessary to point out that eros is already a desire to raise oneself from the perceptible to the intelligible and that only in agape does eros find its meaning. Eros without reason is blind, and reason without eros healed by agape is cold. It is not by chance that our time, living in the oblivion of reason, has granted full rights to love alone, but it is a love that is often empty, superficial, selfish, squalid. A gradual passage goes from the Enlightenment and modernity to post-modernity, which for many would be a post-Christianity.

> The irresponsible cultivation of a totally unaffective modern *logos* fits perfectly with the violent eruption of a totally irrational post-modern *eros*. And it attracts "political", and even "religious", passions in its involutive spiral without reason and without affections. Therefore without justice. Powerful children of an *eros* without logos nor *agape*, therefore falsely deified and humanly destructive.[12]

We live in a world and at a time when concupiscence, which ought to be the horse to the chariot, has become the charioteer. It is largely dominated by an irrational eros, which dilutes the most important things in life into banality. In a world so drowned in concupiscence, it is necessary to first purify eros by showing the healing path of agape. The person who loves God will begin to love themselves truly and therefore to love love, where God and humanity

---

12   Pierangelo Sequeri, "Il Dio della rivelazione cristiana: Logos e Agape," *L'Osservatore Romano*, June 16–17, 2006, 7.

come together. With the truth of love — the driving force of humanity, that *copula mundi* — thus reestablished it will be easier to look at the relationship between reason and faith, the relationship which we must now indicate as reason-love and faith. With eros healed in agape, which in a certain sense is the rationality or truth of love, and the aporias of an erotic-irrational culture resolved, reason will rediscover its decisive role in the life of humanity. Reason postulates the need for God. Without God we grope in the darkness and end up building our existence on the mere banality of the irrational. Now reason, no longer at the mercy of tastes and whims because of an eros-measure of things, can calmly face the discourse about God since it will be open to the contemplation of reality in its totality. Reason together with love postulates the existence of God, of a God who is Reason and who can also love in freedom. Faith finally reveals to us the face of this God: Christ, the Good Shepherd is the face of the Logos-Agape. In Him God is made man. In Christ God has taken our face and gives truth to our reason and foundation to our love.

The synergy of reason-love and faith is an apologia for the uniqueness of Christianity, the one *religio vera*. If Christ is the agapic, incarnate Logos, only in Him is there the full and definitive response to the question of who God is and who man is. In Christ men and women discover the foundation of themselves and understand their reason and love, because they see themselves made in the image of their Creator and their Redeemer. The Creator and Redeemer, then, asks to be known in the freedom of love. The *religio vera* will have the characteristic of imposing itself in freedom, asking to love religious truth. God asks me to love truth and welcome it in freedom. Only that religion which asks for the freedom of my love to open me toward the truth will be the *religio vera*, because it asks me to be fully myself, giving reason to myself and to reality in its totality. Believing in Christ and loving Christ gives full foundation to reason and love, and so faith opens the doors to charity. Faith and charity become the supernatural fullness and perfection of my reason and my love.

Thus, only Christ is the *verus Deus*, only Christianity is the *religio vera*. These statements imply that in Christ and in Christianity is the fullness of what humanity is, too. If, in the end, humanity and God converge precisely in the reality of love,[13] the *religio vera* will be the religion of love, the religion of *Deus-Caritas*. Charity becomes a manifestation of the truth of God, of God who is love.[14] The Good Shepherd is the God of love. Violence in the name of religion is a powerful force of falsehood.

Looking at the image of the Good Shepherd from the Catacombs of Priscilla, how can we not recall the mystery of redemption? Christ is the Redeemer of humanity. In that sheep which He carries on His shoulders, with two others at his feet, one sees the image of she who was redeemed in a unique way, the Immaculate Conception, and who became in Christ the Immaculate Co-redeemer — she who *with* Christ, crouched on His shoulders, participates in a unique way in the redemption of us all. Standing at the feet of Jesus, we receive everything from Him and from His Mother. Mary has never come down from the shoulders of Christ; she never touches the earth although she is fashioned from the earth. She is the only sheep who always remains with Christ, who is always with Him in suffering and in love. She becomes the standard of our redemption, the standard of our reason-love and faith.

---

13 See Pope Benedict XVI, *Deus Caritas Est*, 2.31/c.
14 Ibid., 31/c.

The Good Shepherd

Finally, the Good Shepherd recalls another theme of notable topicality: ecumenism. We remember the Lord's words: "I have other sheep that do not belong to this fold. I must bring them also, and they will listen to my voice. So there will be one flock, one shepherd" (Jn 10:16). There are sheep still not in communion with the flock of Christ, because there is a lack of obedience to the one pastor, the pope, who makes the Good Shepherd visible. We are confident and believe in the words of Christ. His flock gathered around Him can only have one shepherd, the one designated by Christ ("*You* are Peter" and not *I* am Peter), and only one Mother, his Mother, the Immaculate Co-Redeemer.

We follow Christ, the Good Shepherd, the Logos-Love, who unites His Church and carries us to the pastures of eternal life. The words of St. Gregory the Great summarize my own thoughts:

> So our Lord's sheep will finally reach their grazing ground where all who follow him in simplicity of heart will feed on the green pastures of eternity. These pastures are the spiritual joys of heaven. There the elect look upon the face of God with unclouded vision and feast at the banquet of life for ever more. Beloved brothers, let us set out for these pastures where we shall keep joyful festival with so many of our fellow citizens. May the thought of their happiness urge us on! Let us stir up our hearts, rekindle our faith, and long eagerly for what heaven has in store for us. To love thus is to be already on our way.[15]

These green pastures of eternity have a pledge on earth. The Good Shepherd gives us food for the journey that

---

15   St. Gregory the Great, *Homily 14*, 3–6; PL 76, 1130.

is truth and love in one Bread. This is the Holy Eucharist. With the Eucharistic mystery, the discourse about a personal circularity of truth and love is brought to completion.

"Sacramentum Caritatis" *in* Veritate

THE LOGOS-LOVE IS THE "BREAD OF LIFE"

THE EUCHARIST IS THE "SACRAment of charity," Benedict XVI writes (quoting the *Summa Theologiae*, III, q. 73, a. 3) in his first Post-Synodal Apostolic Exhortation, which brings together the proposals, suggestions, and reflections that emerged during the Synod of Bishops which took place in October 2005. A clear thread can be followed in the life and doctrinal animus of the Church in recent years. One recalls the Encyclical of St. John Paul II, *Ecclesia de Eucharistia* (April 17, 2003). Then, the Year of the Eucharist so desired by the Pope was inaugurated at the International Eucharistic Congress in Guadalajara (October 2004). The Apostolic Letter of John Paul II which accompanied the celebration of the Year of the Eucharist, *Mane Nobiscum Domine* (October 7, 2004), desired to break with the considerable liturgical abuses in Eucharistic matters, already denounced in the same Pope's Eucharistic Encyclical. We remember, too, the valuable Instruction of the Congregation for Divine Worship and the Discipline of the Sacraments, *Redemptionis Sacramentum* (March 25, 2004) and finally Benedict XVI's *Sacramentum Caritatis* (February 22, 2007), on which we wish to focus, highlighting especially the links that bind this Post-Synodal Exhortation with the Encyclical *Deus Caritas Est*. In fact, a doctrinal continuity, as the Pope himself confesses,[1] is resolved via the same theological understanding of love as the unity and truth of God and humanity. The Eucharist is the agape of God who gives Himself "to the end" (Jn 13:1): the truth of love. Benedict XVI writes in *Sacramentum Caritatis*:

> In the sacrament of the Eucharist, Jesus shows us in particular the *truth about the love* which is the very essence of God. It is this evangelical truth which challenges each of us and our whole being. For this reason, the Church, which finds in the Eucharist the very centre of her life, is constantly concerned to proclaim to all, *opportune importune* (cf. *2 Tim* 4:2), that God is love. Precisely because Christ has become for us the food of truth, the Church turns to every man and woman, inviting them freely to accept God's gift.[2]

1. THE FOOD OF TRUTH

The Eucharist, the food of truth, is the mystery of Christ, the Logos become flesh to become bread. In the mystery of the Eucharist the truth of God unfolds before the dumbfounded faith of humanity: "There the *Deus Trinitas*, who is essentially love,[3] becomes fully a part of our human condition."[4] Christ gives Himself under the sacramental-sacrificial species of bread and wine,[5] bringing with Himself the gift of divine life — the very being of *Deus-Caritas* — and inviting men and women to partake in this banquet of love by eating the Truth. What does humanity desire if

---

1 Pope Benedict XVI, *Deus Caritas Est*, 5.
2 Ibid., 2.
3 See 1 Jn 4:7-8.
4 Pope Benedict XVI, *Deus Caritas Est*, 8.
5 See Lk 22:14-20.

"Sacramentum Caritatis" in Veritate

not the truth? How can it be reached if not in the fullness of the reality which is love? It seems that these are the two passages which are the background to the document on Eucharist-Charity. The Eucharist is the truth of God who is love, and in the Eucharist is the gift of the truth of love.

The Eucharist is therefore the totality of being because it is the Truth of Love. In the white Eucharistic fragment, we can glimpse the reality of God made flesh — the incarnation of the Logos in a body given even to the consummation of self, the incarnation of the Truth in Love because the Logos is the Son who reveals the Father[6] in an agapic communion without end, which is the Holy Spirit. Truly everything resides in the fragment (the truth of love in the bread and wine consecrated for the salvation of the world), so that humanity itself nourished by the Logos-Love might eat charity by eating truth.[7] The Eucharist is the Church's treasure; it is the greatest good which must be accepted without any compromise. It is the fundamental possibility of communicating with God, of knowing Him and loving Him by eating of Him. Is it not perhaps because people do not know God, do not truly welcome Him in their lives, do not dialogue with Him as a living Person who is alongside us and loves us, that the most serious delusions of humanity occur? Above all, the delusion that one can believe in God without knowing Him, without experiencing the One whose being is love? The Eucharist is the experience of the presence of the "God who is close," that God who, even though transcendent and omnipotent, is not distant, is not an ignorant arbiter of human events,

---

6   See Jn 14:9.
7   "The ancient world had dimly perceived that man's real food — what truly nourishes him as man — is ultimately the *Logos*, eternal wisdom: this same *Logos* now truly becomes food for us — as love" (Pope Benedict XVI, *Deus Caritas Est*, 13).

but is with us, is the Love who becomes the food of truth. Only when we are able to bring the Eucharist to every man and woman — and every man and woman to the Eucharist — will the truth of humanity which yearns for God, and the truth of God who loves humanity and wants humanity with Him eternally, be revealed. The Eucharist is the God-Man who brings the gift of the Trinitarian life of God with Him and inserts humanity in God because God definitively became man. To see the Eucharist is to see God. To speak to the Eucharistic Jesus is to speak with God. The yearning to see God that is written in the heart of every man and woman is fulfilled: God reveals Himself under the Eucharistic veil. He manifests Himself, attracting us to Himself, while living in the apophatic mystery of the totally other. Love breaks the veils of mystery and touches the heart of God, while a white veil continues to make us sigh for the Blessed Motherland where there will no longer be any veil, but we will see God "face to face" (1Cor 13:12).

2. THE EUCHARIST DRAWS US INTO CHRIST'S OBLATION

The Eucharist, in its natural elements (bread and wine), transubstantiated by virtue of the creative-sanctifying power of God into the Body and Blood of Christ, is the start of the transformation of reality in its totality. Creation stained by sin and by corruption becomes a new creation.[8] We become in Christ a new creation,[9] that is, able to transfigure our lives in God and only thus become like God. Being itself is changed in its intimate nature and transformed into *being love* which gives life. The Eucharist elevates the whole of creation in a surge of perfection that

---

8   See Rm 8:19, 23.
9   See 2 Cor 5:17; Gal 6:15.

introduces this earth and this heaven into the dimension to come, that of the new heaven and the new earth.[10] The Eucharist transforms reality in its intimate depths and brings it to the bosom of God. Only the Eucharist can transfigure truth — every truth — into a spotless purity, and transfigure men and women — every man and woman. Thus, the Eucharist participates in the gift of Christ, of His own life; it draws us to Him and transfigures us in Him and with us the whole of creation. To use an image dear to Benedict XVI, here is a sort of nuclear fission which starts a change in reality. Yes, we can change the world because we ourselves can be changed in our most intimate depths; we can become God through eating God. The world will be pure when we ourselves begin to be so. We can be so! That is why the Eucharist is the totality of being:

> The Eucharist draws us into Jesus' act of self-oblation. More than just statically receiving the incarnate Logos, we enter into the very dynamic of his self-giving". He "draws us into himself". The substantial conversion of the bread and the wine into his body and blood places within creation the start of a radical change, like a sort of "nuclear fission", to use an image well-known to us today, brought into the most intimate depth of being, a change destined to create a process of transformation of reality, whose ultimate end will be the transfiguration of the whole world, to the point of that condition where God will be all in all (See 1Cor 15:28).[11]

---

10   See Rev 21:1–2.
11   Pope Benedict XVI, *Deus Caritas Est*, 11. See also Pope Benedict XVI, "Homily on the Solemnity of Corpus Domini" (June 15, 2006), *L'Osservatore Romano*, June 16–17, 2006, 4–5.

3. THE EUCHARIST AS SPOUSAL GIFT

Another important characteristic of the Eucharist, which seems to be the manifestation of that inseparable link between God and humanity repeatedly underlined in the magisterium of Benedict XVI, is the *spousal dimension* of the Eucharist, which has roots in the spousal dimension of love.[12] Here, in effect, is a strong bond between love as spousal gift of God, who in Christ unites Himself to His Spouse, the Church, and perpetuates this spousal gift in the Eucharist, the gift of the Bridegroom to His Spouse. This same Eucharist is the cause of the mystery-sacramental being of the Church. In effect, the wonderful biblical novelty — illuminated by Benedict XVI in *Deus Caritas Est* — lies in a new image of God and consequently of humanity. God is the Creator of everything and, at the same time, a Person who loves with all the ardor and passion of a bridegroom. God loves His people, chooses them and binds them to Himself in a mysterious covenant that prepares the way for the definitive messianic covenant. To the image of God's faithful and spousal love — to which the response is, unfortunately, the unfaithful love of His people — corresponds a radical novelty for men and women, too. Married individuals are called to love in truth the one whom the Lord has placed alongside them in the unity and indissolubility of the one flesh. The unity and indissolubility of marriage corresponds to God's unity and faithfulness.

---

[12] Here one is largely indebted to the teaching of John Paul II who deepened the dimension of love in reference to marriage, as a sacramental reflection of Christ's love for His Church. On the spousal dimension of the Eucharist and its union with sacramental marriage, see his Apostolic Letter *Mulieris Dignitatem* (August 15, 1988), 26. On the other hand, for a reflection on the spousal and redemptive dimension of love, see his "Catechesis at the General Audience" (December 15, 1982).

"Sacramentum Caritatis" in Veritate

So, marriage becomes a sign of God's love, the human place where God-Love manifests Himself. Finally, through the Christ event, God's love assumes a perceptible meaning. Christ draws close to every man and woman; He Himself takes flesh and blood to give flesh and blood to the love of humanity through God. He is the true Bridegroom who loves and unites His Church to Himself in a definitive way.[13] His spousal love, which reaches a climax in the gift of Self in the Body and the Blood, will be a *type* — in the patristic sense of the word, that is, causal example — of every love which will have its natural-sacramental foundation in matrimony. The Eucharist, therefore, summarizes the truth of spousal love. In the Eucharistic banquet we taste the nuptial banquet of the Lamb.[14] Pope Benedict writes:

> The Eucharist inexhaustibly strengthens the indissoluble unity and love of every Christian marriage. By the power of the sacrament, the marriage bond is intrinsically linked to the eucharistic unity of Christ the Bridegroom and his Bride, the Church (cf. *Eph* 5:31-32). The mutual consent that husband and wife exchange in Christ, which establishes them as a community of life and love, also has a eucharistic dimension. Indeed, in the theology of Saint Paul, conjugal love is a sacramental sign of Christ's love for his Church, a love culminating in the Cross, the expression of his "marriage" with humanity and at the same time the origin and heart of the Eucharist.[15]

---

[13] See Pope Benedict XVI, *Deus Caritas Est*, 9-14. Note the intimate link with *Sacramentum Caritatis* on this matter, as I will try to demonstrate.
[14] See Rev 19:9.
[15] Pope Benedict XVI, *Deus Caritas Est*, 11.

The Eucharist, which pours forth from the sacrifice of Christ, from the nuptial chamber of Christ, is a fundamental love for the Church and has its first and fundamental human visibility in Christian marriage. Here one sees the inseparable link between divine love and human love. According to the hermeneutic principle of the *truth of love*, this Eucharistic spousal love of Christ for the Church is the Love that, as radical gift, is the origin of every other gift: it is the truth of love. Thus, the Eucharist can become measure of the sacraments, measure of the liturgy, measure of our being *iuxta dominicam viventes*. Love, in its intrinsic connotation as spousal and redemptive gift, becomes the truth of the Church: the Eucharist is the truth of the Church. The Eucharist is the origin of the Church as causal principle[16] and consequently is the origin of the sacraments shaped and finalized by it. The origin of the Church is the love of the One who always precedes us because He loved us first. "The causal influence of the Eucharist at the Church's origins definitively discloses both the chronological and ontological priority of the fact that it was Christ who loved us "first". For all eternity he remains the one who loves us first."[17]

4. THE INTERTWINING OF FAITH, LITURGY AND LIFE IN THE EUCHARIST

The whole Post-Synodal Apostolic Exhortation is a clarification of the Eucharist, which is the root of truth for the whole Church in its triple dimension of mystery believed, mystery celebrated and mystery lived: the three parts that constitute the whole document. The spousal-agapic

---

16   See Pope Benedict XVI, *Deus Caritas Est*, 14.
17   Ibid.

"Sacramentum Caritatis" in Veritate

dimension of the Eucharist becomes the criterion of truth for every aspect of faith and for the whole Church. The Eucharist is the gift of the Bridegroom to His spouse. As a gift which precedes us, it is greater than us. To place oneself in the dimension of the Church which receives and welcomes the love of the Bridegroom, it is necessary to understand theologically the adorable mystery of the consecrated bread. As the gift of love that becomes the food of truth—through that circularity of truth and love—the Eucharist bestows truth to the Church and to the sacraments in which the Church *receives* and *expresses* what she herself is.[18]

Having spoken incidentally about marriage, we will make some reference to celibacy as an expression of the spousal love of Christ with the Church. Celibacy, in fact, is a spousal mystery. "It is a profound identification with the heart of Christ the Bridegroom who gives his life for his Bride"[19] and finds its center and its summit in the Eucharist. Celibacy cannot be lived as a functional priority—because it is not a function or even a managerial facilitation—but it is the love of the Bridegroom to the consummation of self, who ultimately expresses the fullness of love by giving His own Flesh and Blood in the Eucharist, offered *in Persona Christi*, that is, in the person of Christ Himself as the Head. Celibacy has a fundamental theological foundation and is not just a disciplinary custom: its foundation is Christ Himself. How can one be sacramentally part of Christ without Christ Himself being Head and Pastor? While the practice of the Eastern Churches remains valid—and even there, celibacy remains in force for bishops (whose example is followed by many

---

18 See Pope Benedict XVI, *Deus Caritas Est*, 16.
19 Ibid., 24.

priests) — the practice of the Latin Church, wisely confirmed by the popes, is by far superior and theologically irreproachable.

The Eucharist, then, is the criterion of truth in our liturgy. It is the rule of our celebration of the mystery of Christ. If Christ is the gift of spousal love, we cannot betray this love, which is His gift of being, by ultimately distorting the Eucharist itself. Liturgical abuses are never a simple yearning for novelty — perhaps arising from the good faith of those who believe that the most original inspirations would create more enthusiasm and more participation — but are always a sign of distance from the spousal love of the Eucharist and lack of faith in the mystery. If I believe in Christ and love Him, I celebrate Christ believed and loved — the One who gives me the gift of Himself. I celebrate Him, not me. "The truest beauty is the love of God, who definitely revealed himself to us in the paschal mystery."[20]

Finally, the Eucharist, because its being is self-giving love, gives truth to our identity as Christians. Our lives are informed by the love of the One who loves us and gives Himself in the Sacrament, and therefore cannot but express Him. In Christ we ourselves become a "living sacrifice" (Rom 12:1) and begin to live according to the Lord, according to the Lord's Day, *iuxta dominicam viventes,* to use the expression of St. Ignatius of Antioch. Whoever eats of the Lord will always live for Him, and will become transformed in Him. "Anyone united to the Lord becomes one spirit with him" (1Cor 6:17) and is already participating in eternal life:

> This 'eternal life' begins in us even now, thanks
> to the transformation effected in us by the gift of

---

20   Pope Benedict XVI, *Deus Caritas Est,* 35.

the Eucharist: 'He who eats me will live because of me' (Jn 6:57). These words of Jesus make us realise how the mystery 'believed' and 'celebrated' contains an innate power making it the principle of new life within us and the form of our Christian existence.[21]

The indispensable "eucharistic consistency"[22] when applied in a social context, is the new way of being Christian: a being love in truth. Today, everyone wants to be love — think of the many sentimentalisms because of which the most inane manipulations of the sacrosanct dignity of humanity and the essential foundation of the family are overturned — but often it is a love devoid of truth — a pure morality, a sterile moralism. The Eucharist as truth of love gives truth to Christian conscience. It suggests that conscience is not arbitrary judgment, but a moral judgment that can never prescind from truth and goodness.

5. EUCHARIST AND THE CHURCH'S MISSION

Finally, let us turn to two references which we willingly offer again in an alethic-agapic tone, the first to the evangelization of cultures and the second to the truth of the binding proclamation of Christ, the one Savior. The new Christian worship, the *logiké latreía* and the *rationabile obsequium*,[23] which is worship of the Logos made flesh in love, becomes the leaven that ferments every culture, bringing it to Christ in fullness. It leads to what is truly human because it is rooted in what is truly divine. The evangelizing mission as the leaven of truth begins with the Eucharist:

---

21 Pope Benedict XVI, *Deus Caritas Est*, 70.
22 Ibid., 83.
23 See Rm 12:1.

The intercultural character of this new worship, this *logiké latreía*, needs to be recognized. The presence of Jesus Christ and the outpouring of the Holy Spirit are events capable of engaging every cultural reality and bringing to it the leaven of the Gospel. It follows that we must be committed to promoting the evangelisation of cultures, conscious that Christ himself is the truth for every man and woman, and for all human history. The Eucharist becomes a criterion for our evaluation of everything that Christianity encounters in different cultures[24]

Thus, one arrives at what is intimately bound to the missionary nature of the Church, namely, the universal soteriological dimension of Love that bestows the truth of God. One is Love, one is Truth. Why does the Eucharist lead the Church to all peoples? Because Christ is the one Savior, "yesterday, today and always" (Heb 13:8):

Emphasis on the intrinsic relationship between the Eucharist and mission also leads to a rediscovery of the ultimate content of our proclamation. The more ardent the love for the Eucharist in the hearts of the Christian people, the more clearly will they recognise the goal of all mission: *to bring Christ to others*. Not just a theory or a way of life inspired by Christ, but the gift of his very person. Anyone who has not shared the truth of love with his brothers and sisters has not yet given enough. The Eucharist, as the sacrament of our salvation, inevitably reminds us of the unicity of Christ and the salvation that he won for us by his blood. The mystery of the Eucharist,

---

[24] Pope Benedict XVI, *Deus Caritas Est*, 78.

"Sacramentum Caritatis" in Veritate

believed in and celebrated, demands a constant catechesis on the need for all to engage in a missionary effort centred on the proclamation of Jesus as the one Saviour. This will help to avoid a reductive and purely sociological understanding of the vital work of human promotion present in every authentic process of evangelization.[25]

6. THE EUCHARIST, TRUTH OF LOVE

These reflections on the Eucharist as the *truth of love* can be summarized in the following statement: *the Eucharist is love that gives truth because it is the truth of God who is love*. The Eucharist is the heart of truth because it is the source of love. Isn't truth love? The Eucharist is the Love which gives truth to the Church, to the Christian, to every man and woman of goodwill. To love the Eucharist, to adore it, to live it, means to be in the Truth. Only the Eucharist gives us the Truth because the Eucharist is Jesus-Love. May the Immaculate Virgin, the "first tabernacle in history,"[26] always give us this Love!

At this point we need to consider the risk of preventing truth and love from meeting and engaging in dialogue. Each member of society might wish to advance their own truth, especially in matters of religious belief. If we did so, we would end up with relativism on the one hand and religious fundamentalism on the other. Is this not the case nowadays? Should we not confirm the model of religious freedom adopted in the light of this circularity of truth and love? This will be the subject of our next and final investigation.

---

25 Pope Benedict XVI, *Deus Caritas Est*, 86.
26 Pope John Paul II, *Ecclesia de Eucharistia*, 55.

PART THREE
The Oblivion of Faith

When Reason and Love Do Not Meet

BEYOND POST-MODERN LEVELLING

1. IF REASON AND LOVE NO LONGER LOOK AT EACH OTHER

At the end of our journey, a sort of *pericoresi* around two pillars of the whole of reality — truth and love — some questions remain. We must ask ourselves what would happen if truth and love failed, if they were drastically separated or put in contradiction. We have already considered various aspects along the way. Faith is founded on reason; it is not opposed to reason, but superior to it. Only when faith begins from reason and remains open to its rational logic of inquiry and testing, will it not be reduced to cold sentiment or an optional fideism. If faith starts out from reason and rests on it, charity will truly be the fulfilment of faith, like love which brings everything to fullness. Just as reason is open in love to an intimate desire for fulfilment, beyond rigorous inquiry, so faith moves internally toward charity, which everything finally establishes in the vision of God. Faith works through charity.[1] The verb used by St. Paul and St. James (5:16) is *energéo*, which literally signifies work, that is, to operate. Faith per se is

---

1   See Gal 5:6.

charitable tension, a loving activity in its stretching out toward God and toward one's neighbor in service, just as reason is tension toward the other, not just understood as being, but as being-in-relation, and if possible as person. Reason and love are the rational presupposition; faith and charity, the revelatory fulfilment.

If truth and love fail because we drastically separate them, we will have caused the most heartfelt and lethal wound to Christianity. It would lead to a polarization which, because of the winds and fashions, would one minute exalt only faith, and the next only charity. We have already seen this in the course of history. A faith without charity — because it originates without reason and love — is pure fideistic subjectivism, typical of Luther and many others who think that God's grace is not enough to help us to overcome all the obstacles, temptations, and difficulties of life or to make us live according to the norms of the Gospel. Faith without charity is a Christianity that claims good intentions but is thoroughly closed to the very demands of Christian doctrine. This faith, which can be pastoral, quickly falls into a laborious self-seeking, unconcerned about the true good of the other, of his or her eternal salvation.

Conversely, a charity without faith — since at its root it is devoid of love and reason — is a relativistic moralism. Christianity becomes a charity headquarters for everyone but it lacks faith and a clear identity. This is convenient for the State, which shows no interest in religion and the Church, even tending to put all religious claims on the same level. To relieve itself of its social responsibilities toward the less well-off, the State even gives the patronage of them to some Christian non-profit organization. How many pastoral workers committed in our charitable activities do not have faith in Christ! Yet they willingly lend a hand to serve as volunteers. Strangely, the demand to do voluntary work is growing, while the desire to believe in God lessens. Many prefer to speak about individual religious experiences. Volunteering without God, without the truth, easily turns to self-seeking charity. Charity falls into mere philanthropy, a service of neighbor dictated by love of self; the other becomes simply the one in the mirror. In this logic of "do good" Christianity, one must hasten to help everyone, and yet remain vague about one's own identity to avoid offending the sensitivity of others. While people are relativistic from the dogmatic point of view, they quickly become lax from a moral point of view. Christ is not proclaimed, and even though there is service of neighbor, especially in rough areas, many are quick to compromise on morality. For example, contraception is rejected as a principle, but it is good to distribute contraceptives and condoms to prevent further illness. The gnat is strained out, but the camel is swallowed. Charity without faith and without truth is a mess of good sentiments that are sterile and contradictory. In this collective and relativistic moralism the word of the day is *love*, but its true meaning is *euphoric and undisciplined eros*.

The drastic nature of the separation between reason and love on the one hand, faith and charity on the other, is seen above all in inter-religious dialogue. A rather recent example is the debate in Italy about the possibility of a mosque in some important cities. The whole discussion seems to be focussed on whether a mosque should be erected or not. Whether it is possible to conduct a *dialogue* between the applicants and the residents that is not reduced to a monologue between the deaf is overlooked. Should we not begin by discerning principles, for example, whether religious freedom is considered by both sides as a non-negotiable, rational, and human good? Should we not examine how religious freedom unravels within a civil society with the presence of multiple religious subjects? Even before tackling the burning issue of religious freedom, should we not above all confirm that reason and love are a rational presupposition of the dialogue partners, to arrive at a common understanding on fundamental rational principles, such as common sense, the truth of the human person, the dignity of the woman, and marriage? In a society of *doing* that sets God aside the whole of this discourse is enigmatic and distant from the theme under consideration, which prefers to concentrate on praxis.

Furthermore, the approach of the Italian prelates, who stumble along requesting a mosque, seems to be quite weak. In the best of hypotheses, the mosque would be inappropriate, not just because Islam is insufficiently integrated in the culture or because a mosque could hide Islamic fundamentalism or even terrorist cells. If, instead, the request was motivated by a pure desire to worship God, should the mosque be built? Is it sufficient to claim a rational desire to worship? Is there not a need to demonstrate that such a desire is good and true, not from the Koran or the Bible, but from reason and love, that is, from a presupposition common to both Islam and Christianity?

The neuralgic point and the question to be settled in advance of dialogue with Islam and with all other religious representatives is the problem of religious freedom.

What is freedom of religion, and what is its foundation? Is it a right that stems from human nature? In the final analysis, the problem of religious liberty is the problem of God. Who is God and how can I know Him? Let us examine this issue in light of our discourse about the circularity of reason and love to offer the most complete conclusion possible.

2. RELIGIOUS FREEDOM COMPARED WITH REASON AND LOVE

Benedict XVI's address to the Roman Curia on December 22, 2005, illuminates the issue at hand. In this address he suggested the correct hermeneutic of the Second Vatican Council should be placed on two different levels: continuity in the unchanging principles and discontinuity regarding the historical forms which have borne those principles. The latter are relative; the former, on the other hand, remain. True reform is born from the correct harmony and synchronization of continuity and discontinuity. In the case of the Second Vatican Council, some people have been concerned about responding to the new circumstances of the modern world (rather than an inappropriate "opening to the world"), including redefining the relationship between the Church and the modern State and therefore responding to the new concept of freedom in relation to the plurality of religions within a civil community itself, preserving impartial behavior toward them and guaranteeing peaceful co-existence. The pope said:

> Basic decisions, therefore, continue to be well-grounded, whereas the way they are applied to new contexts can change. Thus, for example, if religious freedom were to be considered an expression of the human inability to discover the truth and thus become a canonisation of relativism, then this social and historical necessity is raised inappropriately to the metaphysical level and thus stripped of its true meaning. Consequently, it cannot be accepted by those who believe that the human person is capable of knowing the truth about God and, on the basis of the inner dignity of the truth, is bound to

this knowledge. It is quite different, on the other hand, to perceive religious freedom as a need that derives from human coexistence, or indeed, as an intrinsic consequence of the truth that cannot be externally imposed but that the person must adopt only through the process of conviction.[2]

So, to see the continuity of the Church's teaching on freedom of religion—which the Council did not abolish, and was not able to—and the discontinuity which designates the novelty and reform, it is necessary to establish the nucleus of religious freedom.

The discontinuity is given primarily by the new approach to religious freedom which begins from the modern concept of State. At a public level, the right of freedom of religion places all religious subjects on the same level; the State will exercise impartiality toward all, without favoring one religion over another and guaranteeing everyone, within the limits of what is reasonable, the right to public worship. There is a new concept of freedom in the modern era, in which the role of the subject's choice of the good is emphasized more, and consequently a new concept of freedom is applied to religion. So, the State attempts to be indifferent toward religions, and therefore it is no longer possible to speak of tolerance toward the false religions (which do not provide rational and revelatory elements to justify their social plausibility). Instead, there is religious freedom for everyone and therefore the consequent freedom of worship of religious groups. The truth or otherwise of religion is replaced by the primacy of the religious subject, and therefore by his or her freedom.

---

2   Pope Benedict XVI, "Address *Expergiscere, homo*" (December 22, 2005): *AAS* 98 (2006), 50.

2.1 A dual dimension of religious freedom

Nevertheless, there is an important distinction to be made between religious freedom as freedom of conscience (in religious matters) and religious freedom as freedom of worship. The two freedoms are not homogenous, and we cannot always pass from one to the other indiscriminately. Here, too, Vatican II is limited.[3]

The journey of the Second Vatican Council to a new paradigm of religious freedom, by a change not in men and women but in civil society, enforces a check and critique of the new principle that is so characteristic of the Council: the principle of realizing religious freedom in freedom of worship for a religious group, since religious freedom is personal and communal freedom of worship. In truth, in a civil society the same religious freedom in the external forum, in an individual or associate form, cannot be recognized without falling into the principal that one religion is the same as another.

The *religio vera* and the one Church of Christ cannot remain just a statement of principle[4] when, by virtue of the *immunity from coercion* — which is in fact the nucleus of religious freedom[5] — the possibility that all religious beings and all religious groups have an equality in the exercise of their religious right is justified by right and not in fact. The only exception is public order; the truth and goodness per se of religions is left to the sphere of the religious sentiment of each person, to be respected always and in every case.[6]

In reality, it is not religious freedom as such which is

---

3 See Second Vatican Council, Declaration on Religious Freedom *Dignitatis Humanae* (December 7, 1965), 7..
4 Ibid., 1.
5 Ibid.
6 Ibid., 2.

inscribed in humanity's nature but freedom from coercion in religious matters. In other words, what is inscribed human nature is the right to not suffer violence and the freedom to adhere to the religion which in conscience individuals believe to be true. However, the right to profess any religion is not inscribed in the nature of humanity. For God would have inscribed both truth and falsehood if all religions were true and good; then, all religious beings must profess their religious faith impartially. It is necessary to choose the truth. Religious freedom is a question of truth and love.

The agreement of continuity and discontinuity encouraged an important reform in Vatican II, which was seeking to descend into the modern era and respond to changing times. However, the Council established that the same conciliar reform of religious freedom was not definitive, but only provisional and bound to the change of the cultural paradigm of that time. The nucleus of the discourse about religious freedom will always be preserved, but its realization can change. So, we preserve the truth of the Second Vatican Council, while driving its vision further, open to new acquisitions and above all to the new commitment in evangelization.

Our time is already radically different from that of the 1960s. Society is strongly relativistic. Relativism has emphasized the phenomenon of secularization, and the concept of freedom is increasingly manifested as a rejection of God. In a Europe now intolerant not just of religions but also of God Himself, of goodness and reason, it is necessary to restate with a clarity grounded in reason that God is necessary. The modern world's concept of freedom is a concept which has shown itself to be closed to God. To recover it, it is necessary for us to recall the need for God and, in the face of growing religious relativism, we must remind others of the need for the true God and the true religion. The debate about freedom of religion should point to the truth about God — and consequently about humanity and freedom in matters of religion — rather than unilaterally to personal or collective freedom to exercise public worship. We must point out the truth about freedom, that is, the truth about love, rather than freedom as a subject's right.

2.2 The State and religious freedom

Moreover, the responsibility for religious freedom cannot, in the final analysis, be simply transferred to the democratic and modern State, as *Dignitatis Humanae* seems to do when it solemnly declares: "Consequently, to deny the free exercise of religion in society, when the just requirements of public order are observed, is to do an injustice to the human person and to the very order established by God for human beings."[7]

Does the constitutional State no longer have any duty toward truth and the true religion? Here it seems that *Dignitatis Humanae* prefers the idea of a modern State so democratic that, out of respect for public order, it relegates religious choice to the mere peaceful co-existence of different entities. According to *Dignitatis Humanae*, provided that public order is respected, the right to freedom of religion "is not to be impeded."[8] But how can we ever suppose that a state judges freedom of religion to be *true*, freedom — as we have said — to choose in conscience without coercion the religion believed to be true, when the state itself is soaked in relativism or when it has great difficulties in affirming indisputably non-negotiable principles and relegates them

---

7   *Dignitatis Humanae*, 3.
8   Ibid., 2.

to the private sphere? How can freedom be true when truth is threatened by the State itself? How can a State guarantee the exercise of freedom of religion when it does not even recognize truth and the absolute priority of moral values? This is the risk of a too-optimistic entrusting of the Church of the Second Vatican Council to the modern concept of the constitutional, free, and democratic State.

In our current situation, the State does not recognize religious freedom but only implies it, respecting it to crush the religious sphere into the circle of the private and questionable. The State would confirm religious relativism. If the Church were to submit to this logic, no longer making an *apo-logia* for the true religion or demanding that the State favor the religion founded on reason and love, and therefore the common good of everyone, it would become a friend of this way of thinking and doing, which contributes to the disappearance of religion. Today it is necessary to restore the concept of true religion and guarantee religious freedom for everyone in the internal forum while privileging in the external forum only those who provide guarantees of openness to the values of rationality upon which they base their revealed faith. Room must be made for Judeo-Christianity. The other religious cults can be respected and tolerated but not be justified on principle. This is precisely the point: in religious matters, too, the State must favor and protect that religion which is good for everyone. It is good because it is founded on reason and love, on truth and on communion, on intelligence and on dialogue, that latter only because it is based on the truth.

The truth directs religious freedom, while love affirms its uniqueness in (apologetic) dialogue with other subjects. Love encourages peaceful co-existence of different religious subjects within the same State, based in religious truth, in the truth about God and humanity. A concept of religious freedom founded on truth and on love, on the one hand encourages the affirmation of the true religion and so the true meaning of religious liberty — which is not relativism but choice without any coercion concerning the truth about God — and on the other hand is open to respect and social admissibility differentiated from other cults. These other cults should not be simply aligned in their mutltiplicity and placed alongside one another but should be acknowledged by virtue of the truth of the human person and their freedom to act publicly, always respecting social order and the good of all. Of course, it will be difficult for the state to venture into a discourse more theological than political. Nevertheless, if that is difficult for the state, it should not be so for the Church, which, for its part, should not simply hand over the question of freedom of religion to the constitutional state, believing it to be sovereign in the administration of justice in matters of religion. Caesar has his power from God and here is called, according to the truth of the one God (and the true humanity), to regulate the most public, external exercise of religious freedom. To regulate the exercise of religious activity according to reason, according to truth and love, will not collide with the democracy of the modern State, because it is a mandate faithful to truth and therefore to the promotion of the true good of all.

The Church should be more committed so that the State might promote the true religion while respecting the presence of other religions, subordinating them to the truth of the Gospel, ready to evangelize them so that all people of goodwill may encounter Christ. It does not seem that the Second Vatican Council or the later Episcopal Conferences have done very much to affirm the supremacy of Christ at a social level or to evangelize the different religious presences to bring them to Christ. Rather, they have promoted a generic affirmation that religious freedom is a good for everyone and that the state is its guarantor, causing all the consequences that we must manage today, such as unawareness of God and human respect supplanting respect for the religious freedom of others.

There is another question that seems fundamental in our situation as a global village: how can freedom of worship be recognized for people who do not recognize the right to freedom of conscience in religious matters as universal, as part of human nature? If freedom of conscience does not exist, as in Islam, what meaning does freedom of religion have for these groups when it is understood as freedom of worship in their own places of worship? In other words, how can one ask for a right to freedom when the duty to respect this same freedom is not recognized? This request for rights without duties fits well in the secularized and permissive West, which demands so many rights but does not assume the obligations of the corresponding duties. When faith excludes reason and therefore love, it also excludes itself and is easily transformed into violence. Violence is not necessarily the use of weapons and terrorism but is simply the use of faith detached from reason and from love, detached from life and from the non-negotiable human principles. The same is true for every other religion or religious philosophy which does not begin with reason and non-negotiable principles.

Some might object: on the back end of this, how will the other religions behave toward Christian minorities, especially in Islamic countries? Here, too, the Christian is fighting for freedom in truth, pressing for a dialogue on human values even before the dialogue about religious ones. Christians ask for permission to publicly exercise their worship, only if that does not harm civil society by conflicting with the achievement of common good. Finally, based on rationality, they ask to resist fear of dialogue, thus encouraging respectful and mutual awareness. If dialogue concerning inviolable principles is lacking, then true freedom of worship will always be missing. Therefore, both here among us and elsewhere, we call for respect and dialogue, primarily a rational dialogue and only secondarily a religious one.

Benedict XVI's words offer us an important directive and a cue to recovering the true meaning of religious freedom and consequently of evangelization in truth and love for everyone:

> A missionary Church known for proclaiming her message to all people must necessarily work for the freedom of the faith. She desires to transmit the gift of the truth that exists for one and all. At the same time, she assures peoples and their Governments that she does not wish to destroy their identity and culture by doing so, but to give them, on the contrary, a response which, in their innermost depths, they are waiting for — a response with which the multiplicity of cultures is not lost but instead unity between men and women increases and thus also peace between peoples.[9]

The Lord said, "Go, therefore, and make disciples of all nations, baptizing them in the name of the Father, and of the Son, and of the Holy Spirit, teaching them to

---

9   Pope Benedict XVI, "Address *Expergiscere, homo,*": *AAS* 98 (2006), 50–51.

observe all that I have commanded you" (Matt 28:19-20). His words have not gone out of fashion and are not to be archived because of pastoral updates. They are the reason why we are disciples of Christ. Only by following them can we build up the Church, His mystical Body.

Conclusion

FAITH IS AN ABSURDITY IN TODAY'S post-Christian environment. By now, even within the Church, it is seen as a leftover from the past, something from which we should distance ourselves for the sake of pastoral care and a pragmatic approach to reality. Reason would no longer be able to furnish us with certainties, such as the foundational role of truth in each area of knowledge. Consequently, God would be nonsense.

After reflecting on the importance of reason and its role in relation to faith in light of recent philosophical and theological contributions, we see that while reason has been brought to the brink of oblivion, an attempt to replace its role as *ancilla fidei* with love has arisen. Love would mean and do more than truth. But love without truth, lacking a natural bond with reason, is empty, as truth without love, without a link to freedom and will, is a cold calculation and is distant from life. Therefore, reason and love either go hand in hand or both fail. Their circularity on a natural level, which includes the harmonic relation between truth and love, intellect and will, is the condition for faith and charity to meet and find their indispensable complementarity. The paradigm of reason and love is therefore propaedeutic to verifying issues such as the correct relationship between doctrine and pastoral care. If ignored, the paradigm produces dangerous effects, such as religious fundamentalism or a religious freedom that easily prefers social stability to the necessity of seeking out the true God and the true religion in light of common good

The paradigm of reason and love becomes personal in Christ. Truth and love meet definitively in the Person of the Word incarnate, in whom we share by faith and charity, and of whom we are partakers in the mystery of the Holy Eucharist. Truth and love are one Person, Christ.

Fundamental theology's apologetic discourse on the existence of God can benefit from a new insight that reinforces the role of reason as a solid foundation to faith. However, it is necessary to point out that God, insofar as He is the object of faith, can be believed only if He is also lovable. The fact that He is lovable goes together with the initial impulse to seek Him out in creation as the First Cause of everything. This solution could regain the importance of reason without forgetting the predominance of love, as today's society vehemently demands.

By correctly coordinating the relationship between reason and love, we can indeed address the whole of reality: all that is thinkable and an object of love. This is why reason and love together can do great things, especially in restoring to a post-Christian society the possibility of addressing the core of all problems: God.

Index of names

Aristotle, 177
Athanasius (Saint), 55n
Augustine (Saint), 5, 39–41, 41n, 128–129, 129n, 158n, 159n, 176–177, 177n

Bellandi, Andrea, 119n, 145n
Bellarmine Robert (Saint), 147
Benedict XVI, xxiv, xxiv n, xxvi, 17n, 25, 25n, 29, 29n, 30n, 59, 59n, 61, 89, 90n, 116, 116n, 118, 118n, 120, 120n, 121, 130–132, 134, 134n, 135n, 136, 136n, 137n, 138n, 139n, 140n, 141n, 142, 142n, 143n, 149n, 150n, 157n, 161n, 187n, 196n, 200, 201n, 206n, 209–210, 210n, 213, 213n, 214, 215n, 216n, 217n, 218n, 219n, 220n, 221n, 229, 230n, 237, 237n
Bentham, Jeremy, 186
Bernard of Clairvaux (Saint), 60, 60n, 110, 120
Bisconti, Fabrizio, 198n
Blanco, Arturo, 148n
Botturi, Francesco, 181, 182n
Bugnini, Annibale, 71
Bulgakov, Sergej, 21
Bultmann, Rudolf, 53
Buonaiuti, Ernesto, 10, 10n

Camus, Albert, 20, 98, 98n
Catherine of Siena (Saint), 104
Chenu, Marie-Dominique, 70, 70n

Chesterton, Gilbert Keith, xv, xv n, xxiii, xxiii n
Cicero, Vincenzo, 202n
Coda, Piero, 13n, 191n, 192n
Congar Yves, 68, 70
Crociata, Mariano, 154n
Cyril of Alexandria (Saint), 92, 92n, 93n, 98, 99n

Daniélou, Jean, 70
Davidson, Donald, 178
Davies, Paul, 37, 37n, 38, 38n
De Chardin, Teilhard, 78–79, 79d
De Lubac, Henri, 70
Denis, Brian, 27n
Descartes, 31, 176, 183
De Unamuno, Miguel, 3, 3n, Dilthey, Wilhelm, 176–177
Döpfner, Julius, 68
Dossetti, Giuseppe, 68
Dostoevsky, Fyodor, 174, 175
Dupuis, Jacques SJ, 54

Eicher, Peter, 150n
Einstein, Albert, 26, 27n
Evdokimov, Pavel, 20

Fabris, Rinaldo, 156n
Faricy, Robert, 79, 79n
Fazzini, Lorenzo, 29n
Feuerbach, Ludvig, 9
Fisichella, Rino, 119n
Forcellini, Egidio, 85n
Forte, Bruno, 15, 167n

Frings, Josef Richard, 67–68

Geissler, Hermann, 145n
Giorello, Giulio, 167n
Gotti, Tedeschi Ettore, 27, 28n
Gregory, the Great (Saint), 207, 207n
Grillmeier, Alois, 70

Habermas, Jürgen, 178
Hadjadj, Fabrice, 29, 29n
Hegel, Georg Wilhelm Friedrich, 9, 13n, 94, 94n, 95, 95n, 152, 152n, 191n
Heidegger, Martin, 5, 5n, 31, 75, 170–173, 177
Hermes, 198, 203
Hilberath, Bernd Jochen, 150n, 190n
Hume, David, 202, 202n
Huxley, Aldous Leonard, xv

Ignatius of Antioch (Saint), 218
Irenaeus of Lyons (Saint), 95, 147
Jedin, Hubert, 67–68, 68n, 69, 69n, 71, 71n, 72, 72n, 73, 73n
John Chrysostom (Saint), 101, 101n, 103
John XXIII (Pope Saint), 66–67, 69
John Paul II (Pope Saint), 34, 34n, 45–46, 46n, 47n, 54, 54n, 87, 88n, 150n, 209, 214n
Jonas, Hans, 15–16
Justin (Saint), 147, 157n

Kant, Immanuel, 3–4, 113, 113n, 114, 114n, 176–177, 183
Kasper, Walter, 15

Kessler, Count, 26
Kierkegaard, Søren, 9
König, Franz, 63
Küng, Hans, 70

Labourdette, Marie-Michel, 70
Latourelle, René, 53n
Lehmann, Karl, 190n
Leo the Great (Saint), 55n
Lévinas, Emmanuel, 178
Lewis, Clive Staples, xix, xx n
Livi, Antonio, xvi n, 78n, 119n, 181, 182n
Loisy, Alfred, 10, 10n
Lorizio, Giuseppe, 148n, 149, 149n, 153n
Luther, Martin, 6, 94, 94n, 95n, 150, 226

Machovec, Milan, 18
Mancuso, Vito, 11, 11n, 12, 12n, 13, 13n, 14
Marcion, 95
Martini, Carlo Maria, 32
Marucci, Corrado, 11n
Marx, Karl, 141
Melloni, Alberto, 66, 67n
Metz, Johann Baptist, 17, 17n, 18
Mohammed, 183
Moltmann, Jürgen, 15, 19, 53
Mura, Gaspare, 188n, 195n

Newman, John Henry Cardinal (Saint), xiv, xiv n, 144–145, 145n
Nietzsche, Friedrich, 31, 84, 135, 141, 165, 169, 170–173, 175, 175n, 177–178, 183, 185, 187, 187n, 188

Ocáriz, Fernando, 148n
Onfray, Michel, 172, 182–188, 183n, 184n, 185n, 186n, 187n
Orlando, Federico, 168n, 181
Ott, Ludwig, 95n
Ottaviani, Alfredo, 69, 73–75

Pannenberg, Wolfhart, 53
Pascal, Blaise, 4, 5n
Paul VI (Pope Saint), 67
Pavlou, Telesphora, 21n
Pearse, Roger, 101n
Philips, Gérard, 68, 70
Pizzardo, Giuseppe, 68
Plato, 116, 144n, 159n, 177–178
Pope Francis, 121
Possenti, Vittorio, 188n, 195n

Rahner, Karl, 17, 63, 63n, 64, 68, 70, 73–75, 74n, 75n
Rondet, Henri, 70
Rorty, Richard, 5
Rossé, Gérard, 19, 19n, 20n
Ruggeri, Giuseppe, 179n

Sabatier, Louis Auguste, 10, 10n
Sarafoni, Paolo, 21n
Schelling, Friedrich, 9, 191n
Schillebeeckx, Edward, 70
Schneider, Theodor, 150n, 190n
Schopenhauer, Arthur, 84
Schütz, Achim, 9n
Semmelroth, Otto, 70
Sequeri, Pierangelo, 179n
Serini, Paolo, 5n
Sewell, Bryson, 101n
Socrates, 116, 175
Spicq, Ceslas OP, 156n
Spinoza, Baruch, 174, 186

Staffa, Dino, 68
Stuart Mill, John, 186

Tertullian, 147
Thayer, Joseph Henry, 127n
Thibon, Gustave, 28
Thomas Aquinas (Saint), 5, 96, 118
Tillich, Paul, xvi
Trembelas, Panagiotes N., 20

Vannini, Marco, 158
Vattimo, Gianni, 5, 168n, 170–178, 170n, 172n, 173n, 174n, 176n, 177n, 178n, 179n, 180–182, 181n, 185–186, 187n, 188
Vendemiati, Aldo, 182n
Volk, Hermann, 70
Von Balthasar, Hans Urs, 15, 153n
Von Drey, Johann Sebastian, 147
Von Harnack, Adolf, 10, 10n, 122
Von Hildebrand, Dietrich, 202n
Von Stockhausen, Alma, 94n, 95n
Vorgrimler, Herbert, 63n

Ware, Kallistos, 20
Weil, Simone, 11
Wiederkehr, Dietrich, 191n
William of Saint-Thierry, 7–8, 8n, 110, 110n, 111n, 112, 112n

Zabala, Santiago, 168n, 170, 181n
Zoroaster, 59

ABOUT THE AUTHOR

Fr Serafino M. Lanzetta STD is resident in the Diocese of Portsmouth (England) where he exercises his priestly ministry. He is lecturer in Dogmatic Theology at the Theological Faculty of Lugano (Switzerland) and editor-in chief of the Theological Journal *Fides Catholica*. He has facilitated the organisation of several Theological Conferences—the last one on The Fatima Message in its 100th Anniversary, and has written for *L'Osservatore Romano*. His published works include his post-doctoral habilitation, *Vatican II, a Pastoral Council: Hermeneutics of Council Teaching* (Gracewing, 2016), *Fatima at the Heart of the Church: God's Vision of History and Oblative Spirituality* (2018) and *The Symphony of Truth: Theological Essays* (Arouca Press, 2020).

www.ingramcontent.com/pod-product-compliance
Lightning Source LLC
Chambersburg PA
CBHW021423070526
44577CB00001B/35